The Map Book™
Presented by DonTech

W9-COS-086

Table of Contents

Community Map Index

© DonTech, Chicago, IL 1992

All maps in The Map Book™ created exclusively for DonTech
by R.R. Donnelley Cartographic Services

West Edition Coverage Map

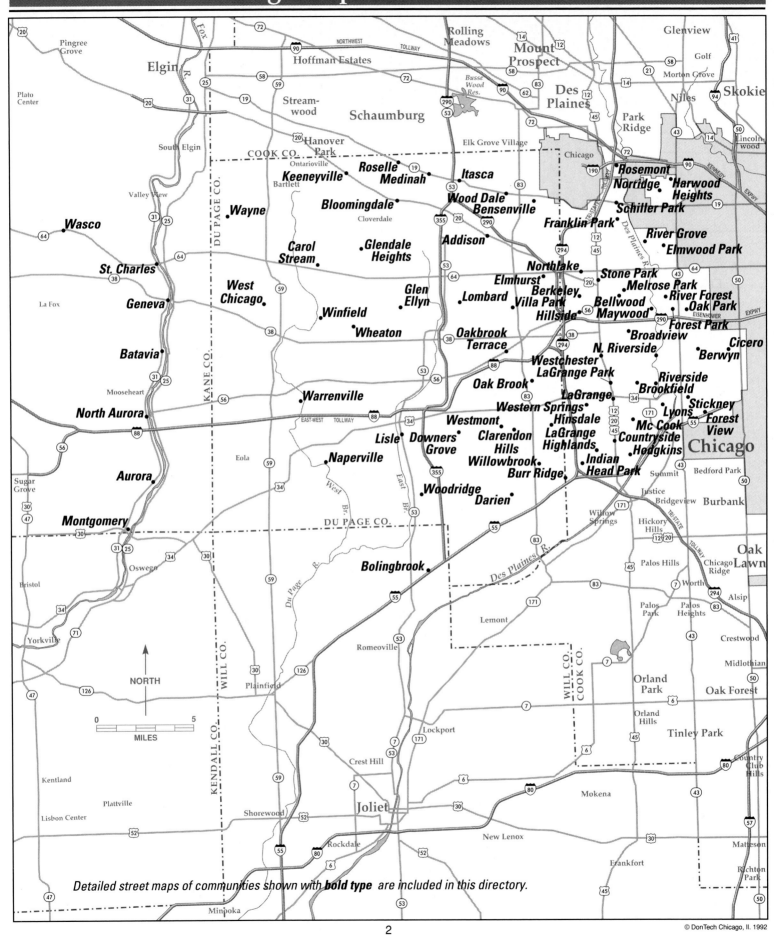

*Detailed street maps of communities shown with **bold type** are included in this directory.*

© DonTech Chicago, Il. 1992

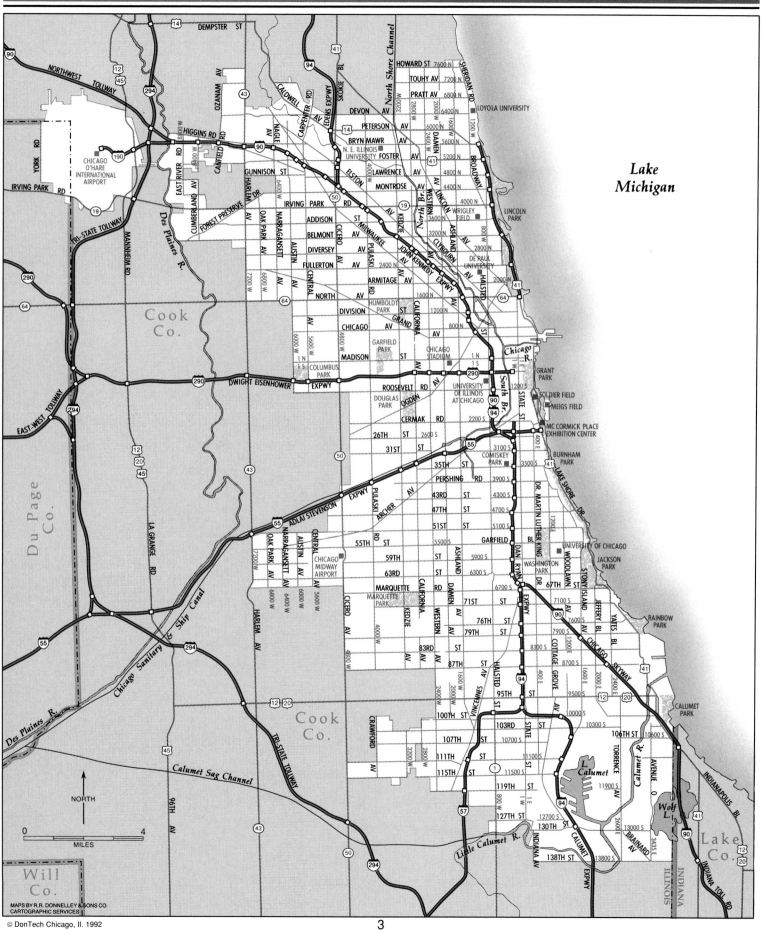

MAPS BY R.R. DONNELLEY & SONS CO.
CARTOGRAPHIC SERVICES

© DonTech Chicago, Il. 1992

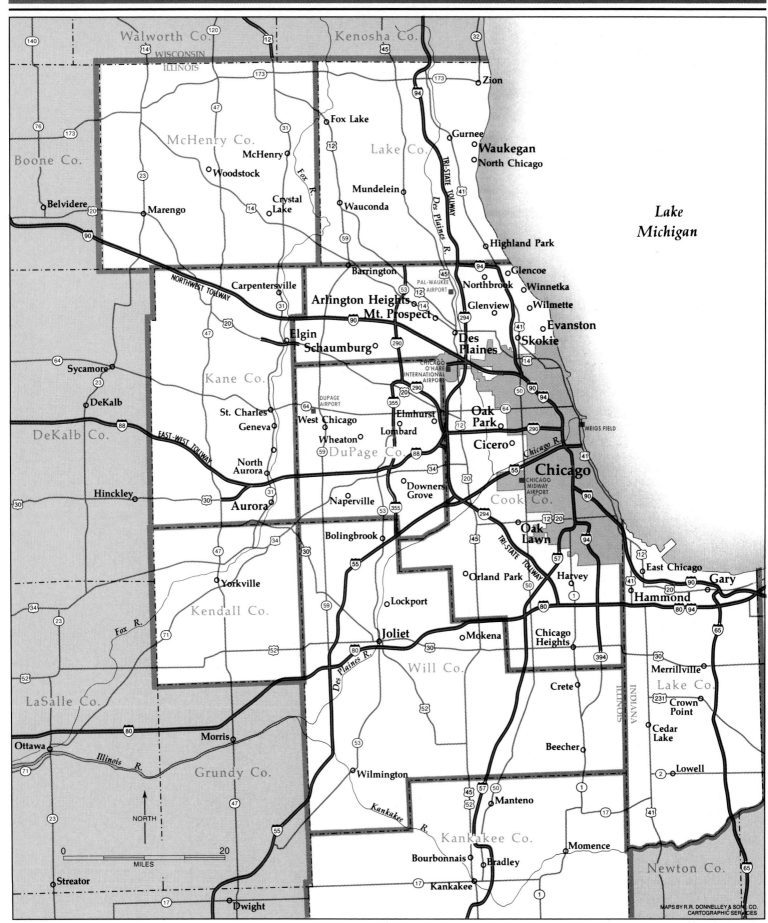

MAPS BY R.R. DONNELLEY & SONS CO. CARTOGRAPHIC SERVICES

© DonTech Chicago, Il. 1992

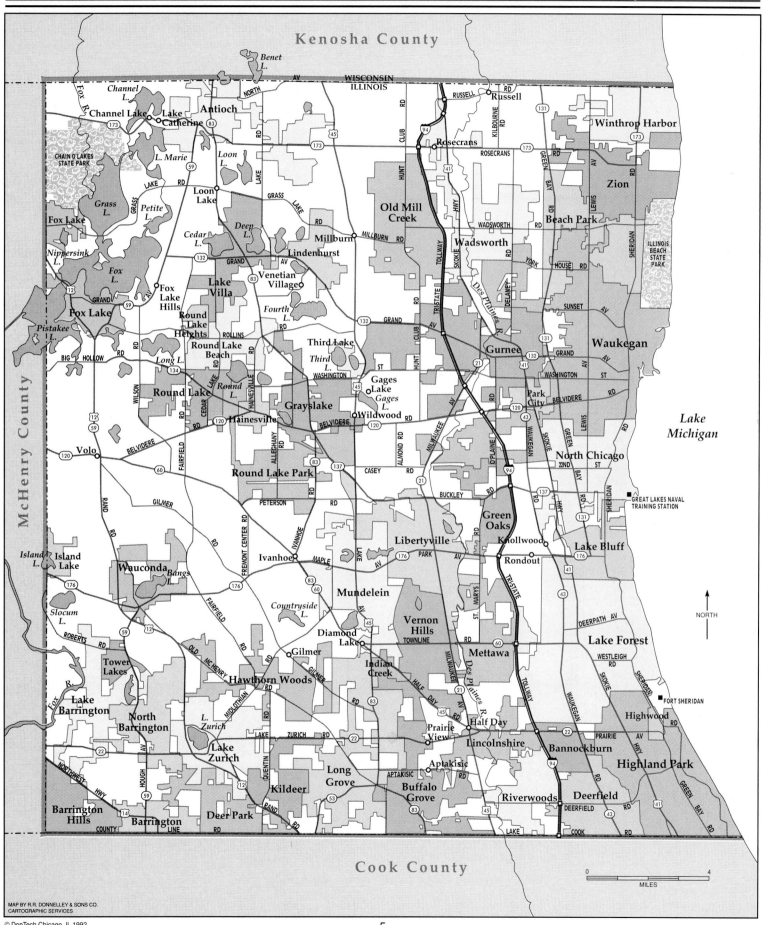

MAP BY R.R. DONNELLEY & SONS CO.
CARTOGRAPHIC SERVICES

© DonTech Chicago, Il. 1992

McHenry County

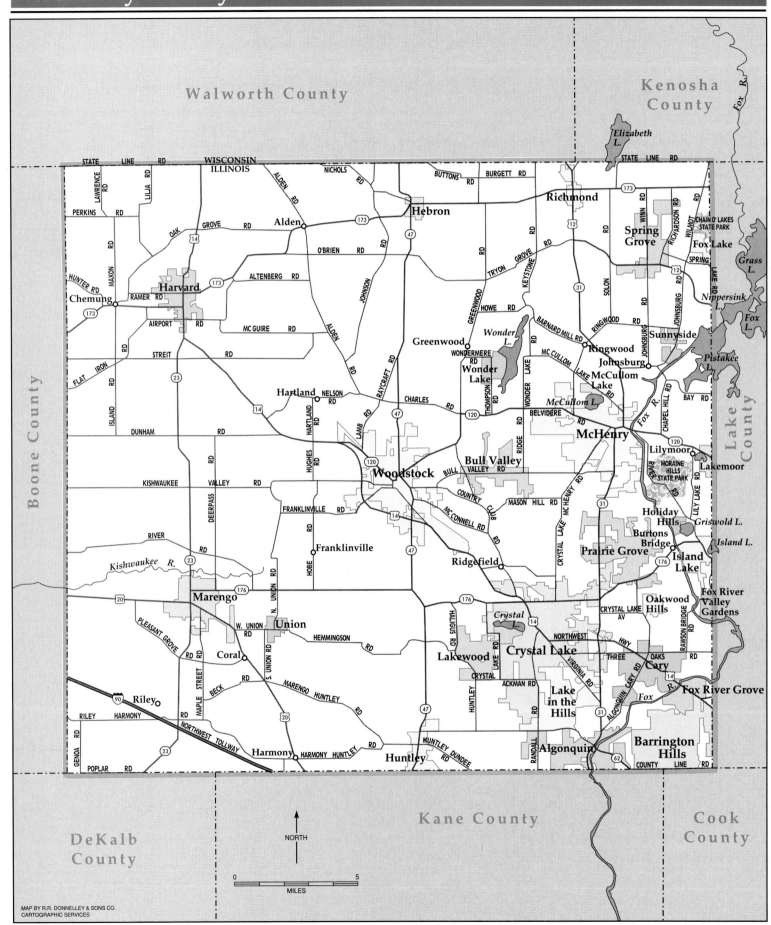

Walworth County

Kenosha County

Boone County

Lake County

DeKalb County

Kane County

Cook County

NORTH

0   5
MILES

MAP BY R.R. Donnelley & SONS CO.
CARTOGRAPHIC SERVICES

© DonTech Chicago, Il. 1992

MAP BY R.R. DONNELLEY & SONS CO.
CARTOGRAPHIC SERVICES

© DonTech Chicago, Il. 1992

Kane County

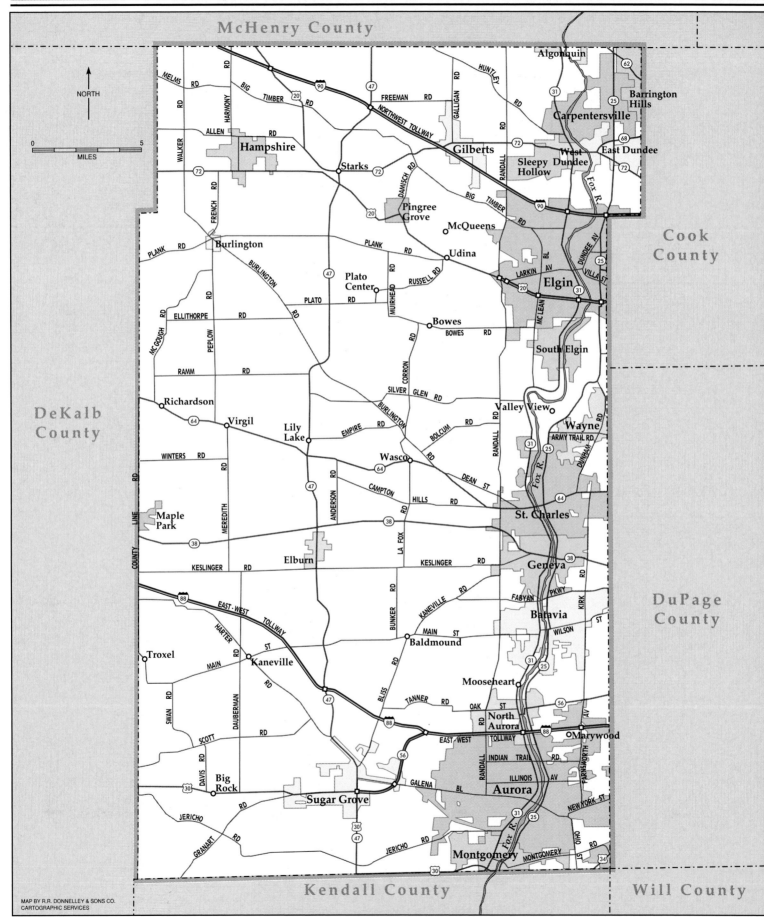

NORTH

0 — MILES — 5

McHenry County

Cook County

DeKalb County

DuPage County

Kendall County

Will County

Algonquin
Barrington Hills
Carpentersville
West Dundee
East Dundee
Sleepy Hollow
Gilberts
Hampshire
Starks
Pingree Grove
McQueens
Udina
Burlington
Plato Center
Bowes
Elgin
South Elgin
Richardson
Virgil
Lily Lake
Wasco
Valley View
Wayne
Maple Park
St. Charles
Elburn
Geneva
Troxel
Kaneville
Baldmound
Batavia
Mooseheart
North Aurora
Marywood
Big Rock
Sugar Grove
Aurora
Montgomery

MELMS RD
HARMONY RD
BIG TIMBER RD
ALLEN RD
WALKER RD
FREEMAN RD
HUNTLEY RD
GALLIGAN RD
NORTHWEST TOLLWAY
RANDALL RD
DUNDEE AV
VILLA ST
FOX R.
PLANK RD
FRENCH RD
BURLINGTON RD
PLANK RD
DAMISCH RD
MUIRHEAD RD
RUSSELL RD
PLATO RD
ELLITHORPE RD
McGOUGH RD
PEPLOW RD
RAMM RD
CORRON RD
BOWES RD
LARKIN AV
McLEAN BL
SILVER GLEN RD
WINTERS RD
MEREDITH RD
BURLINGTON RD
BOLCUM RD
ARMY TRAIL RD
DUNHAM RD
EMPIRE RD
CAMPTON HILLS RD
ANDERSON RD
DEAN ST
LA FOX RD
KESLINGER RD
KESLINGER RD
COUNTY LINE RD
EAST-WEST TOLLWAY
HARTER RD
MAIN ST
BUNKER RD
KANEVILLE RD
FABYAN PKWY
KIRK RD
WILSON ST
DAUBERMAN RD
SWAN RD
SCOTT RD
DAVIS RD
BLISS RD
TANNER RD
OAK ST
INDIAN TRAIL RD
FARNSWORTH AV
JERICHO RD
GRANART RD
GALENA BL
ILLINOIS AV
NEW YORK ST
MONTGOMERY RD
OHIO ST
JERICHO RD

MAP BY R.R. DONNELLEY & SONS CO.
CARTOGRAPHIC SERVICES

© DonTech Chicago, Il. 1992

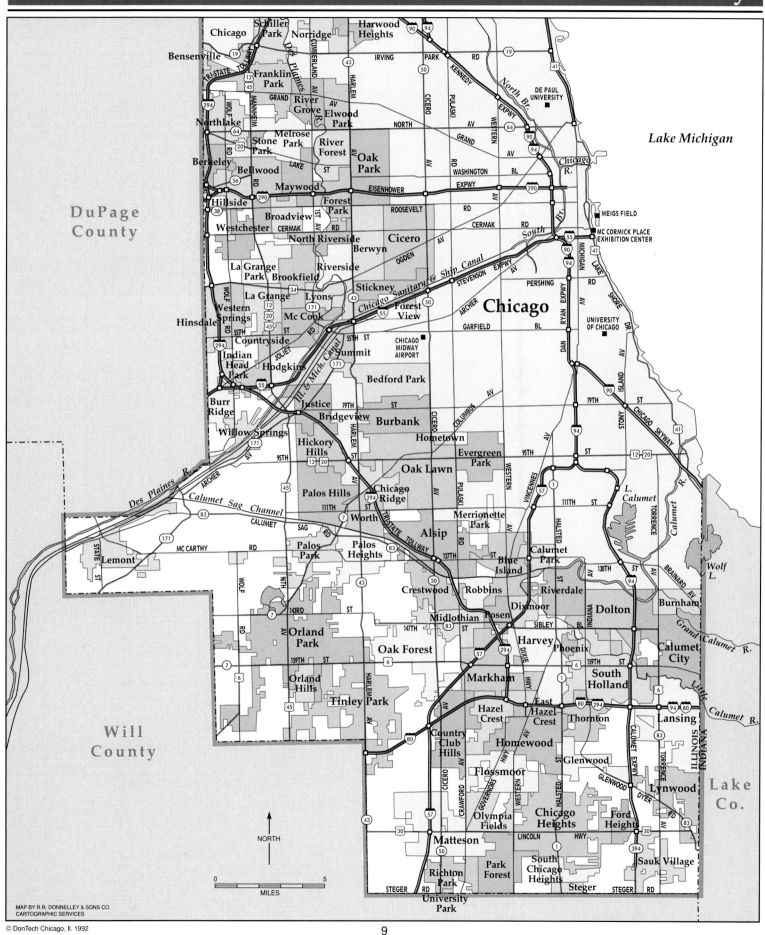

MAP BY R.R. Donnelley & Sons Co.
CARTOGRAPHIC SERVICES

© DonTech Chicago, Il. 1992

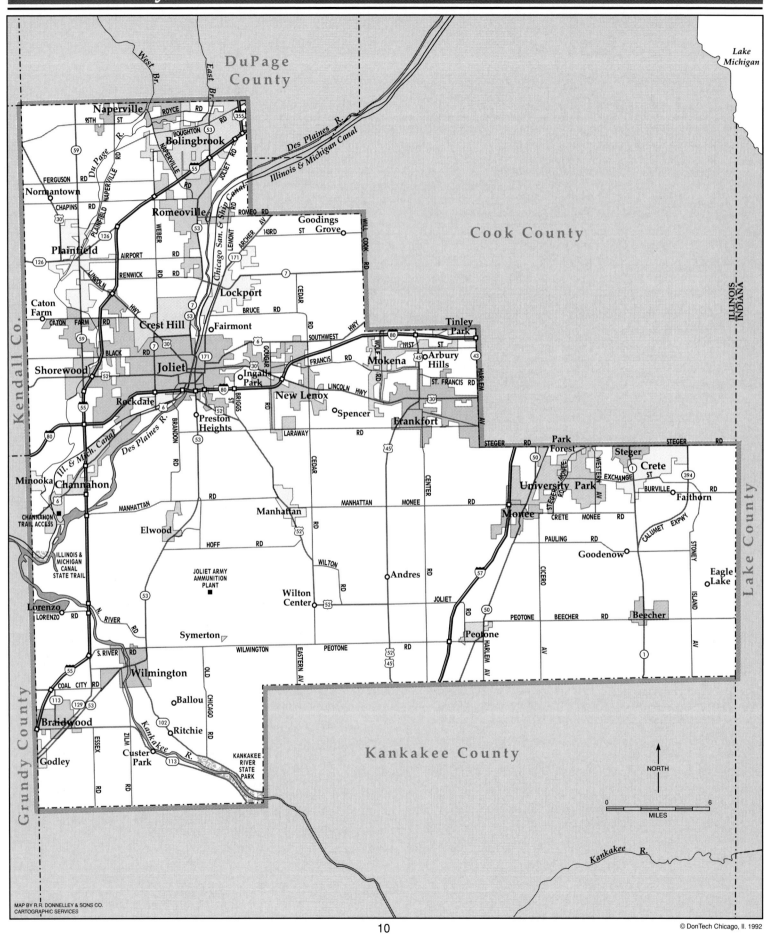

Will County map

DuPage County

Cook County

Kankakee County

Grundy County

Kendall Co.

Lake County

ILLINOIS
INDIANA

Lake
Michigan

Naperville
Bolingbrook
Romeoville
Normantown
Plainfield
Caton Farm
Crest Hill
Fairmont
Lockport
Goodings Grove
Shorewood
Joliet
Ingalls Park
Rockdale
New Lenox
Mokena
Arbury Hills
Tinley Park
Frankfort
Spencer
Preston Heights
Minooka
Channahon
Manhattan
Elwood
Park Forest
Steger
Crete
University Park
Faithorn
Monee
Goodenow
Burville
Eagle Lake
JOLIET ARMY AMMUNITION PLANT
Andres
Symerton
Wilton Center
Peotone
Beecher
Lorenzo
Wilmington
Ballou
Ritchie
Braidwood
Custer Park
Godley

ILLINOIS & MICHIGAN CANAL STATE TRAIL
CHANNAHON TRAIL ACCESS
KANKAKEE RIVER STATE PARK

Kankakee R.

NORTH

0 MILES 6

MAP BY R.R. DONNELLEY & SONS CO.
CARTOGRAPHIC SERVICES

© DonTech Chicago, Il. 1992

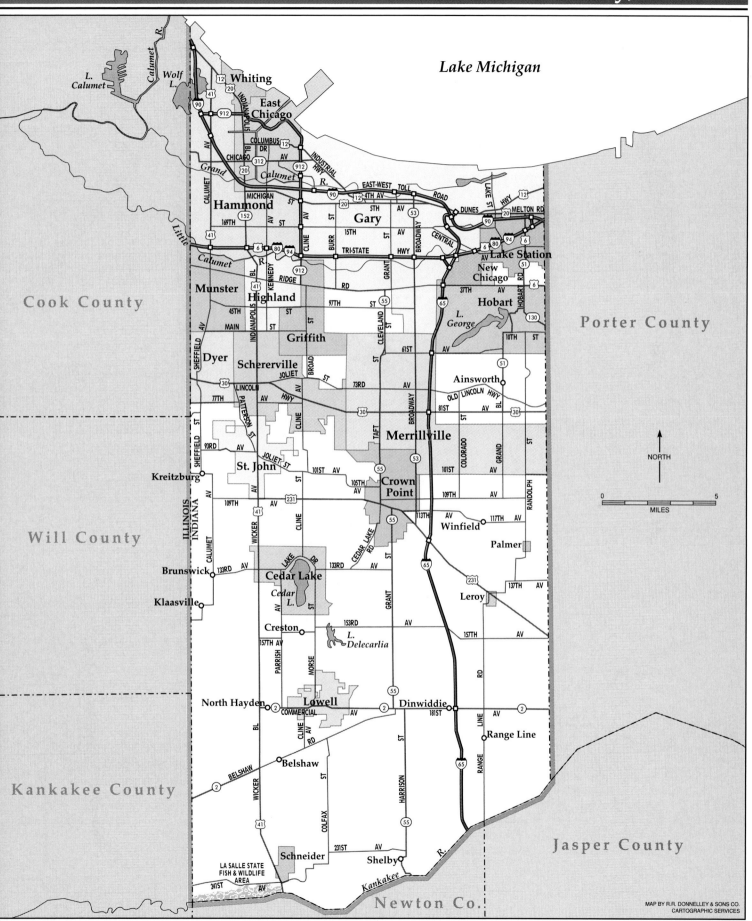

MAP BY R.R. DONNELLEY & SONS CO.
CARTOGRAPHIC SERVICES

© DonTech Chicago, Il. 1992

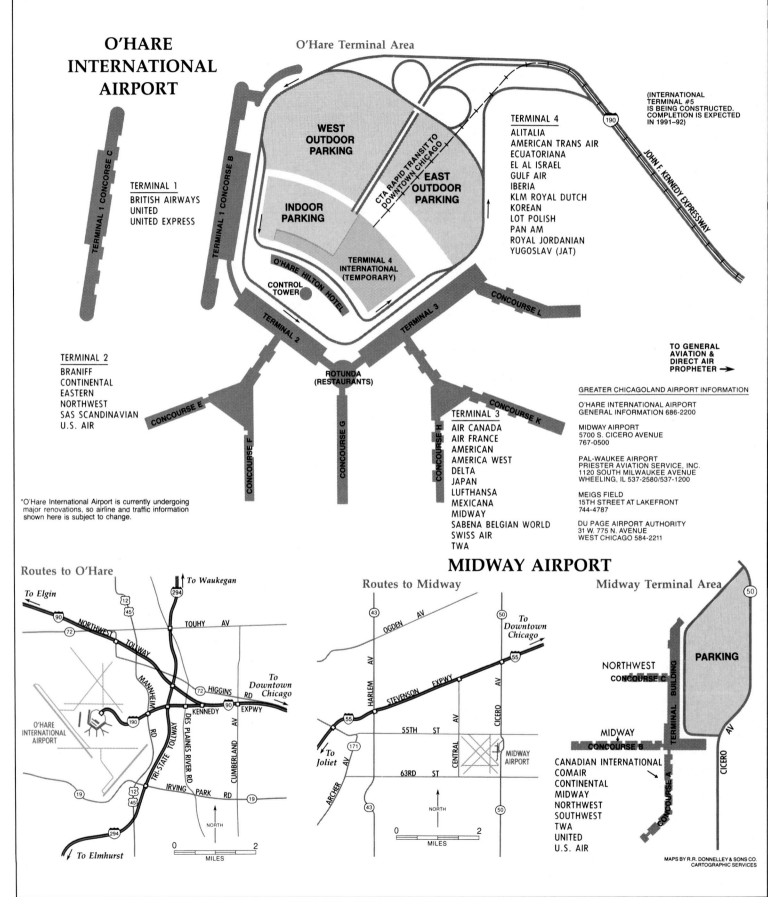

O'HARE INTERNATIONAL AIRPORT

O'Hare Terminal Area

WEST OUTDOOR PARKING

INDOOR PARKING

EAST OUTDOOR PARKING

CTA RAPID TRANSIT TO DOWNTOWN CHICAGO

TERMINAL 1 CONCORSE C

TERMINAL 1 CONCORSE B

TERMINAL 1
BRITISH AIRWAYS
UNITED
UNITED EXPRESS

O'HARE HILTON HOTEL

CONTROL TOWER

TERMINAL 4 INTERNATIONAL (TEMPORARY)

TERMINAL 2

TERMINAL 3

ROTUNDA (RESTAURANTS)

TERMINAL 2
BRANIFF
CONTINENTAL
EASTERN
NORTHWEST
SAS SCANDINAVIAN
U.S. AIR

CONCOURSE E

CONCOURSE F

CONCOURSE G

CONCOURSE H

CONCOURSE K

CONCOURSE L

TERMINAL 4
ALITALIA
AMERICAN TRANS AIR
ECUATORIANA
EL AL ISRAEL
GULF AIR
IBERIA
KLM ROYAL DUTCH
KOREAN
LOT POLISH
PAN AM
ROYAL JORDANIAN
YUGOSLAV (JAT)

TERMINAL 3
AIR CANADA
AIR FRANCE
AMERICAN
AMERICA WEST
DELTA
JAPAN
LUFTHANSA
MEXICANA
MIDWAY
SABENA BELGIAN WORLD
SWISS AIR
TWA

(INTERNATIONAL TERMINAL #5 IS BEING CONSTRUCTED. COMPLETION IS EXPECTED IN 1991–92)

JOHN F. KENNEDY EXPRESSWAY

190

TO GENERAL AVIATION & DIRECT AIR PROPHETER →

GREATER CHICAGOLAND AIRPORT INFORMATION

O'HARE INTERNATIONAL AIRPORT
GENERAL INFORMATION 686-2200

MIDWAY AIRPORT
5700 S. CICERO AVENUE
767-0500

PAL-WAUKEE AIRPORT
PRIESTER AVIATION SERVICE, INC.
1120 SOUTH MILWAUKEE AVENUE
WHEELING, IL 537-2580/537-1200

MEIGS FIELD
15TH STREET AT LAKEFRONT
744-4787

DU PAGE AIRPORT AUTHORITY
31 W. 775 N. AVENUE
WEST CHICAGO 584-2211

*O'Hare International Airport is currently undergoing major renovations, so airline and traffic information shown here is subject to change.

Routes to O'Hare

To Elgin
To Waukegan
294
12
45
90
72
NORTHWEST TOLLWAY
TOUHY AV
MANNHEIM RD
72
HIGGINS RD
190
DES PLAINES RIVER RD
KENNEDY EXPWY
90
CUMBERLAND AV
TRI-STATE TOLLWAY
To Downtown Chicago
O'HARE INTERNATIONAL AIRPORT
19
12
45
IRVING PARK RD
19
294
To Elmhurst

NORTH

0   2
MILES

Routes to Midway

43
OGDEN AV
50
To Downtown Chicago
HARLEM AV
STEVENSON EXPWY
55
55
CENTRAL AV
CICERO AV
55TH ST
MIDWAY AIRPORT
171
To Joliet
ARCHER
63RD ST
43
50

NORTH

0   2
MILES

MIDWAY AIRPORT

Midway Terminal Area

50

PARKING

NORTHWEST
CONCOURSE C

MIDWAY
CONCOURSE B

TERMINAL BUILDING

CICERO AV

CANADIAN INTERNATIONAL
COMAIR
CONTINENTAL
MIDWAY
NORTHWEST
SOUTHWEST
TWA
UNITED
U.S. AIR

CONCOURSE A

MAPS BY R.R. DONNELLEY & SONS CO. CARTOGRAPHIC SERVICES

© DonTech Chicago, Il. 1992

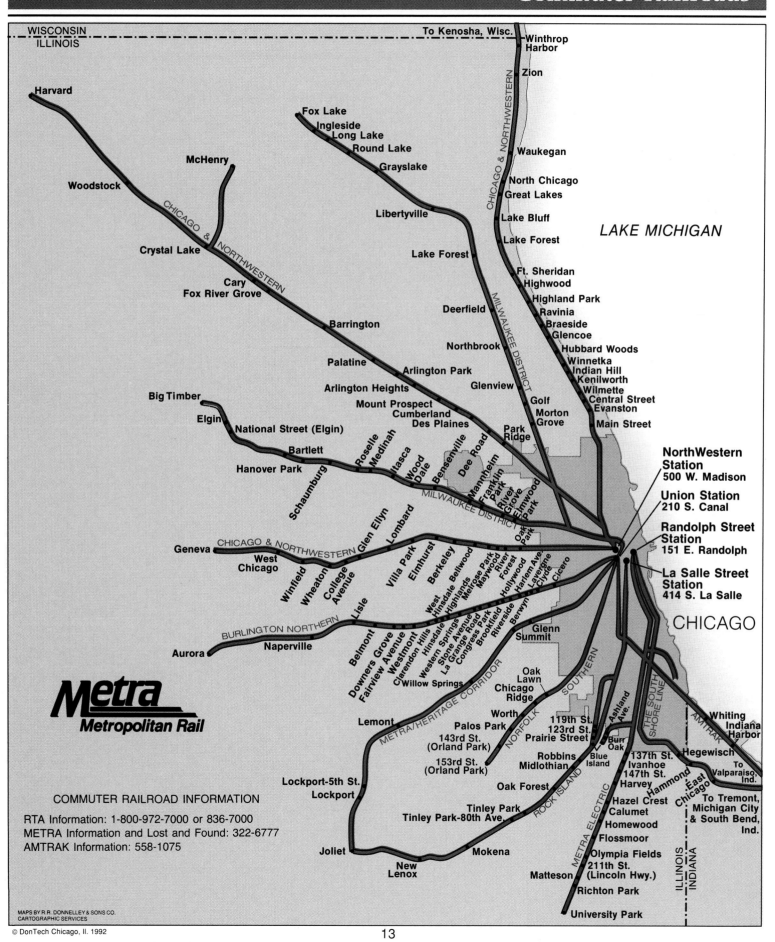

WISCONSIN
ILLINOIS

To Kenosha, Wisc.
Winthrop Harbor
Zion

Harvard

Fox Lake
Ingleside
Long Lake
Round Lake
Grayslake

Waukegan

North Chicago
Great Lakes

LAKE MICHIGAN

McHenry

Woodstock

CHICAGO & NORTHWESTERN

Libertyville

Lake Bluff
Lake Forest

Crystal Lake

Lake Forest

Ft. Sheridan
Highwood
Highland Park
Ravinia
Braeside
Glencoe
Hubbard Woods
Winnetka
Indian Hill
Kenilworth
Wilmette
Central Street
Evanston
Main Street

Cary
Fox River Grove

Barrington

Deerfield

Northbrook

Golf
Morton Grove

MILWAUKEE DISTRICT

Palatine

Arlington Park

Glenview

Arlington Heights

Big Timber

Mount Prospect
Cumberland
Des Plaines

Park Ridge

NorthWestern Station
500 W. Madison

Elgin

National Street (Elgin)

Bartlett

Roselle
Medinah
Itasca
Wood Dale

Bensenville

Dee Road

Union Station
210 S. Canal

Hanover Park

Schaumburg

Mannheim
Franklin Park
River Grove
Elmwood Park

MILWAUKEE DISTRICT

Oak Park

Randolph Street Station
151 E. Randolph

Geneva

CHICAGO & NORTHWESTERN

Glen Ellyn
Lombard

Elmhurst

La Salle Street Station
414 S. La Salle

West Chicago

Winfield
Wheaton
College Avenue

Villa Park

Berkeley

West Hinsdale
Highlands
Hinsdale
Western Springs
Stone Avenue
La Grange Road
Congress Park
Brookfield
Riverside
Hollywood
Berwyn
Harlem Ave.
Laverne
Clyde
Cicero

Bellwood
Melrose Park
Maywood
River Forest

CHICAGO

Lisie

BURLINGTON NORTHERN

Belmont
Downers Grove
Fairview Avenue
Westmont
Clarendon Hills

Glenn
Summit

Aurora

Naperville

Willow Springs

METRA/HERITAGE CORRIDOR

Oak Lawn
Chicago Ridge

SOUTHERN

Metra
Metropolitan Rail

Lemont

Worth
Palos Park
143rd St. (Orland Park)
153rd St. (Orland Park)

Prairie Street

119th St.
123rd St.

Ashland Ave.

THE SOUTH SHORE LINE

Whiting
Indiana Harbor

AMTRAK

Robbins
Midlothian

Burr Oak
Blue Island

137th St.
Ivanhoe
147th St.
Harvey

Hegewisch

To Valparaiso, Ind.

Lockport-5th St.
Lockport

Oak Forest

NORFOLK

Hazel Crest
Calumet
Homewood
Flossmoor

Hammond
East Chicago

To Tremont, Michigan City & South Bend, Ind.

ROCK ISLAND

METRA ELECTRIC

Tinley Park
Tinley Park-80th Ave.

Joliet

New Lenox

Mokena

Matteson

Olympia Fields
211th St. (Lincoln Hwy.)
Richton Park

ILLINOIS
INDIANA

University Park

COMMUTER RAILROAD INFORMATION

RTA Information: 1-800-972-7000 or 836-7000
METRA Information and Lost and Found: 322-6777
AMTRAK Information: 558-1075

MAPS BY R.R. DONNELLEY & SONS CO.
CARTOGRAPHIC SERVICES

© DonTech Chicago, Il. 1992

Addison

Street	Grid
ADAMS DR-N	G4
ADDISON RD-N	**G5**
ADDISON RD-S	**G2**
ADELINE AV	F4-F2
ALDEN DR	H4
AMELIA LN	B6-C6
ANNORENO DR	E3
ANVIL CT	E7
ARDMORE AV	H1
ARDMORE TERR	H3
ARI CT	B3
ARMITAGE AV-E	H2
ARMITAGE CT-W	C2
ARMY TRAIL RD	**A5-E4**
ASCOT PL	C8
ASHLEY LN	D7
ASHWOOD CT	D7
ASPEN WAY	D7
AUTUMN TR	C8
BABBITT AV-N	E7
BABCOCK AV	I3
BARNWALL DR	D4
BAYBROOK CT	D7
BAYNARD RD-N	E5
BEACH DR	E7
BELDEN AV-E	H2
BELDEN AV-W	F2
BELMONT AV	I5
BELMONT PL-W	C5
BERNARD DR	C3
BEVERLY AV	H2
BLECKE AV	G2
BRASHARES DR	E5
BRIARHILL LN	E6
BRIDLE TERR	C7
BROADVIEW AV	C5-C4
BRUCE AV	I4-I5
BYRON AV	D6-F6
CAMBRIDGE ROW	B6
CAPITOL DR	D3
CARDINAL AV	I4-I5
CARMELA CT	C6
CASTLE RD	C5
CATALPA	I5
CEDAR ST	I5
CENTRAL AV-N	G4
CENTRAL CT	C5-C4
CENTRAL RD	C7
CHATHAM AV	H2
CHERRY HILL CT	H3
CHERRY HILL DR	H3
CHESTNUT ST	G5
CHURCH ST	G3
CIRCLE DR	F3
CLAREDON AV-S	F4-F1
CLOVER CT	D8
COLLINS AV	B3
COMMERCIAL RD	G2
COMPTON PT-W	D5
COMSTOCK AV	H2
CONGRESS AV	H3
COPORATE DR	A4
CORTLAND CT-W	C2
COUNTRY CLUB DR	E5
CRAIG PL	F6
CROCKETT AV	I2
DALE AV	F4
DALE DR	F4
DENISE CT	G5
DIVERSEY AV-E	E4-G4
DIVERSEY AV-W	C4
DIVERSEY BL	I4
DOUGLAS AV	I2
DRAKE AV	H3
DU PAGE AV	C5
DU PAGE CT	C5
EDGEWOOD AV	F1
EDGEWOOD AV-N	F2
EGGERDING DR	E7
ELIZABETH DR-W	G5
ELIZABETH ST	F2
ELLSWORTH AV	I2-I5
ELM ST	B1
ELMWOOD AV	H5
EVERGREEN AV-N	F4
EXECUTIVE DR	A4
FACTORY RD	E2-F2
FAIRBANK ST	D3
FARMWOOD DR	D7
FAY AV-E	H2
FAY AV-W	F2
FIENE DR	G2
FISCHER DR-N	E7
FLORA PKWY-N	D4
FOREST CT-N	I5
FOREST DR	I5
FOXDALE DR	C8
FRIARS CT-N	D5
FULLERTON AV-E	**G4**
FULLERTON AV-W	**C4**
FULTON AV	**I2**
GERRI LN	F1
GLADYS AV	H2-I2
GOLDEN GATE CT	C6
GOLDEN GATE DR	C6
GRACE ST	E2
GRAMERCY LN-W	D4
GRANT DR-N	G6
GRANT DR-S	F4
GREEN MEADOW DR	G5
GREEN OAKS CT-E	F5
GREEN OAKS CT-N	F5
GREEN OAKS CT-S	F5
GREEN RIDGE ST	C5
GROVE AV	F4
HADDON PL-N	D5
HALE ST-S	G3
HARROW CT	B6
HARVARD AV-S	H3
HEATHER CT	E7
HERITAGE CT	E4
HERITAGE DR	E4
HICKORY PL	E7
HICKORY TRAIL	D7
HIGHVIEW AV-N	F6
HIGHVIEW AV-S	F4
HIGHVIEW BL	F5
HILTON AV	H3
HOLLY CT-E	I5
HOLTZ AV-W	B6-D6
HONEY HILL RD	E7
HOWARD AV	F6
HORSESHOE CT	D4
HUNTER CT	D7
INDUSTRIAL RD	G3
INTERSTATE RD	F2
IOWA AV-N	G4
IOWA AV-S	G2
IRMEN DR	F3
ITASCA RD	D7
JAMEY LN	I5
JANICE LN	G6
JEFFREY DR	D3
JOSEPH LN	E7
JOYCE LN	H4
JUSTIN CT	I5
KAY AV-S	F2
KEEBLE CT	E7
KENDALL TRAIL-W	D5
KENMORE ST	B5
KENNEDY DR-N	G5
KINGERY CT	I3
KINGS POINT DR EAST	C6
KINGS POINT DR NORTH	B6
KINGS POINT DR SOUTH	B6
KINGS POINT DR WEST	B6
KINGSTON DR-N	D5
KRAGE DR	I3
LAKE ST-E	**H4**
LAKE ST-W	**A8-D6**
LAKE MANOR DR	E3
LAKE PARK DR-W	F3
LA LONDE AV	E3
LA PORTE CT	H4
LA PORTE DR	H4
LANCERS DR	C5
LAURA DR	F2-G2
LAWLER AV-N	B6
LENORE ST	G6
LILAC LN	D8
LINCOLN AV-N	F5-F2
LINCOLN AV-S	F4-G4
LINCOLN CT-N	F5
LINCOLN ST	F6
LINDA LN	C6-C4-F6
LOIS AV-N	E6
LOMBARD RD-N	C4
LOMBARD RD-S	C1
LORRAINE AV-E	H3-I3
LULLO DR	G6
MACIE CT-N	G5
MAPLE AV	H4
MAPLE CT	H4
MAPLE ST-N	I5
MARE BARN LN	E7
MARILYN TERR	G6
MAVIS LN	G6
MAY ST-N	G4
MC NAIR AV	I3
MEADOW AV	A4-F6
MEADOWS BL	B6
MEMORY LN	F4
MEYER DR-W	D6
MICHAEL LN	G5
MICHIGAN AV-N	H3
MICHIGAN AV-S	H2
MICHIGAN CT	H3
MILL MEADOWS LN	E4
MILL RD-N	F6
MILL RD-S	F4
MILLINS CT	F7
MILLINS LN	F7
MITCHELL CT	B3
MONARCH LN	C5
MORELAND AV-E	C4-G4
MORELAND AV-W	E5
MORRIS AV	E5
MULLOY DR	B6-C6
MYRICK AV-E	G4
MYRICK AV-W	F4
NATALIE LN	F4
NATIONAL AV-W	D4
NATOMA ST-E	G4
NATOMA ST-W	F4
NEVA AV	F6
NORDIC BLVD	B6
NORMANDY DR	H4
NORTH AV	H5
NUGENT AV	G5
OAK ST-E	H5
OAK ST-W	F5
OAKLEAF DR-N	I5
OFFICIAL RD	G3
OLD FENCE RD	E7
OLD GRAND AV	I4
OVERKAMP AV	G5
PALMER AV-E	G3
PARK AV	F3
PARK PL	F6
PARKVIEW DR	F3
PFUND AV	I4
PIONEER DR	D5-E5
PLAMONDON DR-N	C5
PLEASANT DR	F6
POWER CT	G3
PRAIRIE DR	D4
PRINCETON ST-S	H3
RACQUET CLUB DR	E3
RAMPART RD	C5
REED CT	B6
REGAL CT	C5
REPUBLIC DR	D3
RICHARD CT	F4
ROHLWING RD	**B2-C6**
RONALD DR	E6
ROSE AV	F4
ROSEBUD LN	D8
ROUTE 53-N	**C4**
ROUTE 53-S	**C1**
ROUTE 83-S	**I1-5**
ROYAL DR	C7
ROZANNE CT	G6
ROZANNE DR	G6
RUGA CT	G4
RUGELEY CT-W	D5
RUMPLE LN	B6
SABLE DR	D7-E7
SADDLE RD	C8
ST AUBIN DR	E7
SCARLET CT	C7
SCARLET DR	C7
SCHOOL ST-N	G4-G6
SHARON DR	F6
SHERRY LN	B5
SHERWOOD DR-E	I5
SIDNEY AV	B1-G1
SIDNEY CT	I1
SQUIRE LN	C8
STATE ST	H5
STEVENS DR	F6
STEWART AV	E3
STILES DR	F2
STONE AV	F5
STONE MILL AV	E5
SUMNER ST	F6
SUNRISE RD	I3
SUNSET DR	I4
SURREY RD	D7
SWIFT RD	**A4-A7**
SWIFTON COMMONS BL	A6
TALLYHO CT	C8
TALLYHO DR	D8
THATCHER LN	D7
TRINITY DR	D8
VALERIE LN	G5
VICTORY PKWY	H4
VILLA AV-S	**I2-H3**
VISTA AV	F4-F2
WAVELAND AV	F7
WESLEY DR	E5
WESTGATE ST	G2
WESTRIDGE PL	D7
WESTVIEW CT	H2
WESTWOOD AV-S	F2
WESTWOOD DR	D5
WHITE FENCE LN	E7
WILLOW GLEN ST	F6
WINDSOR CT	A4
WINTHROP AV-E	H2
WINTHROP AV-W	E1-F1
WISCONSIN AV-N	G3
WISCONSIN AV-S	G2
WOOD AV	D7
WOOD ST	D7
WOOD DALE RD	H6
WOOD DALE RD-N	H7
WOODLAND AV	H4
WRIGHTWOOD AV-E	E3-H6-H3
WRIGHTWOOD AV-W	C5
WRIGHTWOOD CT-W	C3
WYNCROFT PL	B6
YALE AV-S	H3
1ST AV	E6
2ND AV	E6
3RD AV	E6
8TH AV	D6
9TH AV	D6
10TH AV	D6
11TH AV	D6

Unincorporated Addison Area

Street	Grid
ADELE AV	H1
ADELE CT	I1
ANN CT	C6
ARTHUR AV	H5
BARRY AV	E6
BYRON AV	C6
DUPAGE AV	D1
EDWARDS DR	A5
FAIRFIELD AV	E1
GROVE AV	D8
HILLCREST AV	H5
JO ANN LN	C6
JO CT	C6
JOYCE AV	F1
LA LONDE AV	E1
LYDIA RD	A4
MAIN ST	D1
MEADOW RD	A4
MEDINAH RD	A7-A8
NILES AV	C6
NORTH AV	**D1-H1**
PARK AV-W	A3
PETERSEN AV	B1
PRINCETON AV	H1
PROGRESS RD	D1
RIDGE AV	D1
ROBBIE LN	A5
STONE AV	A5-H5
VALLEY VIEW RD	A5
VERRILL AV	H5
WALTER DR	A5
WOODLAND AV-E	H6
YALE AV-S	H1
4TH AV	E6
5TH AV	E6
6TH AV	E6
7TH AV	E6

© DonTech Chicago, Il. 1992

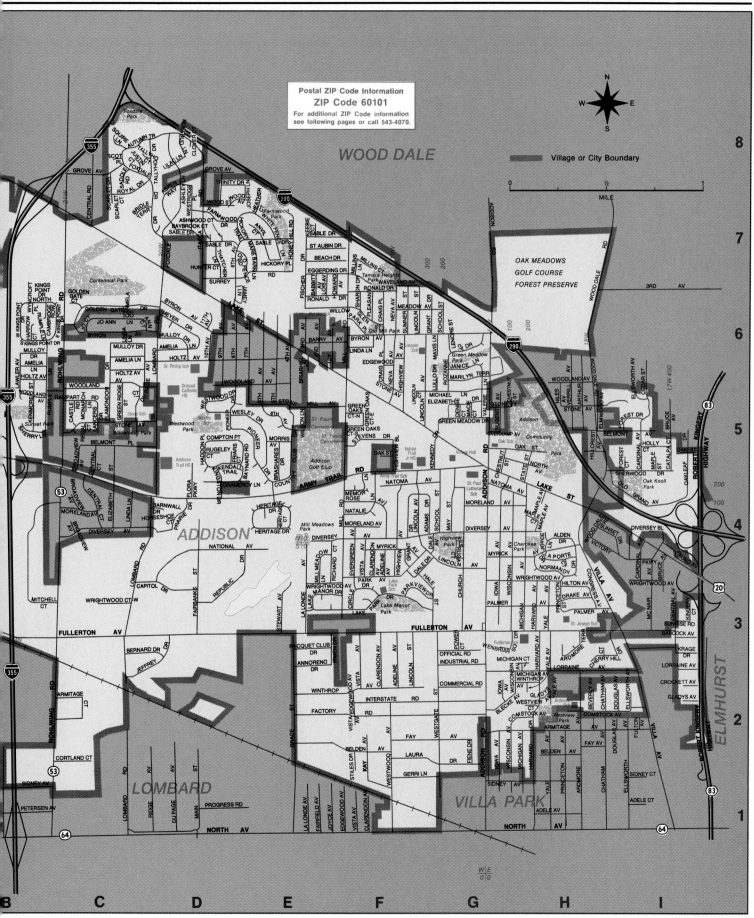

WOOD DALE

Postal ZIP Code Information
ZIP Code 60101
For additional ZIP Code information
see following pages or call 543-4070.

Village or City Boundary

0   ½   1
MILE

OAK MEADOWS
GOLF COURSE
FOREST PRESERVE

ADDISON

LOMBARD

VILLA PARK

ELMHURST

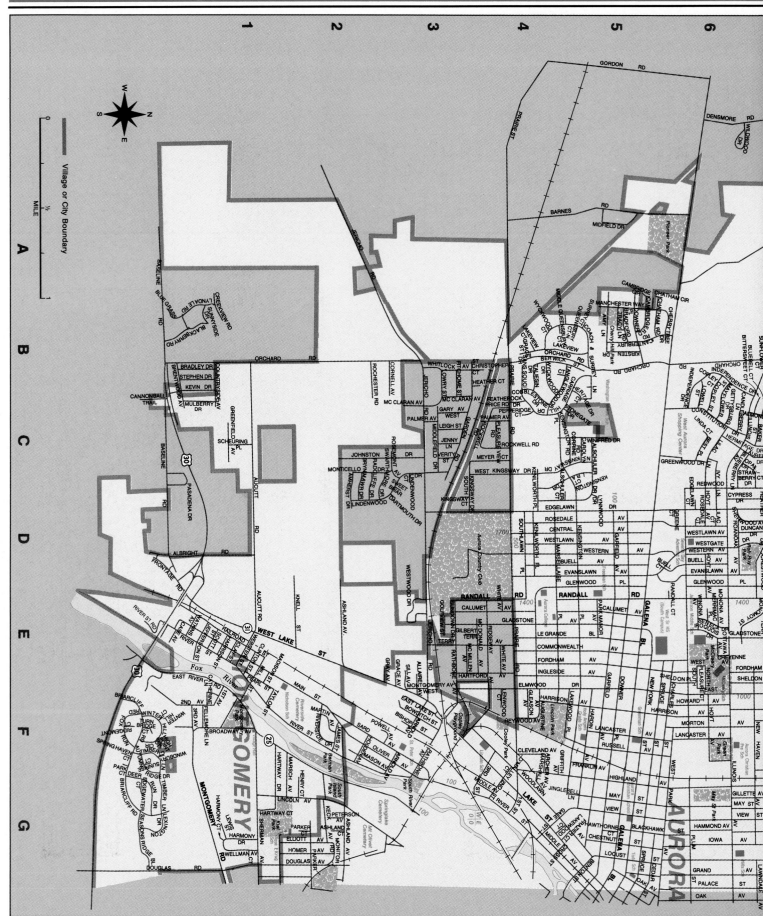

© DonTech Chicago, Il. 1992

Aurora post office lock box patrons ZIP Code is 60504
Rural routes ZIP Code is 60507

60542
60506
60538
60538
60505
60504

AURORA
NORTH AURORA
MONTGOMERY
Fox River

For additional ZIP Code information see following pages or call:

Aurora	897-2221
Montgomery	897-0153
North Aurora	896-3836

Village or City Boundary

© DonTech Chicago, Il. 1992

© DonTech Chicago, Il. 1992

Village or City Boundary

© DonTech Chicago, Il. 1992

© DonTech Chicago, Il. 1992

Aurora Area Street Guides

Aurora

© DonTech Chicago, Il. 1992

PERSIMMON CT P4
PETERSON AV G2
PHEASANT RUN LN O2
PHOENIX CT I6
PIERGE ST I6
PIN OAK TR E8
PINE AV I7
PINE CONE CT N12
PINE GROVE CT N2
PINE LAKE DR Q1
PINELAND CT O2
PINETREE CT M12
PINEY AV G4
PLAIN AV K6
PLEASANT PL I1
PLEASANT TERR J7
PLEASURE CT EAST E6
PLEASURE CT NORTH E6
PLEARURE CT SOUTH E6
PLEASURE CT WEST E6
PLUM ST G6
PORTLAND CT O4
PORTLAND LN O4
PORTSMOUTH M1
POST RD F8
POWELL AV F3
PRAIRIE PATH J8
PRAIRIE RD C4
PRAIRIEVIEW N11
PRESTON CT N11
PRIMROSE P4
PRIMROSE CT P5
PRINCETON AV P4
QUAIL CT O12
QUEENSBURY CT-N B4
QUINCY CT O1
QUINCY LN O1
RADCLIFF LN O8
RAINTREE CT P4
RAINWOOD DR D7
RANDALL CT D6
RANDALL RD-N E5
RANDALL RD-S E4
RATHBONE AV F3
RECKINGER RD K8
REDBUD CT N12
REDBUD LN N12
REDWOOD DR C6
REGENCY CT Q3
REISING ST I6
RESERVE CT N8
RICHARD AV K9
RICHARD ST C7-F7
RICHLAND CT O4
RICHLAND LN O4
RICHMOND LN N4
RIDGE AV M1
RIVER ST H5
RIVERWOOD CT N12
ROANOAK AV D6
ROBERT CT C7
ROBERT ST C7-F7
ROBINHOOD DR I9
ROBINWOOD DR F8
ROOSEVELT CT I5
ROOT ST I4-I6
ROSE ST J4
ROSEDALE AV-N D5
ROSEDALE AV-S D4
ROSEDALE CT D6
ROSEWOOD AV G4
RUMFORD CT O2
RURAL ST I6
RUSSELL AV-N F7
RUSSELL AV-S F5
RUSSELL CIR F7
RUSSELL CT F7
RUSSELL DR F7
ST JOSEPH AV I6
SALEM CT O3
SANDBURG ST C7
SANDPEBBLE P4
SANDPIPER P4
SANDPIPER CT P5
SANDY LN F9
SANS SOUCI DR B4
SAPPHIRE LN C7
SARAH LN M7
SARD AV F3
SCARLET OAK CIR E8
SCHILLER AV J5
SCHOMER AV I3
SELMARTEN RD L9
SEMINARY AV H3
SENECA DR E6
SEQUOIA DR D9
SEXTON ST G3
SHADY LN B7
SHADYBROOK LN P4
SHAMROCK CT K9
SHANNON DR J7
SHAWANO DR L7
SHEFFER RD J7-N7
SHEFFIELD M1
SHELDON AV E6
SHELDON PL E6
SHERIDAN ST J6
SHERMAN ST J7
SHERWOOD AV D6
SHERWOOD DR I9
SILL AV E3
SILVER CREEK CT Q1
SIMMS ST I2
SIRIUS AV E7
SIVIS RD F6
SMITH BL-S J3
SMITH ST-N J5
SMITH ST-S J4
SOCIETY HILL LN Q1
SOLFISBURG AV K6
SOMERSET CT P5
SOUTH AV H3
SOUTH RD O4
SOUTH BRIDGE DR F8
SOUTHGATE CT N2
SOUTHLAWN PL D4
SPENCER ST-N I4
SPENCER ST-S I1
SPERRY CT H3
SPRING ST I5
SPRINGBROOK DR F9
SPRING LAKE LN P4
SPRUCE ST F5
SQUIRE CT J9
SQUIRE DR J9
STANTON CT N11
STAR AV J8
STATE ST-N I4
STATE ST-S J2
STOLP AV-N H5
STOLP AV-S H5
STONE AV H4
STONEBRIDGE BL N9
STONEGATE DR C4
STONEYBROOK LN N11
STRATFORD CT P3
STRAWBERRY CT C6
STREAMWOOD LN N11
STUART AV J5
STUBBLEFIELD CT N11
SULLIVAN RD E8-H9
SUMMIT AV J4
SUMNER AV-N K5
SUMNER AV-S K3
SUNFLOWER CT B6
SUNLIGHT CT N12
SUNSET AV G7
SUNTREE CT P1
SUPERIOR ST J6
SURREY CT B5
SUSSEX AV Q6
SWEET BRIAR C3
SYCAMORE LN M1
T ST H4
TALIESIN DR B4
TALL OAKS DR L9
TALMA ST H2
TANGLEWOOD CT B4
TANGLEWOOD DR B4
TANNER RD C7
TAYLOR AV F7
TERRY AV E3
THORNLY CT N3
THURSTON CT M8
TIMBER HILL CT O2
TIMBER HILL LN O2
TIMBERLAKE CT D7
TINLEY DR F9
TITSWORTH CT G4
TOLLVIEW TERR K7
TRACY LN B6
TRADE ST Q4
TRAFALGAR M1
TRALEE CT P1
TRASK RD J7
TRASK ST J5
UNION ST-N I5
UNION ST-S I3
UPPER BRANDON DR F8
VALAYNA CT N1
VALAYNA DR N1
VALLEY AV I5
VAUGHN CT N1
VAUGHN RD M3-N6
VERMONT AV K5
VIEW ST G5
VIEW ST-N G6
VILLAGE CT N2
VILLAGE GREEN DR O3
VINE ST H5
VIOLET ST L9
WALCOTT RD M2
WALDEN CIR D8
WALTER AV J3
WARDIN CT N1
WARREN AV G3
WASHINGTON ST H4
WATER ST H5
WATERBURY DR M3
WATERFORD CT N11
WATSON ST I3
WEBSTER AV J4
WEBSTER AV-S J3
WELSH DR M5
WENNMACHER LN I7
WENTWORTH LN M9
WEST ST I4
WEST HAMPTON CT P4
WEST LAKE ST E2
WEST PARK AV G6
WEST PARK PL H5
WESTBROOK DR Q4
WESTERN AV-N D6
WESTERN AV-S D5
WESTGATE DR D6
WESTLAWN AV-N D6
WESTLAWN AV-S D4
WESTLEIGH M1
WESTMOOR CT M4
WESTON AV H3
WESTWOOD DR E3
WEXFORD PL Q1
WHEATFIELD FERRY N11
WHEATLAND LN O2
WHITEBARN RD N11
WHITE EAGLE DR P1
WHITE EAGLE DR-W P1
WHITE HALL CT N3
WHITTINGHAM ST L1
WILDER ST H6
WILLIAMS ST H6
WILLOUGHBY LN N12
WILLOW CT N2
WILLOW FALLS CT O3
WILLOWVIEW LN O3
WILSHIRE CT N11
WINBERIE AV Q1
WINBERIE CT Q1
WINCHESTER CT-E O1
WINDMERE CT N2
WINDMERE LN N2
WINDSOR AV J3
WINDSTREAM P5
WINGATE CT N11
WINIFRED DR C5
WINONA AV E6
WOOD ST J6-J7
WOOD CREST CIR M9
WOODLAND AV L5
WOODLAWN AV G4
WOODLYN DR I9
WOODRUFF ST J5
WRIGHT CT M5
WYCKWOOD CT B4
WORCESTER LN O2
WYCKWOOD DR B4
WYNDHAM LN M3
YORKSHIRE CT N11
ZENGELE AV I6
ZENNER AV I7
ZIEGLER AV J3
1ST ST G4
2ND AV I4
2ND ST F4
3RD ST-N F4
4TH AV I3
4TH ST-N I5
4TH ST-S H2
5TH AV I3-M3
5TH ST H3
6TH AV I3
7TH AV I3
75TH ST Q3
83RD ST O1
87TH ST O1

Unincorporated Aurora Area

ADELINE CT K9
AMHERST DR D2
ANDY LN J6
ANN'S LN J6
ARLENE DR I9
AUCUTT RD D1
AUDREY AV J9
AUGUSTA DR H12
BARTSON LN L7
BASELINE RD C1
BECKER LN K7
BIRCHWOOD RD K7
BLACKBERRY RD B1
BLUE GRASS DR B1
BRADLEY DR B1
BRYANT ST E9
BRYN MAWR DR C2
CALIFORNIA CT E7
CAMBRIDGE CIR A5
CAMBRIDGE RD B5
CAMEL RD J8
CANNONBALL TRAIL C1
CANTIGNY CT H12
CAROL PL J1
CAROL LYNN ST L10
CAROLYN DR I9
CAROLYN DR EAST L10
CHATHAM CIR A5
CHATHAM RD B5
CHERRYTREE DR B6
CONNIE CT K9
CORNELL AV C3
CRANE AV L6
CREEKVIEW RD A1
CYPRESS CT H12
DARTMOUTH DR C3
DAWES ST E9
DEAD MAN LN A5
DEERPATH RD A7
DENSMORE RD A7
DIEHL RD K9
DORAL LN H12
DOUGLAS ST E9
EASTVIEW DR F12
EDGEWOOD AV L4
ELIZABETH LN K9
EOLA RD M1
EXPOSITION AV E9
FARNSWORTH AV K2
FELTES LN I10
FIDLER RD K1
FITCHOME ST B3
FOREST DR N4
FORREST DR K7
FREEMAN ST K6
FRIAR DR I9
FRONTENAC RD P5
GARDEN RD C3
GARDINER ST J6
GARY AV K9
GARY AV WEST C3
GERTEN AV J9
GILBERT TERR E3
GILMORE ST E9
GRANDVIEW DR L4
HANKES RD A7
HART RD I12
HARTFORD AV E4
HASTINGS AV L8
HEATHER CT B3
HILL AV K2
HILLTOP DR F12
INDIANA ST E9
JENNY LN C3
JOHNS LN J6
JOHNSON DR C3
KEVIN DR B1
KINGSTON AV J1
KINGSWAY CT C3
KINGSWAY DR SOUTH C3
KREEZ RD L7
LEIGH ST C3
LENWOOD CT F4
LINDENWOOD CT C3
LINDENWOOD DR C3
LOWRY ST B3
LYNDALE RD B1
MAPLE ST E9
MARGARET'S LN J9
MARILYN LN J9
MARION AV K9
MARYWOOD AV-W J8
MC CLARAN AV C3
MC DONALD AV E4
MC MILLEN AV E3
MEADOW RD Q11
MERIDIAN RD Q11
METTEL RD I9
MEYER CT C4
MIDDLEFIELD DR C3
MONTICELLO DR C2
NAN ST L10
OAK CREST DR H12
OAK MANOR RD J8
OAKVIEW AV L4
OAKWOOD AV J8
PALMER AV C4
PARKSIDE AV L4
PARKVIEW DR L11
PERSHING ST E9
PINEHURST CT H12
PINEHURST DR H12
PLEASURE VIEW RD C4
POSS RD O7
PRAIRIE ST E9
PRICE RD C4
RADCLIFFE DR C2
RADDANT RD J12
RED OAK DR L8
REID PL O7
RIDGEWAY AV E4
ROCHESTER RD B2
ROCKWELL RD C4
ROSEMONT AV C3
SADDLE LN I8
SAWGRASS ST H12
SHAGBARK LN A7
ST CHRISTOPHER CT B3
SARTOR LN M6
SCHOMER RD J9
SPYGLASS CT H12
STEPHEN ST B1
STEPHENS RD L7
SUNDOWN DR E3
SUNNYSIDE DR B1
SUNRISE RD Q11
SWARTHMORE DR C2
THOMPSON LN L3
TURNBERRY DR H12
TURNER RD I8
VALLEY RD F12
VERITY ST C3
VICTOR RD J8
WABANSIA AV H1
WERMES AV K4
WEST RIDGE RD A7
WHITE AV E4
WHITLOCK AV B3
WILDWOOD DR A6
WINGFOOT DR H12
WOODLAND DR J8
WOODLAWN AV L4
WOODSIDE LN L8
YOUNGS AV K4
4TH ST O7

Montgomery

ALBRIGHT RD D1
ALL STEEL DR E2
AMBER DR J1
AUCUTT RD D1
AUTUMN RIDGE DR F1
BRENTWOOD AV B1
BRIARCLIFF RD F1
BROADWAY AV-S F1
CASE AV E1
CATHERINE LN F1
CLAY ST E1
CLINTON ST E1
COUNTRYSIDE AV B1
CROWN ST J1
DAWN AV J1
DEER RUN DR F1
DOUGLAS RD G1
EAST RIVER RD-S E1
EDGEWATER CT F1
FELLEMORE LN F1
FRONTAGE RD F1
GREENFIELD AV C1
HARMONY CT G1
HARMONY DR G1
HARRISON ST E1
HARTWAY CT F1
HARTWAY DR G1
HENRY CT G2
HIGH POINT CT F1
HINCKLEY ST H1
JAMES ST F2
JEFFERSON ST E1
KECK AV G2
KIMBERLY LN J1
KNELL ST E2
LEWIS ST G1
LEXINGTON DR G1
LINCOLN AV-S G2
MADISON ST E1
MAIN ST-N E1
MAIN ST-S E1
MARSCH AV F2
MARTIN AV F2
MILL ST E1
MONTGOMERY RD G1
MULBERRY DR C1
PARK CT F1
PARK DR J1
PARKER AV G2
PARKER CT G2
PASADENA DR E1
PEARL ST E1
RAILROAD ST-N E1
RAILROAD ST-S E1
RAYMOND DR J1
RED FOX RUN F1
RIDGEMONT CT F1
RIVER ST E1
RIVER ST RD E1
RIVERSIDE DR F2
ROYAL DR J1
SARD AV G2
SCHEURING PL C1
SCOTT ST E1
SEASONS RIDGE BL G1
SHERMAN AV G1
SPRING HAVEN CT F1
SUNRISE CT F1
TAYLOR ST F1
TIMBER LN DR F1
TURNBRIDGE CT F1
WATKINS AV E1
WEBSTER ST E1
WELLMAN AV G1
WELLMAN CT G1
WEST LAKE ST E1
WINDBURY CT F1
WINTER HILL CIR F1
WINTER HILL CT F1
1ST AV F1
2ND AV F1
3RD AV F1
4TH ST H1
14TH AV J1

North Aurora

ABBEYWOOD LN F11
ACCESS RD E11
ACORN DR E11
ADAMS ST-N G11
ADAMS ST-S G11
AIRPORT RD-E G10
AIRPORT RD-W E10
ALDER DR E10
ANNA ST G12
APRIL CT G12
APRIL LN H12
ARROWHEAD ST EAST H11
ARROWHEAD ST NORTH H12
ARROWHEAD ST WEST H11
BANBURY RD H12
BASSWOOD DR E11
BELL ST E11
BIRCHWOOD DR E11
BRIAR LN G12
BUCKTHORN DR E11
BUTTERFIELD RD H11
BUTTERNUT DR E11
CANDLEWICK CT F11
CEDAR DR F10
CHANTILLY LN F11
CHARLOTTE ST G11
CHERRY TREE CT-N F11
CHERRY TREE CT-S F11
CHERRYWOOD DR E11
CHESTNUT RD H12
CLEARWATER DR H9
CONCO ST G10
COTTONWOOD DR E11
CYPRESS LN-N E11
CYPRESS LN-S E11
DEE RD H12
EAST-WEST TOLLWAY F10
ELM AV F12
EVERGREEN DR G9
FAIRVIEW DR G9
FARVIEW CT F11
FARVIEW DR F11
GIBSON ST G11
GRACE AV-N F11
GRACE AV-S F11
GRACE CT F11
GRANT ST-N G10
GRANT ST-S G10
HARMONY DR F11
HAWTHORNE DR F10
HETTINGER LN G11
HICKORY ST H12
HILL AV G12
HILLSIDE PL F11
JOHN ST F10
JUNIPER DR E11
KINGSWOOD DR F11
LARCHWOOD DR F11
LAUREL DR H11
LILAC LN G11
LINCOLN WAY G9
LINCOLN WAY-N G12
LINCOLN WAY-S G12
LINN CT H11
LOCUST ST-E H12
LONG AV H12
LOVEDALE LN G9
MAPLE AV F11
MAPLEWOOD DR F11
MARVO ST G11
MISTWOOD LN F11
MONROE ST G11
MOOSEHEART RD F12
OAK ST E11
OAKWOOD DR G10
OFFUTT LN G9
OFFUTT RD G9
PIERCE ST G11
PINEWOOD DR F12
PINOAK F11
POPLAR PL E10
PRINCETON CT F10
PRINCETON DR F10
RANDALL RD E11
REDWOOD CT F11
RIVER RD-N G11
RIVER RD-S G10
RIVERSIDE DR G10
RIVERVIEW DR G10
ROBERT ST F10
ROSE DR H11
SHAGBARK LN E11
SHARON LN H12
SMOKE TREE G9
SOUTH ST H9
SPRUCE ST H11
STAGHORN LN E10
STATE ST-E G11
STATE ST-W F11
STONE AV G11
SULLIVAN RD G9
SYCAMORE LN F11
TIMBEROAKS DR F11
VOLKS CT H11
WALNUT DR E11
WILDWOOD DR F11
WILLOW WAY-N F10
WILLOW WAY-S F10

© DonTech Chicago, Il. 1992

Batavia

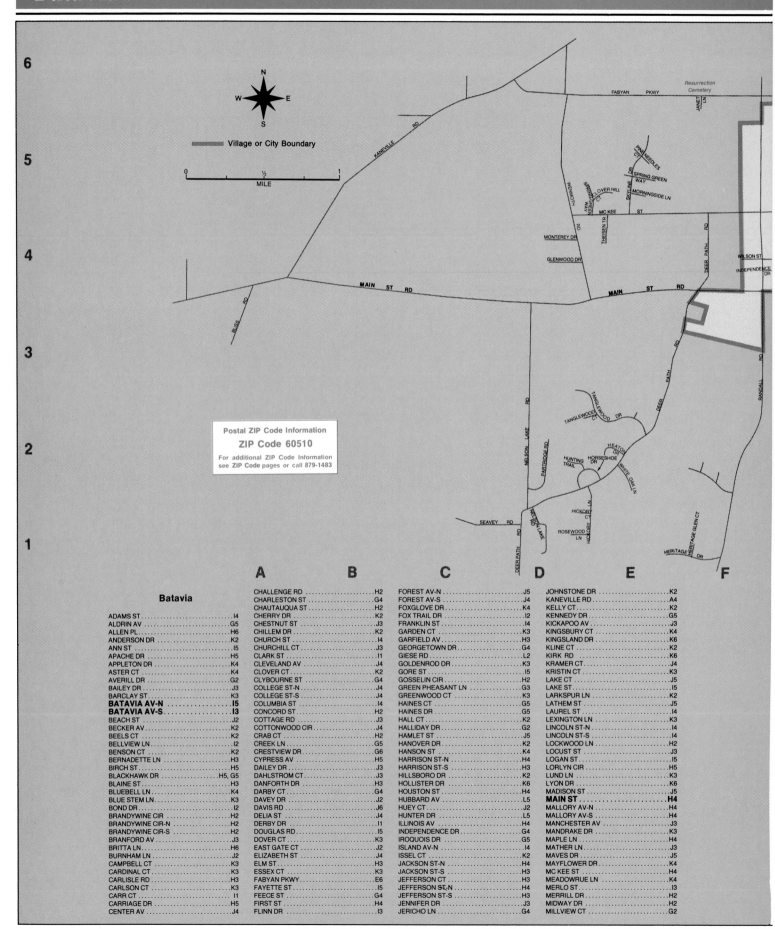

Postal ZIP Code Information
ZIP Code 60510
For additional ZIP Code Information
see ZIP Code pages or call 879-1483

Village or City Boundary

	A	B	C	D	E	F

Batavia

	CHALLENGE RD H2	FOREST AV-N J5	JOHNSTONE DR K2		
	CHARLESTON ST G4	FOREST AV-S J4	KANEVILLE RD A4		
	CHAUTAUQUA ST H2	FOXGLOVE DR K4	KELLY CT K2		
ADAMS ST.........................I4	CHERRY DR K2	FOX TRAIL DR I2	KENNEDY DR G5		
ALDRIN AV.........................G5	CHESTNUT ST J3	FRANKLIN ST I4	KICKAPOO AV J3		
ALLEN PL...........................H6	CHILLEM DR K2	GARDEN CT K3	KINGSBURY CT K4		
ANDERSON DR K2	CHURCH ST I4	GARFIELD AV H3	KINGSLAND DR K6		
ANN ST.............................I5	CHURCHILL CT J3	GEORGETOWN DR G4	KLINE CT K2		
APACHE DR H5	CLARK ST I1	GIESE RD L2	KIRK RD K6		
APPLETON DR K4	CLEVELAND AV J4	GOLDENROD DR K3	KRAMER CT J4		
ASTER CT K4	CLOVER CT K2	GORE ST I5	KRISTIN CT K3		
AVERILL DR G2	CLYBOURNE ST G4	GOSSELIN CIR H2	LAKE CT J5		
BAILEY DR J3	COLLEGE ST-N J4	GREEN PHEASANT LN G3	LAKE ST I5		
BARCLAY ST K3	COLLEGE ST-S J4	GREENWOOD CT K3	LARKSPUR LN K2		
BATAVIA AV-N I5	COLUMBIA ST I4	HAINES CT G5	LATHEM ST J5		
BATAVIA AV-S....................I3	CONCORD ST H2	HAINES DR G5	LAUREL ST I4		
BEACH ST J2	COTTAGE RD J3	HALL CT K2	LEXINGTON LN K3		
BECKER AV K2	COTTONWOOD CIR J4	HALLIDAY DR G2	LINCOLN ST-N I4		
BEELS CT K2	CRAB CT H2	HAMLET ST J5	LINCOLN ST-S I4		
BELLVIEW LN........................I2	CREEK LN G5	HANOVER DR K2	LOCKWOOD LN H2		
BENSON CT K2	CRESTVIEW DR G6	HANSON ST K4	LOCUST ST J3		
BERNADETTE LN H3	CYPRESS AV H5	HARRISON ST-N H4	LOGAN ST I5		
BIRCH ST H5	DAILEY DR J3	HARRISON ST-S H3	LORLYN CIR H5		
BLACKHAWK DR H5, G5	DAHLSTROM CT J3	HILLSBORO DR K2	LUND LN K3		
BLAINE ST H3	DANFORTH DR H3	HOLLISTER DR K6	LYON DR K6		
BLUEBELL LN K4	DARBY CT G4	HOUSTON ST H4	MADISON ST J5		
BLUE STEM LN K3	DAVEY DR J2	HUBBARD AV L5	**MAIN ST** **H4**		
BOND DR I2	DAVIS RD J6	HUEY CT J2	MALLORY AV-N H4		
BRANDYWINE CIR H2	DELIA ST J4	HUNTER DR L5	MALLORY AV-S H4		
BRANDYWINE CIR-N H2	DERBY DR I1	ILLINOIS AV J4	MANCHESTER AV J3		
BRANDYWINE CIR-S H2	DOUGLAS RD I5	INDEPENDENCE DR G4	MANDRAKE DR K3		
BRANFORD AV J3	DOVER CT K3	IROQUOIS DR G5	MAPLE LN J3		
BRITTA LN H6	EAST GATE CT J2	ISLAND AV-N I4	MATHER LN J3		
BURNHAM LN J2	ELIZABETH ST J4	ISSEL CT K2	MAVES DR J5		
CAMPBELL CT K3	ELM ST H3	JACKSON ST-N H4	MAYFLOWER DR K4		
CARDINAL CT.........................K3	ESSEX CT K3	JACKSON ST-S H3	MC KEE ST H4		
CARLISLE RD H3	FABYAN PKWY E6	JEFFERSON CT H3	MEADOWRUE LN K4		
CARLSON CT K3	FAYETTE ST I5	JEFFERSON ST-N H3	MERLO ST I3		
CARR CT I1	FEECE ST G4	JEFFERSON ST-S H3	MERRILL DR H2		
CARRIAGE DR H5	FIRST ST H4	JENNIFER DR J3	MIDWAY DR H2		
CENTER AV J4	FLINN DR I3	JERICHO LN G4	MILLVIEW CT G2		

© DonTech Chicago, Il. 1992

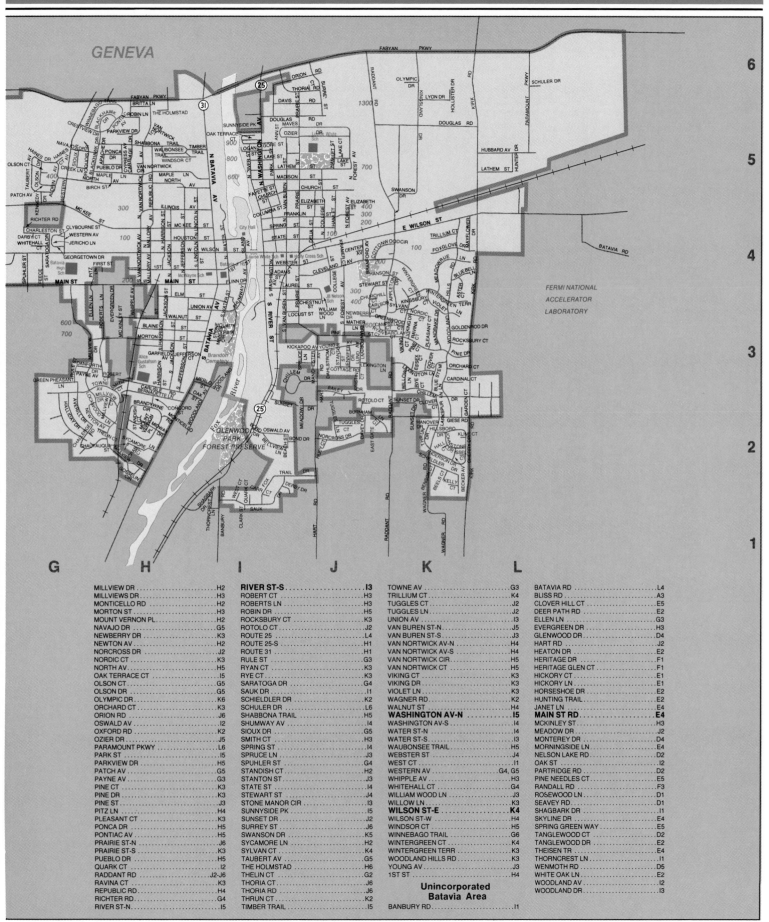

© DonTech Chicago, Il. 1992

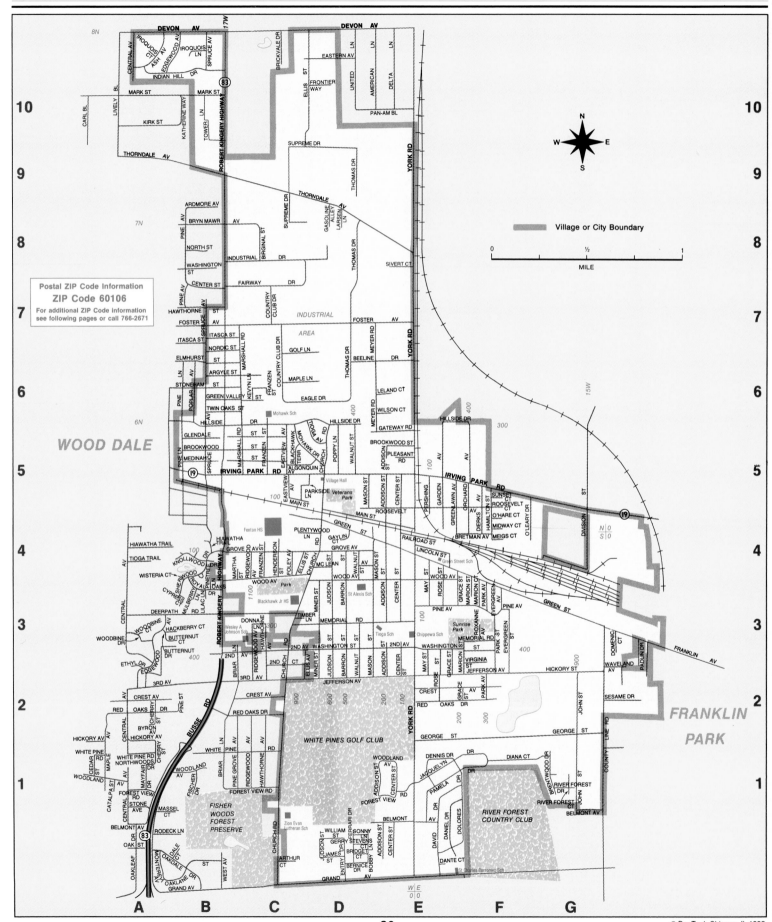

Postal ZIP Code Information
ZIP Code 60106
For additional ZIP Code information
see following pages or call 766-2671

Village or City Boundary

WOOD DALE

FRANKLIN PARK

© DonTech Chicago, Il. 1992

Bensenville

Street	Grid
ADDISON ST-N	D4
ADDISON ST-S	D1
ALGONQUIN AV	C5
ARGYLE ST	B6
ARTHUR CT	C1
ASH AV	A10
BARRON ST-S	D2
BEELINE DR	E6
BELMONT AV-E	E1
BELMONT AV-W	A1-D1
BERNICE DR	D1
BIRGINAL DR	C8
BLACKHAWK TERR	C5
BOBBY LN	D1
BRENTWOOD DR	G1
BRIDGET CT	D1
BROOKWOOD ST	A5-D5
BRYN MAWR AV	B8
CENTER ST-N	E4
CENTER ST-S	E1-E2
CENTRAL AV	A10
CHURCH RD-N	D4
CHURCH RD-S	C1
COUNTRY CLUB DR	C7
DANIEL DR	E1
DANTE CT	E1
DAVID DR	E1
DEERPATH RD	A3
DENNIS DR	E1
DEVON AV-W	A10
DIANA CT	F1
DIERKS AV	F4
DIVISION ST-N	G4
DOLORES DR	E1
DOMENIC CT	G3
DONNA LN	C3
EAGLE DR	C6
EASTVIEW AV	C5
EDGEWOOD AV	A3-A10
ELLIS ST-N	C10
ELLIS ST-S	D4
ELMHURST ST	A7
ENTRY DR	D1
EVERGREEN AV-S	F4
EVERGREEN ST	F3
FAIRWAY DR	C7
FERRARI DR	D1
FOLEY AV	C4
FOREST VIEW RD	A1-D1
FOSTER AV	D7
FRANZEN ST	C5
FRONTIER WAY	D10
GARDEN AV	E4
GASOLINE ALLEY	D8
GATEWAY RD	D6
GAYLIN CT	D4
GEORGE ST-E	E1
GERRY STEVENS CT	D1
GLENDALE ST	A6
GOLF LN	C7
GRACE ST-S	E2
GRAND AV-E	D1
GRAND AV-W	A1
GREEN ST-E	D4
GREEN ST-W	C3
GREENLAWN AV	E4
GREEN VALLEY ST	B6
GROVE AV	B4
HAMILTON ST	F4
HAWTHORNE ST	A7
HENDERSON ST	B4
HICKORY ST	G2
HILLSIDE DR-E	E5
HILLSIDE DR-W	B5
INDIAN HILL DR	A10
INDUSTRIAL DR	B8
IROQUOIS CT	A10
IROQUOIS LN	B10
IRVING PARK RD-E	F5
IRVING PARK RD-W	B5
ITASCA ST	A7
JACQUELYN DR	E1
JAMES ST	D1
JEFFERSON AV-E	E2
JOHN ST	G1
JUDSON ST	D2
KEVYN LN	B6
LARSEN LN	D8
LELAND CT	D6
LINCOLN ST	E4
MAIN ST-W	C4
MAPLE LN	C7
MARION CT	F3
MARION ST	F3
MARK ST	A10
MARSHALL RD	B5
MARTHA ST	B4
MASON ST-N	D5
MASON ST-S	D2
MASSEL CT	A1
MAY ST	E2
MC LEAN AV	D4
MEDINAH ST	A5
MEIGS CT	F4
MEMORIAL RD-E	F3
MEMORIAL RD-W	C3
MEYER RD	D6
MIDWAY CT	F4
MINER ST	C2
MOHAWK DR	C5
NORDIC ST	B6
O'HARE CT	F4
O'LEARY DR	F4
ORCHARD AV	E4
PADLIN DR	G3
PAMELA DR	E1
PARK AV	F3
PARK ST	F3
PARKSIDE LN	C5
PERSHING	E5
PINE AV	A7
PINE AV-E	E3
PINE LN	A5
PLEASANT RD-W	D5
PLENTYWOOD LN	C4
PODLIN DR	G3
POPLAR AV	A6
POPPY LN	C5
RAILROAD ST-E	E4
RED OAKS DR	E2
RIDGEWOOD AV	B1-B4
RIVER FOREST CT	G1
RIVER FOREST DR	G1
ROOSEVELT AV-E	F4
ROOSEVELT AV-W	D4
ROOSEVELT CT	F4
ROSE ST	E2
ROUTE 83-N	B10
ROUTE 83-S	B2
ROXANNE AV	E3
SESAME ST	G2
SIVERT CT	E8
SONNY LN	D1
SPRUCE AV	B2-B10
STONEHAM ST	A6
SUNSET CT	F4
SUPREME DR	C8
THOMAS DR	D8-D9
THORNDALE AV	A9
TIMBER LN	C3
TIOGA AV	C5
TOWER LN	B10
TWIN OAKS ST	B6
VIRGINIA ST	E2
WALNUT ST-N	D5
WALNUT ST-S	D2
WASHINGTON ST-E	E2
WASHINGTON ST-W	B3
WAVELAND AV	G2
WILLIAM ST	D1
WILSON CT	D6
WOOD AV-E	E3
WOOD AV-W	B3
WOODLAND AV-W	A1-E1
YORK RD-N	E5
YORK RD-S	E1
2ND AV-W	B3
2ND CT	B2
3RD AV-W	A2

Unincorporated Area

Street	Grid
AMERICAN LN	E10
ARDMORE AV	A8
BRIAR LN	B1
BRICKVALE DR	C10
BUSSE RD	B2
BUTTERNUT CT	A1
BUTTERNUT DR	A1
BYRON AV	A2
CARL BL	A10
CATALPA ST	A1
CEDAR ST	A1
CENTER ST-W	B7
CENTRAL AV-S	A1
CHERRY ST	A1
COUNTY LINE RD	G1
CREST AV-E	E2
CREST AV-W	A2
CYPRESS CT	B3
DALE CT	A1
DELTA LN	E10
DUNLAY ST	B4
EASTERN AV	D10
EDGEWOOD AVE	A5
ETHYL DR	A2
FISCHER DR	B1
FOREST ST	B5
FRANKLIN AV	G4
GREEN ST	B4
HACKBERRY CT	B3
HAWTHORNE AV-S	B1
HIAWATHA TRAIL	A4
HICKORY AV	A1
KATHERINE WAY	B10
KIRK ST	A10
KNOLLWOOD DR	B4
LILAC LN	B3
LIVELY BL	A10
MAPLE ST	A1
MAYFAIR DR	A1
MONTEREY AV	A1
MULBERRY LN	B3
NORTH ST	A8
NORTHWOODS DR	A1
OAK LN	B1
OAK ST	A1
OAKDALE DR	A1
OAKLANE ST	A1
OAKLEAF DR	A1
PAN-AM BL	E10
PINE AV-N	A7
PINE ST	A2
PINETREE LN	B4
PINE GROVE AV	B1
POTTER ST	B5
RED OAKS DR-W	A2
RODECK LN	A1
ROYAL OAKS DR	B3
SHERWOOD DR	B4
STONE AV	A1
TIOGA TRAIL	A4
UNITED LN	E10
WASHINGTON ST-NORTH	A8
WEST AV	B1
WHITE PINE RD	A1
WISTERIA CT	B4
WOODBINE CT	A3
WOODBINE DR	A3

© DonTech Chicago, Il. 1992

Street Guide

ADAMS ST	C1
BELLWOOD AV	B1
BOHLAND AV	C1
BOHLANDER AV	A3
BUTTERFIELD RD	B2
CASTLE DR	A3
CERNAN DR	C1
CONGRESS ST	B1-D1
DAVIS DR	A3
EASTERN AV	C2

EISENHOWER EXPWY	A1
ENGLEWOOD AV	B2
ERIE ST	A3
FREDERICK AV	B2
GENEVA AV	A2
GLADYS AV	B1
GLOS ST	D3
GRANT AV	D3
GRANVILLE AV	B2
HARRISON ST	C1
HYDE PARK AV	B2
JACKSON ST	B2
KORRELL AV	C3
LINDEN AV	C2

MADISON ST	C1
MANNHEIM RD	B1-B3
MARIK DR	B1
MARSHALL AV	B2
MARSHALL CT	B3
MAYWOOD DR	D1
MIAMI RD	B3
MONROE ST	C1
MORRIS AV	B3
OAK ST	A2-D2
PARK CT	B3
RANDOLPH ST	A2-D2
RICE AV	C2

ST CHARLES PL	B3
ST CHARLES RD	B3
ST PAUL AV	B2
TWINING AV	A3
VAN BUREN ST	C1
WARREN AV	B2-D2
WASHINGTON BL	C2
WILCOX AV	C1
ZUELKE DR	C3
22ND AV-S	D2
23RD AV-S	D2
24TH AV-S	D2
25TH AV-S	D2
26TH AV-S	D2

27TH AV-S	D2
28TH AV-S	D2
29TH AV-S	D3
30TH AV-S	C1-C3
31ST AV-S	C1-C3
32ND AV-S	C1-C3
46TH AV-S	A2
47TH AV-S	A2
48TH AV-S	A2
49TH AV-S	A2
50TH AV-S	A2
51ST AV-S	A2
52ND AV-S	A2
53RD AV-S	A2

Postal ZIP Code Information

ZIP Code 60104

For additional ZIP Code information
see following pages or call 544-5040

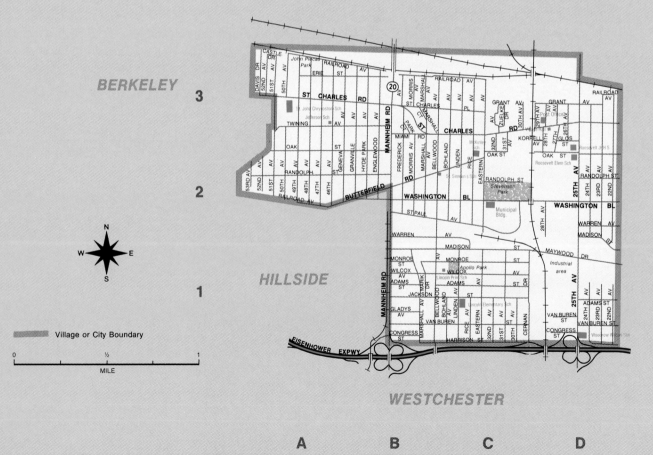

Village or City Boundary

0   ½   1
MILE

© DonTech Chicago, Il. 1992

ALBIN TERR A3	CHICAGO AV A4	HOWARD AV B4	MC DERMOTT DR B4
ARTHUR AV A2-A4	COOLIDGE AV A2	HURON ST B4	MORRIS AV C3
ASHBEL AV B4	**EISENHOWER EXPWY A3**	IRVING AV B4	MURRAY DR B3
ATWOOD AV A1-A3	ELECTRIC AV A2	JERELE AV D3	PARK AV A5
BIRCH DR B3	ELM AV A2	KING DR B3	PROSPECT AV A2
BOHLANDER AV C3	HARDING AV A3	KOUBA DR B2	PROVISO DR C4
BURR OAK AV A3	HAWTHORNE AV B3	LEE BL C3	RICHARD AV A4
BUTTERFIELD RD A1	HERBERT AV B1-B3	LIND AV C4	RIDGE AV B2
CALVIN AV A1	HIGH ST A1	MADISON ST A1	ROHDE AV D3
	HILLSIDE AV B3	MAPLE AV A3	ROSE CT B2

ST CHARLES RD B4
SCHOOL ST A2
SPEECHLEY BL D3
SPENCER AV D3
SUNNYSIDE DR C4
SUPERIOR ST A4
TAFT AV B3
TRI-STATE TOLLWAY A3
VICTORIA AV A3-A5
WOLF RD C3

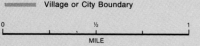

Postal ZIP Code Information

ZIP Code 60163

For additional ZIP Code information
see following pages or call 544-3347

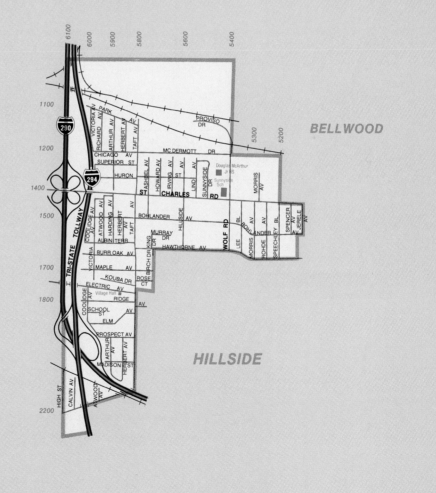

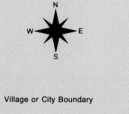

Village or City Boundary

0   ½   1
MILE

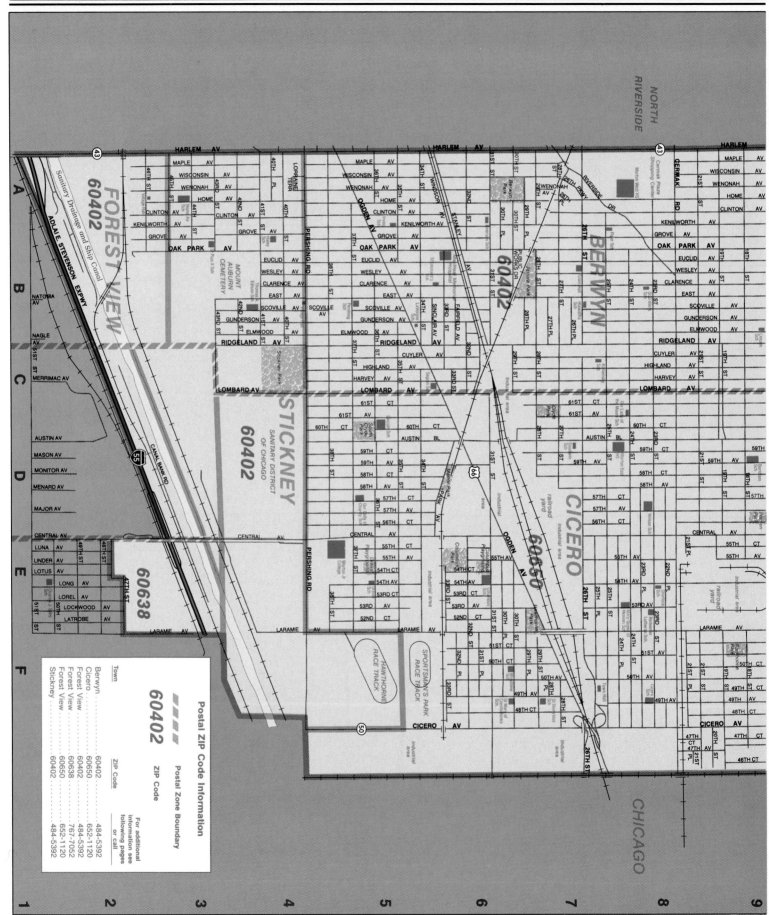

© DonTech Chicago, Il. 1992

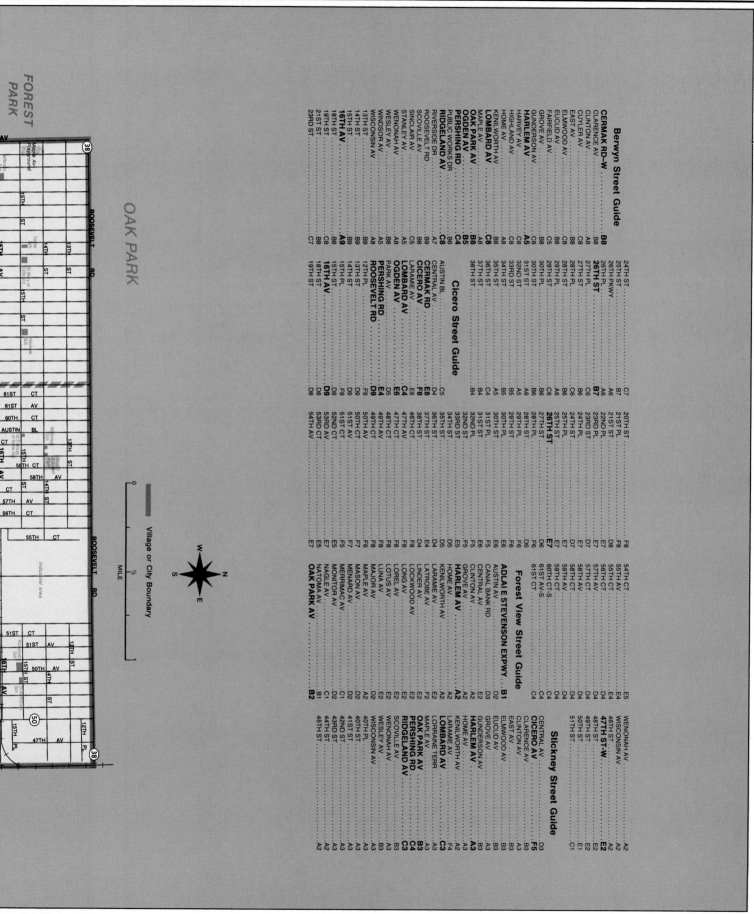

Berwyn Street Guide

CERMAK RD–W	B8
CLARENCE AV	B8
CLINTON AV	B8
CUYLER AV	A8
EAST AV	C8
ELMWOOD AV	B8
EUCLID AV	B8
FAIRFIELD AV	B6
GROVE AV	C5
GUNDERSON AV	B8
HARLEM AV	A5
HARVEY AV	C8
HIGHLAND AV	C8
HOME AV	A8
KENILWORTH AV	B8
LOMBARD AV	C8
MAPLE AV	B4
OAK PARK AV	B8
OGDEN AV	B5
PERSHING RD	C4
PUBLIC WORKS DR	B6
RIDGELAND AV	C8
RIVERSIDE DR	A7
ROOSEVELT RD	B9
SCOVILLE AV	B8
SINCLAIR AV	C5
STANLEY AV	A5
WENONAH AV	A8
WESLEY AV	B8
WINDSOR AV	A5
WISCONSIN AV	A8
13TH ST	B9
14TH ST	B9
15TH ST	B9
16TH AV	A9
18TH ST	B8
19TH ST	B8
21ST ST	B8
23RD ST	C7
24TH ST	C7
25TH ST	B7
26TH PKWY	A6
26TH ST	B7
27TH PL	A6
27TH ST	B6
28TH PL	B6
28TH ST	B6
29TH PL	A6
29TH ST	B6
30TH PL	C6
30TH ST	A6
31ST ST	B6
32ND ST	B5
33RD ST	B5
34TH ST	A5
35TH ST	B5
36TH ST	C4
37TH ST	B4
38TH ST	B4

Cicero Street Guide

AUSTIN BL	C5
CENTRAL AV	D4
CERMAK RD	E8
CICERO AV	F8
LARAMIE AV	E8
LOMBARD AV	C4
OGDEN AV	E6
PARK AV	D5
PERSHING RD	E4
ROOSEVELT RD	D9
12TH PL	F9
13TH ST	D9
14TH ST	D9
15TH ST	D9
16TH AV	F9
19TH ST	D8
20TH ST	F8
21ST PL	F8
21ST ST	D8
22ND PL	D8
23RD ST	E7
24TH ST	D7
25TH PL	E7
25TH ST	E7
26TH ST	E7
27TH ST	D6
28TH PL	F6
28TH ST	D6
29TH PL	F6
29TH ST	E6
30TH PL	E6
30TH ST	E6
31ST PL	E5
31ST ST	F5
32ND PL	E5
32ND ST	F5
33RD ST	E5
34TH ST	D5
35TH ST	D5
36TH ST	D4
37TH ST	E4
38TH ST	D4
46TH CT	F8
47TH AV	F8
48TH CT	F8
49TH AV	F8
49TH CT	E4
50TH CT	F7
51ST CT	F7
51ST ST	F7
52ND CT	F5
53RD AV	E5
53RD CT	E5
54TH AV	E7

Forest View Street Guide

ADLAI E STEVENSON EXPWY	B1
AUSTIN AV	D2
CANAL BANK RD	D3
CENTRAL AV	A2
CLINTON AV	A2
GROVE AV	A2
HARLEM AV	A2
HOME AV	A2
KENILWORTH AV	A2
LARAMIE AV	F4
LATROBE AV	F2
LINDER AV	E2
LOCKWOOD AV	E2
LONG AV	F5
LOREL AV	F5
LOTUS AV	F8
LUNA AV	F8
MAJOR AV	F8
MAPLE AV	F6
MASON AV	F7
MENARD AV	D2
MERRIMAC AV	C1
MONITOR AV	D2
NAGLE AV	E5
NATOMA AV	E5
OAK PARK AV	E7

Stickney Street Guide

CENTRAL AV	D3
CICERO AV	F5
CLARENCE AV	B3
CLINTON AV	A2
EAST AV	B3
ELMWOOD AV	B3
EUCLID AV	B3
GROVE AV	A3
GUNDERSON AV	A3
HARLEM AV	A3
HOME AV	A2
KENILWORTH AV	A2
LARAMIE AV	F4
LOMBARD AV	C3
LORRAINE TERR	A3
MAPLE AV	A3
OAK PARK AV	B3
PERSHING RD	C4
RIDGELAND AV	C3
SCOVILLE AV	B3
WENONAH AV	A2
WESLEY AV	B3
WISCONSIN AV	A2
40TH ST	A3
41ST ST	A3
42ND ST	A3
43RD ST	A3
44TH ST	A2
45TH ST	A2

Village or City Boundary

© DonTech Chicago, Il. 1992

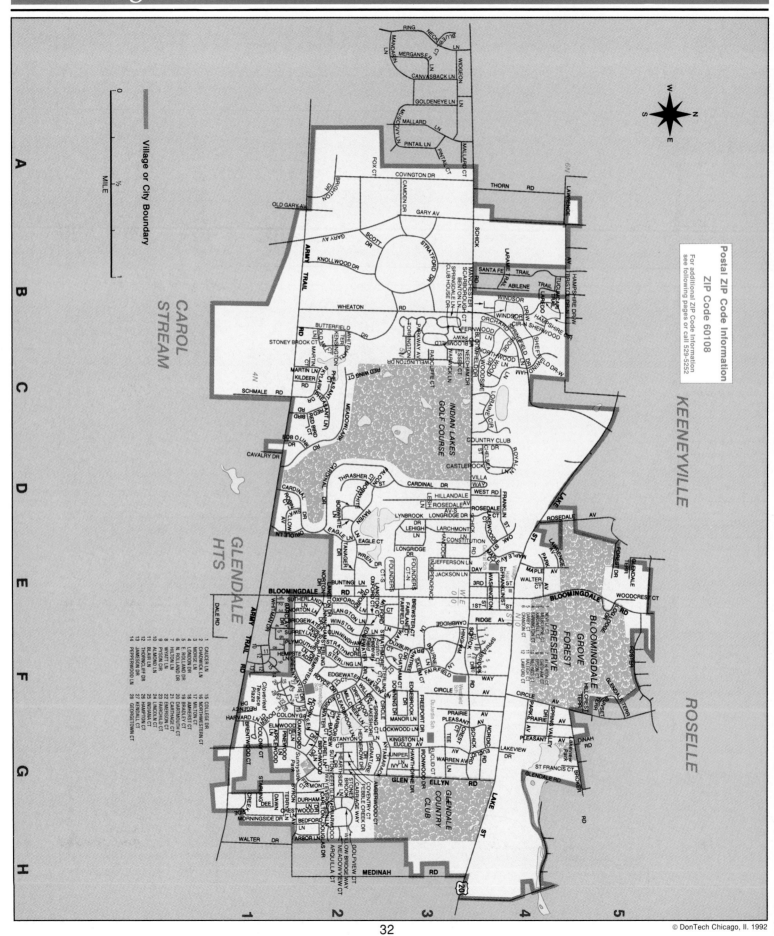

© DonTech Chicago, Il. 1992

© DonTech Chicago, Il. 1992

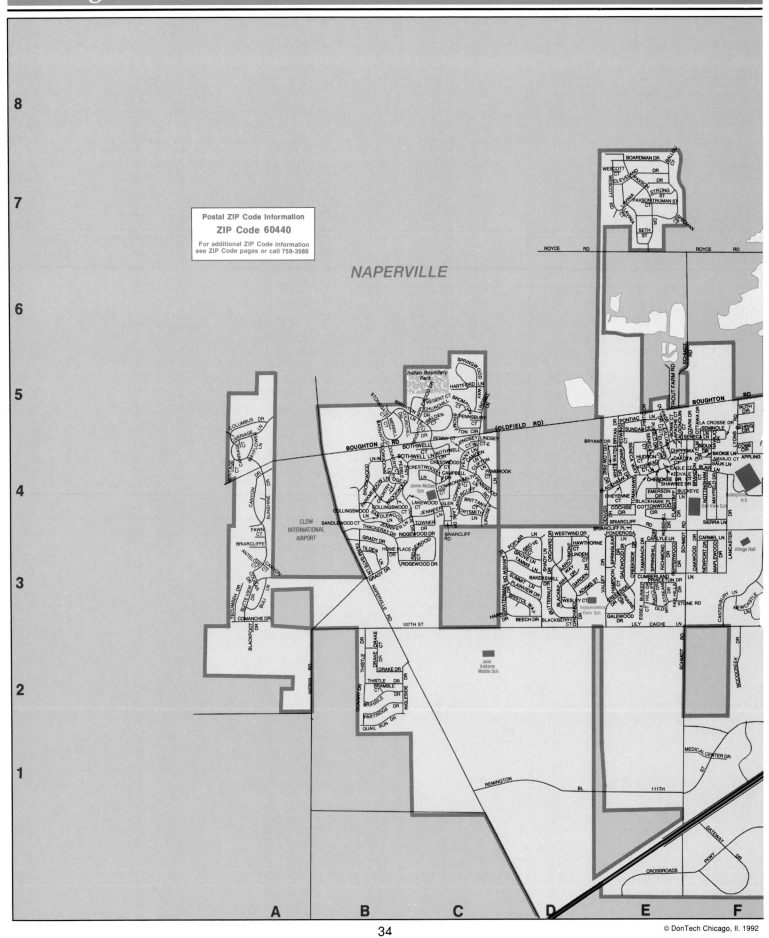

Postal ZIP Code Information
ZIP Code 60440
For additional ZIP Code information
see ZIP Code pages or call 759-3560

NAPERVILLE

© DonTech Chicago, Il. 1992

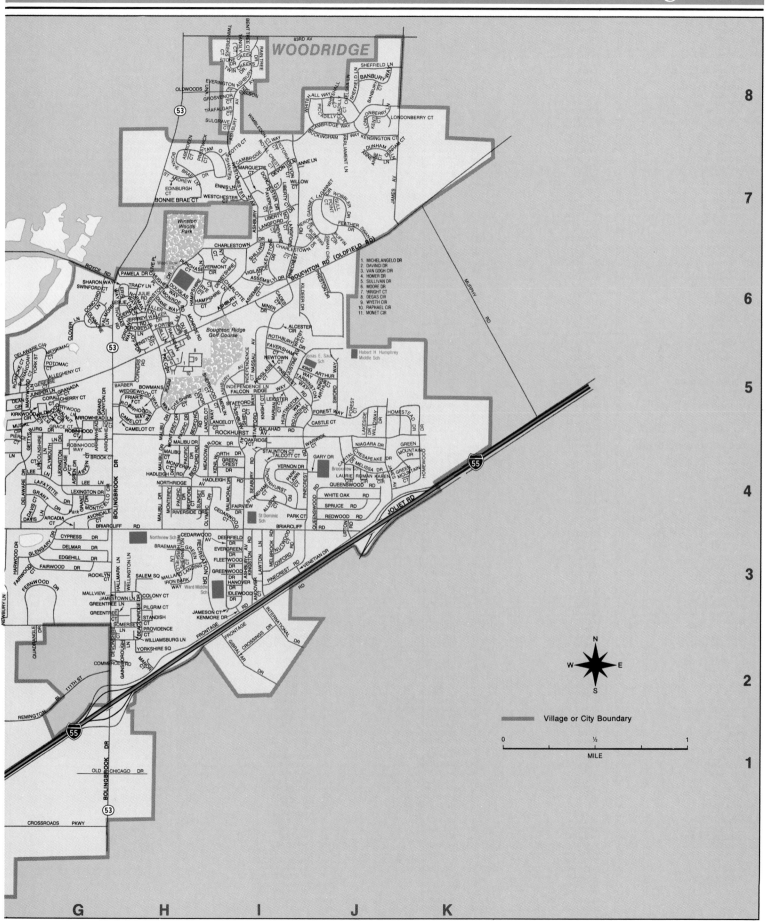

© DonTech Chicago, Il. 1992

Bolingbrook Street Guide

Street	Grid
ABERDEEN CT	H7
ADAMS ST	D3
ALCESTER CIR	I6
ALGONQUIN CT	E4
ALLEGHENY CT	G5
ALLISON CT	I4
ANDOVER CT	I3
ANNE LN	K7-I7
ANTELOPE CT	A3
APACHE CT	E4
APPLEWOOD DR	C5
APPLING LN	F4
ARCADIA CT	G4
ARDGLASS CT	I5
ARROWHEAD CT	G5
ARROWHEAD LN	G5
ARROWHEAD PL	G5
ASHBURY AV	I7
ASHBURY AV-N	I7
ASHBURY AV-S	I3
ASHBURY CT	I6
ASPEN CT	G4
ASPEN DR	G4
ASSEMBLY CT	I6
ASSEMBLY DR	I6
AVONDALE CT	G4
BAKERSMILL DR	D3
BALLOU CT	E8
BALMORAL DR	I4
BANBURY WAY	J8
BANBURY CT	J8
BARNWOOD	B5
BARBER CORNERS RD	H5
BEACONRIDGE DR	H3
BEDFORD CT	H4
BEDFORD RD	H5
BEECH DR	D3
BENT TREE CT	I8
BLACKBERRY CT	D3
BLACKBERRY DR	D3
BLACKFOOT DR	A2
BLACKHAWK LN	E4
BLACKHAWK PL	E4
BLAIR LN	F4
BOARDMAN CT	E8
BOLINGBROOK DR	**G4**
BONNIE BRAE CT	H7
BONNIE BRAE LN	H7
BOTHWELL CIR	C4
BOTHWELL CT	C4
BOTHWELL LN	C4
BOUGHTON RD-E (OLDFIELD RD)	**J6**
BOUGHTON RD-W (OLDFIELD RD)	**B4**
BOWIE CT	E4
BOWMANS CT	H5
BRAEMAR GREEN	H3
BRAMBLE CT	B2
BRAMBLE DR	B2
BRANDON CT	F4
BRIARCLIFF PL	E4
BRIARCLIFF RD	G4, E4, C4
BRIARCLIFFE	A3
BRIARCLIFFE RD	C3
BRIGHTON CT	B5
BRIGHTON LN	B5
BRISTOL WAY	D3
BRITTANY CT	C4
BROMPTON CIR	C5
BROMPTON CT	C5
BROOK CT	G4
BROOKWOOD	B4
BROOKWOOD LN-E	B4
BROOKWOOD LN-W	B4
BRYAN DR	E4
BRYANT DR	E4
BUCKEYE LN	E4
BUCKINGHAM WAY	J8
BULI LN	A3
BUNKER HILL DR	E3
BUNTING CIR	J7
BUTTERNUT DR	D3
BUTTE VIEW DR	A3
CADES CT	I6
CALUMET CT	E4
CAMBRIDGE WAY	J8
CAMDEN LN	C4
CAMELOT CT	H5
CAMELOT WAY	H5
CAMPBELL DR	C4
CANTERBURY LN	F3
CANYON CT	A3
CANYON DR	A4
CAPITAL DR	J4
CARLYLE LN	E3
CARMEL LN	F3
CARRIAGE CT	A4
CARRIAGE LN	A4
CASTLE CT	J5
CEDARWOOD AV	I3
CEDARWOOD CT	I4
CHARLESTOWN CT	H6
CHARLESTOWN DR	I6
CHARLOTTE CT	H6
CHARLOTTE LN	I6
CHASE CT	G4
CHELSEA LN	J8
CHEROKEE DR	E4
CHERRY CT	G5
CHESAPEAKE DR	J4
CHESHIRE CT	H5
CHEYENNE CT	E4
CHIPPEWA CT	E4
CHURCHILL DR	C5
CLEVELAND DR	E7
CLIFTON LN	C4
CLOVER LN	G6
COBB CIR	F4
COCHISE CIR	E4
COLLINGSWOOD CT, LN.	B4
COLONY CT	H3
COLUMBUS DR	A4
COMANCHE DR	A3
COMMERCE RD	G2
COMMONWEALTH CT	C4
CONCORD LN	G6
COPPER CT	C4
CORAL CT	G5
COTTONWOOD CIR	E4
COUGAR DR	A3
COUNTRY CT	B4
COUNTRY RIDGE LN	B4
CREEKSIDE DR	E3
CRESTWOOD CT	C4
CRESTWOOD LN	C4
CROSSINGS DR	I2
CROSSROADS PKWY	F1
CUMBERLAND LN	E3
CYPRESS DR	G3
DAKOTA CT	E4
DAVIS CT	G4
DAVIS LN	G4
DEAN CIR	F5
DEERFIELD DR	I3
DEGAS CIR	H5
DELAWARE CIR	G5
DELAWARE DR	F4
DELMAR DR	G3
DENVER DR	E4
DERBYSHIRE CT	I6
DERBYSHIRE LN	I6
DEVON CT	I7
DEVON LN	I7
DEVONSHIRE CT	G2
DORCHESTER CT	I7
DORCHESTER DR	I7
DOUGLAS WAY	H6
DRAKE CT	B2
DRAKE DR	B2
DU BOIS CIR	H6
DUNHAM CT	K7
DUNHAM LN	K7
DUNMORE CT	G6
DU PAGE DR	E5
EAGLE CT	E4
EDGEHILL CT	D3
EDINBURGH CT	H7
ELKHORN CT	C4
ELM CT	G5
EMERSON CIR	E4
ENNIS LN	I7
ERIC WAY	G6
ESSEX CT	E3
EVERGREEN DR	I3
EVERINGTON CT	I8
FAIRVIEW DR	I4
FAIRWOOD CT	G3
FAIRWOOD DR	G3
FALCON RIDGE WAY	I5
FALMORE LN	G6
FAR HILLS DR	E3
FARM GATE LN	B3
FAVERSHAM CT	I5
FAWN CT	A3
FEATHER SOUND DR	J7
FERNWOOD DR.	G3
FLAGSTAFF DR	E4
FLEETWOOD DR	I3
FOREST CT	J5
FOREST WAY	J5
FOXHEAD CT	E4
FRIAR'S CT	H5
FRONTAGE RD-N	I3
FRONTAGE RD-S	I3
FULLER LN	H6
GAINSBOROUGH CT	H2
GALAHAD RD	I5
GALEWOOD DR	E3
GANNET CIR	J7
GANNET LN	J7
GARDEN DR	D3
GARY DR	J4
GATEWAY DR	F1
GEHRIG CIR	F5
GENESSE CT	G5
GETTYSBURG DR	G4
GIBRALTAR DR	I2
GLEN LAKE DR	H3
GLENGARY RD	G3
GRACE CT	G5
GRADY DR	B3
GRANADA CT	G5
GRAND CANYON DR	A3
GRANT DR	G4
GREENCREST DR	J4
GREEN MOUNTAIN CT	J4
GREEN MOUNTAIN DR	J4
GREENTREE CT	G3
GREENTREE LN	G3
GREENWOOD DR	I3
GROSVENOR CT	I8
GROVE CT	D3
GROVE LN	D3
GULL POINT CT	J7
HADLEIGH RD	H4
HALLMARK LN	G3
HAMPDON CT	E3
HAMPSHIRE CT	H6
HAMPSHIRE LN	H6
HANOVER DR	I3
HARRIS DR	D3
HARTFORD LN	C5
HARWOOD DR	F3
HAVERHILL CT	I7
HAWTHORNE CT	D3
HERITAGE CT	A4
HERON CIR	J7
HOME PLACE DR	B3
HOMESTEAD DR	K5
HOMER DR	H5
HOMEWOOD DR	K4
HUDSON CT	E4
HUGHES PL	H6
HUNTINGTON WAY	I5
HYWOOD LN	G5
IDLEWOOD DR	I3
INDEPENDENCE CT	I5
INDEPENDENCE LN	I5
INGLESIDE DR	B2
INTERNATIONAL DR	I3
IRON BARK WAY	H3
JAMES AV-N	J7
JAMESON CT	I3
JAMESTOWN LN	H3
JANES AV	J4
JEFFREY RD	H6
JENNIFER LN	C4, B4
JEROME LN	H6
JILL LN	H6
JOLIET RD	**J4**
JORDAN WAY	H6
JOY DR	H5
JULIE RD	H6
JUNIPER LN	G5
JUSTINE AV	I5
KAREN CIR	J4
KEDVALE CT	E4
KENILWORTH DR	I4
KENMORE DR	I3
KENSINGTON CT	J8
KENT CT	J8
KEYSTONE DR	I6
KILDEER CT	I6
KING ARTHUR CT	J5
KING ARTHUR WAY	J5
KINGSTON DR	I3
KIRKWOOD CIR	G5
KNIGHT CT	I5
LACROSSE DR	F4
LAFAYETTE DR	G4
LAKESIDE DR	J5
LAKEWOOD CT	B4
LANCASTER DR-N	F4
LANCASTER DR-S	F3
LANCELOT CT	I5
LANCELOT WAY	H5
LANGFORD CT	I7
LANGFORD DR	I7
LARCHMONT WAY	D3
LAURIE CIR	J4
LAVINIA CT	E7
LAVINIA DR	E7
LAWTON LN	I3
LEE LN	G4
LEICESTER CT	I5
LESLIE LN	G6
LEXINGTON DR	G4
LIBERTY CT	I7
LIBERTY DR	I7
LILY CACHE LN	E2
LINCOLNSHIRE CT	G4
LINCOLNSHIRE LN	G4
LINDEN CT	D3
LINDSEY CT-E	C5
LINDSEY CT-W	C5
LINDSEY LN	C5
LONDONBERRY CT	J8
LONDONBERRY LN	J8
LYONS RD	F4
MALIBU CT	H4
MALLARD LANDING	H3
MALLVIEW LN	G3
MANOR CT	H2
MAPLEWOOD DR	F3
MARIAN CT	I5
MARQUETTE CT	I7
MARYWOOD LN	F5
MAYFIELD DR	F4
MAYFLOWER LN	A4
MEADOWBROOK DR	H4
MEDICAL CENTER DR	F2
MELBROOK RD	I3
MELISSA DR	J4
MERLIN CT	I5
MERRILL CT	B5
MERRIMAC CT	G5
MICHELANGELO DR	H5
MILLSTREAM DR	E3
MINER DR	I6
MONET CIR	H5
MONROE RD	H5
MONTEREY CT	H4
MONTEREY DR	H5
MONTICELLO CIR	G4
MOORE DR	H5
MURPHY RD	K6
MUSIAL CIR	F5
NAPERVILLE RD	B3
NASSAU AV	I5
NAVAJO CT	F4
NAVAJO DR	F4
NELSON CT	I8
NEWBURY LN	F3
NEWCASTLE LN	F3
NEWPORT DR	F3
NEWTOWN CT	F3
NIAGARA DR	J4
NORMAN WAY	H6
NORTHRIDGE AV	H4
NOTTINGHAM DR	F4
NUTWOOD CT	I3
OAKRIDGE CT	I4
OAKWOOD DR	F3
OLD CHICAGO DR-W	G1
OLD ELM DR	F4
OLD STONE RD	E3
OLDWOODS	H8
OLIVE PL	H6
OLYMPIC DR	H4
ORCHARD DR	D3
OTTAWA DR	F4
OXFORD RD	I3
OZARK DR	E4
PACIFIC DR	H5
PAMELA DR	H4
PARK CT	I4
PARKLAWN CT	I4
PARKMEADOW LN	B4
PARLIAMENT LN	J8
PARTRIDGE DR	B2
PAXSON CT	I7
PAXSON DR	E7
PEBBLE CT	B4
PEMBROOK CT	C4
PENNSBURY CT	C5
PENNWOOD LN	C4
PENNY CT	C4
PENNY LN	C4
PEPPERWOOD DR	E3
PICCADILLY CT	J8
PICCADILLY LN	J8
PIERCE CT	F4
PILGRIM CT	H3
PINECREST CT	I6
PINECREST RD-N	I6
PINECREST RD-S	I4
PINTO DR	E5
PLAINVIEW DR	D3
PLYMOUTH LN	G4
PONDEROSA LN	E3
PONTIAC LN	E5
POPLAR LN	D3
PORTER LN	H6
PORTSMITH LN	C4
POTOMAC CT	G5
PRAIRIE CIR	E3
PRESTON DR	J6
PRESTWICK CT	I7
PRINCETON DR	E3
PROVIDENCE CT	H2
PUEBLO DR	E4
PUFFIN CIR	J7
PURCHASE CT	H6
QUADRANGLE DR	G2
QUAIL RUN DR	B1
QUARRY DR	B2
QUEENSWOOD RD	J4
RACINE LN	H6
RADCLIFF DR	E3
RAIN TREE DR	I8
RAPHAEL CIR	H5
RECREATION DR	H3
REDWING CT	E4
REDWOOD RD	J4
REGENT CT	B5
REMINGTON BL	G2
REVERE CT	I7
RICHMOND DR	E3
RIDGEWOOD CT	C3
RIDGEWOOD DR	B3
RIVERSIDE DR	H4
ROANOKE CT	G5
ROBERTS LN	H6
ROBINHOOD CT	G5
ROBINHOOD WAY	H5
ROCKHURST RD	I4
ROCKLYN CT	G3
ROMAN CIR	J4
ROSEHILL DR	E4
ROTHBURY DR	I5
ROUNDHILL CT	I5
ROUTE 53	**G1**
ROYAL CREST CT	I7
ROYCE RD	G6, F7
RUTH CIR	F5
RYE CT	H6
SALEM SQ	H3
SANDLEWOOD CT	B4
SANDLEWOOD LN	B4
SAUK LN WEST	F4
SCHMIDT RD-N	I3
SCHMIDT RD-S	E2
SCOTTS CT	I7
SEABURY RD	I4
SEMINOLE LN	F4
SENECA CT	E4
SENECA LN	F4
SENECA WAY	E4
SETH ST	E7
SHADY LN	D3
SHARON WAY	G6
SHAWNEE DR	E4
SHEFFIELD LN	J8
SHENANDOAH CT	G5
SHERINGTON CT	H3
SHERWOOD CT	H5
SHIELD CT	I5
SHILLING CT	I6
SIERRA LN	F4
SIOUX DR	F4
SKOKIE LN	F4
SOMERSET LN	H2
SPECMAN CT	E8
SPRINGHILL DR	E3
SPRINGLEAF DR	E3
SPRINGWOOD WAY	C5
SPRUCE RD	J4
STAFFORD CT	I5
STAFFORD WAY	I5
STANDISH CT	H3
STANDREW DR	H14
STAUNTON CT	I4
STONE CREEK DR	I8
STONEGATE CT	B5
STONEHAM CT	I4
STRONG ST	E7
SULGRAVE CT	I8
SULLIVAN CIR	H5
SUMMIT LN	D3
SUNDANCE CT	E5
SUNSET DR	H4
SUNSHINE DR	A4
SWAN CIR	J7
SWINFORD CT	G6
SWORD WAY	J5
TAHOE DR	C3
TALCOTT CT	I4
TAMARACK DR	E3
TAMMS LN	D3
TAM O'SHANTER	I7
TANGLY CT	I8
TARRINGTON WAY	J5
TECUMSEH DR	A3
THACKERAY DR	B3
THISTLE DR	B2
THOMAS RD	G6
THORNHURST RD	I4
TILDEN LN	B3
TOMAHAWK CT	E4
TOWNER DR	C3
TRACY LN	H6
TRAFALGAR CT	I8
TROUT FARM RD	E5
TRUMAN ST	E7
TUDOR CT	H5
TWIN CREEKS CT	I8
TWIN CREEKS DR	I8
UNA	H8
UPTON RD	J4
VALLEY DR	E3
VAN GOGH CIR	H5
VERNON DR	I4
VENETIAN DR	I3
VERMONT CIR	H6
VICTORIA CT	I7
VIGILANCE CT	I6
WALDEN CT	C5
WALKER DR	H6
WALNUT CIR	G5
WARWICK CT	I8
WATERMAN DR	D3
WEBER RD	A2
WEDGEWOOD WAY	H5
WELLINGTON LN.	H3
WESCOTT CT, RD.	E7
WESTCHESTER CT	I7
WESTCHESTER LN.	I7
WESTLEY CT	D3
WESTWIND DR	D3
WETHERSFIELD LN	H3
WHITBY CT	I5
WHITE OAK RD	J4
WHITEHALL CT	J8
WHITEHALL WAY	J8
WHITEWATER DR	E4
WILDWOOD LN	G5
WILLIAMSBURG LN	H2
WILLOW LN	I7
WILLOWAY DR	H7
WIMBLEDON CT	I8
WINDSOR DR	E4
WINSTON CT	H5
WINSTON DR	H6
WOBBLER DR	J7
WOODCREEK DR	F2
WRIGHT CT	H5
WYETH CIR	H5
YELLOW PINE DR	E4
YORK ST	G5
YORKSHIRE SQ	H2
83RD AV	I8
107TH ST	C2
111TH ST	G2

© DonTech Chicago, Il. 1992

Postal ZIP Code Information

ZIP Code 60153

For additional ZIP Code information
see following pages or call 345-3830

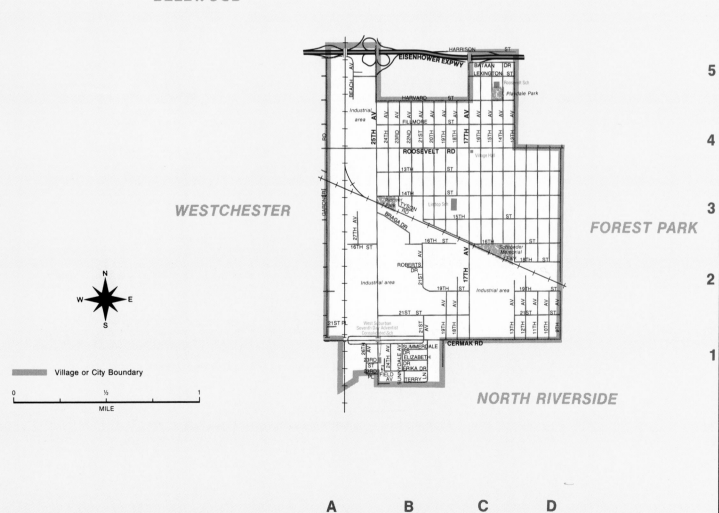

© DonTech Chicago, Il. 1992

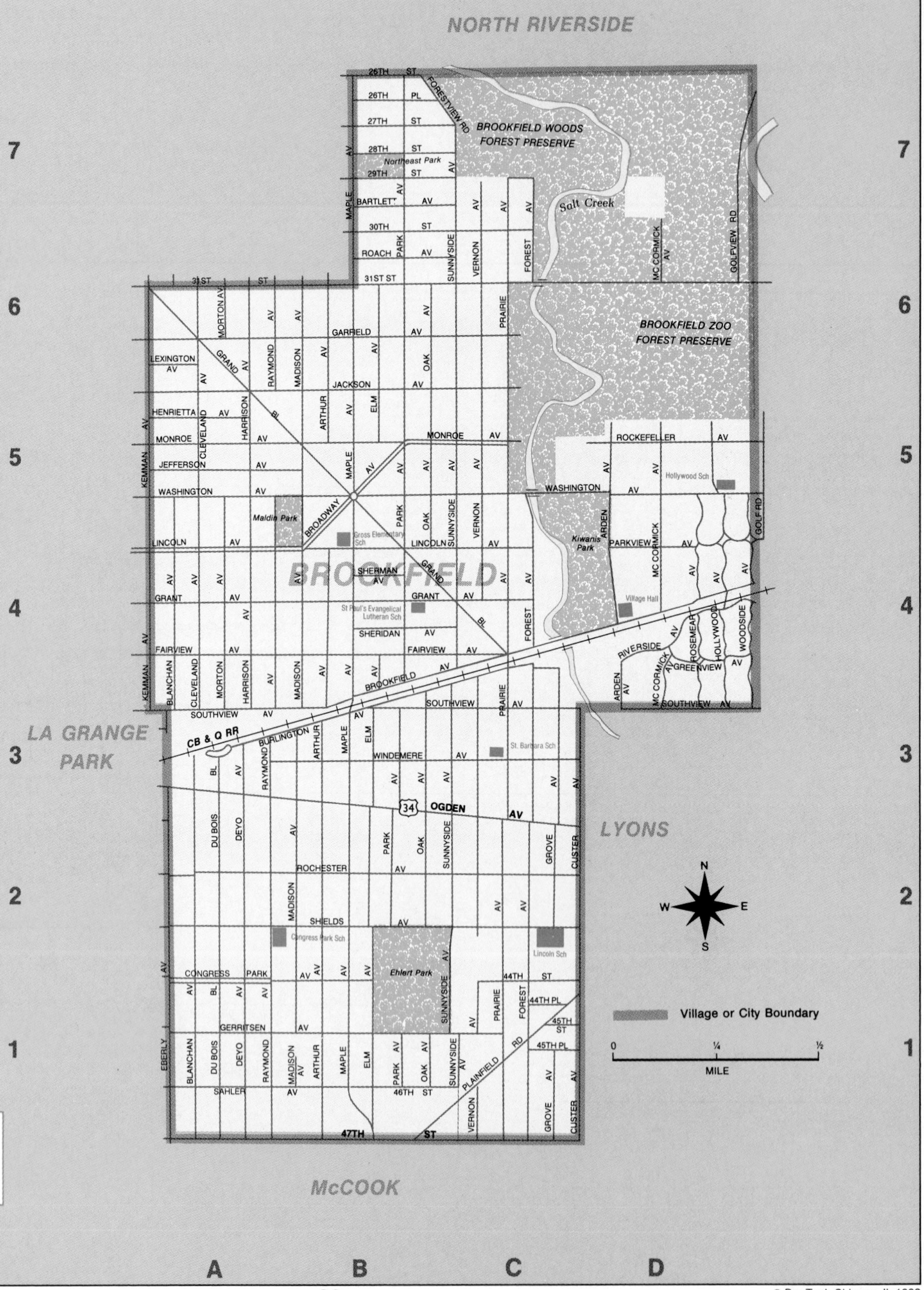

Postal ZIP Code Information

ZIP Code 60513

For additional ZIP Code information
see following pages or call 485-0572

NORTH RIVERSIDE

BROOKFIELD WOODS FOREST PRESERVE

Salt Creek

Northeast Park

BROOKFIELD ZOO FOREST PRESERVE

Kiwanis Park

Maldin Park

Gross Elementary Sch

BROOKFIELD

St Paul's Evangelical Lutheran Sch

Village Hall

Hollywood Sch

Rockefeller

LA GRANGE PARK

LYONS

St. Barbara Sch

CB & Q RR

OGDEN AV

Congress Park Sch

Ehlert Park

Lincoln Sch

McCOOK

Village or City Boundary

0   ¼   ½
MILE

Village or City Boundary

© DonTech Chicago, Il. 1992

WATCH YOUR MAILBOX FOR MONEY-SAVING COUPONS!

Brought To You By

DonTech
A Partnership between Ameritech and Donnelley Directory

For advertising information contact DonTech at **708-449-1350**

© DonTech Chicago, Il. 1992

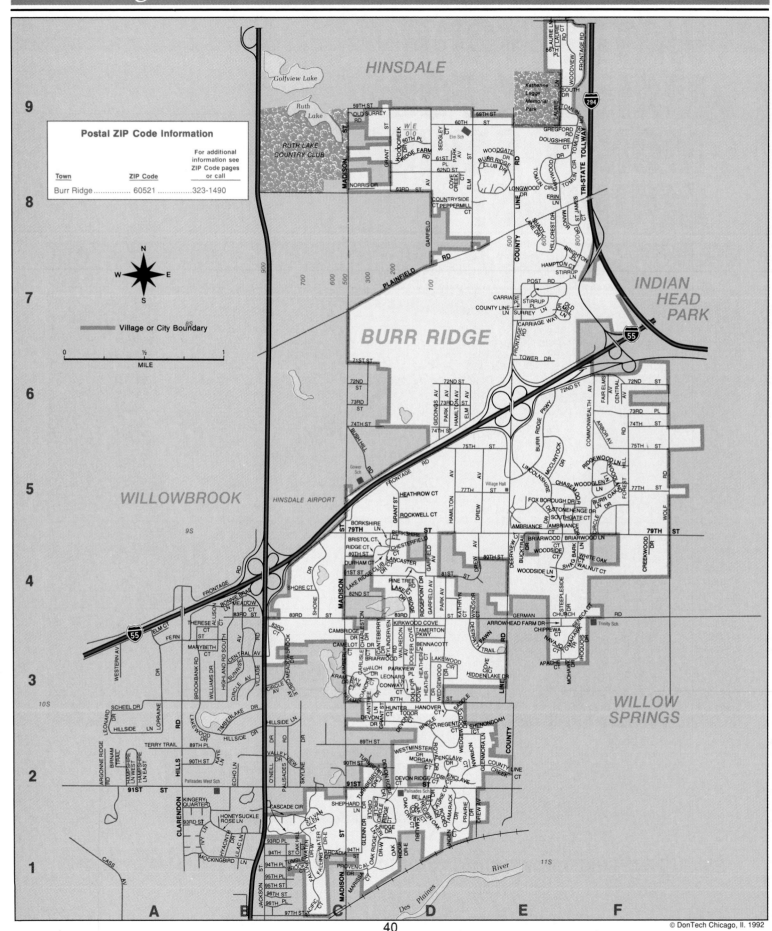

Postal ZIP Code Information

Town	ZIP Code	For additional information see ZIP Code pages or call
Burr Ridge	60521	323-1490

Village or City Boundary

HINSDALE

Golfview Lake

Ruth Lake

RUTH LAKE COUNTRY CLUB

Katherine Legge Memorial Park

BURR RIDGE

INDIAN HEAD PARK

WILLOWBROOK

HINSDALE AIRPORT

WILLOW SPRINGS

Des Plaines River

© DonTech Chicago, Il. 1992

Burr Ridge

AINTREE LN C3
AMBRIANCE CT E5
APACHE CT E3
ARBOR RD.......................F6
ARCADIA CT C1
ARROWHEAD FARM DR E4
BAYRUM CT C3
BEL AIR CT D2
BENNACOTT LN D3
BERKSHIRE CT D5
BORKSHIRE LN C5
BRIARWOOD C3
BRIARWOOD CT E4
BRIARWOOD LN F4
BRIDLE CT D3
BRIGHTON PL....................F7
BRISTOL CT C4
BUCKTRAIL DR E4
BURR OAK LN....................F5
BURR RIDGE CLUB DR E6, E8
BURR RIDGE PKWY E6
BUSH HILL RD C5
CAMBRIDGE DR C3
CAMELOT DR C3
CANTEBERRY DR C3
CARLISLE CT C3
CARRIAGE PL....................E7
CARRIAGE WAY DR E7
CASCADE CIR....................B2
CENTRAL AV F6
CIRCLE DR C2
CHARLESTON DR C3
CHASEMOOR DR E5
CHESTERFIELD CT D4
CHIPPEWA CT E3
CIRCLE RIDGE CT D2
CLYNDERVEN RD D3
COMMONWEALTH AV F6
CONWAY CT D3
COUNTRYSIDE CT D8
COUNTY LINE LN E7
COUNTY LINE RD-S E2, E8
COUNTY LINE CREEK CT E2
COVE CREEK CT D8
COVE CT E3
CREEKWOOD DR F4
DEERPATH TRAIL D3
DEERVIEW CT E4
DEVON CT D3
DEVON DR C3

DEVON RIDGE CT D2
DOLFOR COVE D3
DOUGSHIRE CT E9
DREW AV E2, E5
DURHAM CT C4
ELM AV D6, D8
ENCLAVE CT D2
ENCLAVE DR D2
ERIN LN E8
FAIR ELMS AV F6
FALLING WATER DR-E C1
FALLING WATER DR-W C1
FAWN E3
FOREST HILL AV F5
FOX BOROUGH DR E5
FRONTAGE RD D5, F9
GARFIELD AV D4, D8
GARRYWOOD DR E8
GERMAN CHURCH RD E4
GIDDINGS AV D6
GLENMORA LN E2
GRANT ST C3, D8
GREGFORD RD E9
HAMILTON AV D5, D6
HAMPTON CT E7
HANOVER CT D3
HEATHER CT D3
HEATHER DR D3
HEATHROW CT D5
HIDDEN LAKE DR E3
HILLCREST DR E8
HORE CT C4
HUNTER CT D3
IROQUOIS DR F3
KATHRYN CT D4
KERI LN C1
KIMBERLY CT C3
KIRKWOOD COVE D4
KRAML DR C3
LAKE RIDGE CT D4
LAKE RIDGE DR D4
LAKE RIDGE CLUB DR C4
LAKEWOOD CIR B2, D3
LANCASTER CT D4
LAURIE CT D4
LAURIE LN D2, E9
LEONARD LN A3, D3
LINCOLNSHIRE DR E5
LINDEN CT D1
LONGWOOD DR....................E8
MADISON ST C1, C8
MALIBU CT D1
MANOR DR E8

MARISSA CT C1
MCCLINTOCH DR E5
MOHAWK DR E3
MORGAN CT D2
NAVAJO CT E3
NORMAN CT D2
NORRIS DR C8
OAK CT D2
OAK CREEK DR D2
OAK RIDGE DR-E D1
OAK RIDGE DR-W C1
OLD MILL LN E7
PACIFIC CT C1
PARK AV D4, D8
PARKVIEW PL....................D3
PEPPERMILL CT D8
PIN OAK CT D2
PINE TREE RD D4
PLAINFIELD RD D7
POST RD E7
PRAIRIE DR.....................D2
PROVENCAL CT D2
RED OAK CT D2
REDIEHS CT D3
REGENT CT D3
RIDGE CT C4
RIDGE FARM RD D8
RIDGEPOINT DR D4
RIDGEWOOD LN F5
ROANOKE CT C3
ROCKWELL CT D5
RODEO DR D2
ROYAL DR D2
SADDLE CT D3
ST JAMES CT F8
SEDGLEY CT D9
SENECA CT F4
SHADY LANE DR E8
SHAG BARK LN F4
SHENONDOAH CT E2
SHILOH DR C3
SHORE CT C4
SHORE DR C4
SOUTH DR E9
SOUTHGATE CT E5
STEEPLESIDE DR E4
STIRRUP LN E7
STIRRUP PL E7
STONEHENGE DR E5
SURREY LN E7
SYLVAN GLEN CT C2
TAMARACK DR D2
TAMERTON PKWY D3

TOBI CT D2
TODOR..........................D3
TOMAHAWK TR E3
TOMLIN CIR E8
TOMLIN DR F9
TOWER DR E6
TRI STATE TOLLWAY F8
TUMBLE BROOK CT C1
TURNBERRY CT C2
TURNBERRY DR C2
WALNUT CT F4
WALREDON AV D3
WEDGEWOOD DR D2
WESTMINSTER DR D2
WHITE OAK CT F4
WINDSOR CT D4
WOLF RD F5
WOODGATE DR E9
WOODGLEN LN F5
WOODLAND LN F5
WOODCREEK DR D9
WOODSIDE CT E4
WOODSIDE LN E4
WOODVIEW RD E9
56TH PL E9
60TH PL D9
60TH ST D9
61ST PL D8
62ND ST D8
63RD ST D8
71ST ST C6
72ND ST C6, F6
73RD ST C6
73RD PL F6
74TH ST C6, F6
75TH ST D5, F6
77TH ST D5, F5
79TH ST C5, F5
80TH ST C4
81ST ST C4, D4
83RD CT B4
83RD ST B4, D4
87TH ST D3
89TH ST C2
91ST ST A2

Unincorporated Area

ALLISON CT B4
ARGONNE RIDGE RD A2
BIRNAM TRAIL A2
BONNIE BRAE LN B4
BROOKBANK RD B3

CASS AV A1
CENTRAL AV B3
CIRCLE AV B3
CLARENDON HILLS RD A2
ECHO LN B2
ELM CT A3
FERN ST A3
FRONTAGE RD B4
GLENN DR C1
HAMPSHIRE LN EAST A2
HAMPSHIRE LN WEST A2
HIGHLAND RD SOUTH B3
HILLSIDE DR B2
HILLSIDE LN A2, B3
HONEYSUCKLE ROSE LN B2
HYACINTH DR B1
IVY LN B1
JACKSON ST B1
KAYE LN B2
KINGERY QUARTER A2
LILAC LN B1
LORRAINE DR A3
MARYBETH CT B3
MEADOW CT B4
MEADOWBROOK DR B3
MOCKINGBIRD LN B1
O'NEILL DR B2
OAK HILL CT C1
OLD SURREY RD C9
PALISADES RD B2
SCHEEL DR A3
SHEPHARD LN C2
SKYLINE DR C2
SUNRISE AV B3
TERRY TRAIL A2
THERESE CT B4
TIMBERLAKE DR B3
VALLEY VIEW DR B2
VILLAGE RD B3
WESTERN AV A3
WILLIAMS DR B3
82ND ST C4
89TH PL A2
90TH ST A2, C2
93RD PL B1
93RD ST A2
94TH PL B1
94TH ST B1
95TH PL B1
95TH ST B1
36TH PL B1
96TH ST B1
97TH ST C1

© DonTech Chicago, Il. 1992

Carol Stream

ADAM LN	C5
ADOBE CT	C5
ALABAMA TRAIL	D6
ALAMO CT	D6
ALDRIN CT	D4
ALEUT TRAIL	C6
ALLEGHENY CT	B4
ALTON CT	B4
AMBER CT	H2
AMBER LN	G2
ANDREW LN	C5
ANTELOPE TRAIL	D6
ANTIGO TRAIL	A8
APACHE LN	C4
APPALOOSA CT	C5
APPOMATTOX TRAIL	A8
ARAPAHOE TRAIL	D4
ARMY TRAIL RD	A8
ARROWHEAD TRAIL	D4
ASH CT	A8
ASPEN CT	D7
AZTEC DR	C4
BARTON PL	B4
BASSWOOD CTR	D7
BASSWOOD CT	D7
BAYBROOK LN	B7
BEAR PAW CT	A4
BEDFORD DR	C7
BEECH CT	D7
BELAIR CT	E5
BERKSHIRE DR	B4
BIG EAGLE TRAIL	A6
BIG HORN TRAIL	A8
BILOXIE CT	B4
BIRCH BARK TRAIL	B5
BLACKHAWK DR	E4
BLUFF ST	D5
BOA TRAIL	A7
BONNIE LN	F3
BOONE DR	D6
BOWIE DR	D6
BOWSTRING CT	A8
BRADBURY	D7
BRAVE CT	A7
BRIGHTON DR	B7
BRISTOL DR	C4
BROOKSTONE DR	A6
BUCKINGHAM CT	C7
BUCKINGHAM DR	C7
BUCKSKIN LN	A5
BUFFALO CIR	A5
BURKE DR	D7
BURNETT AV	C3
BURNING TRAIL	A5
BURNS ST	G2
CACTUS TRAIL	A5
CANTERBURY DR	C7
CANYON TRAIL	D6
CARIBOU TRAIL	A7
CARLTON DR	F2
CARRIAGE LN	E3
CARSON CT	D6
CEDAR CT	D8
CHADSFORD	C4
CHALET DR	C7
CHARGER CT	A7
CHATHAM DR	C6
CHATTANOOGA TRAIL	A7
CHEROKEE CT	C4
CHESTER DR	C6
CHETWOOD CT	C7
CHEYENNE TRAIL	C4
CHIPPEWA TRAIL	C5
CIMARRON DR	B5
CLEAR WATER CT	D6
CLIFF CT	C6
CLIFFVIEW LN	A6
COACHLITE TRAIL	D3
COCHISE CT	D4
COCHISE PL	C4
COLORADO CT	B4
COLUMBIA CT	D6
COMMANCHE CT	C5
COMMANCHE LN	C5
COMMERCE	F4
COMMONWEALTH	F2
CONCORD DR	B5
COUNTY FARM RD	B3
COUNTRY GLEN LN	B8
COUNTRYSIDE LN	A8
CREEKWOOD CT	C4
CREST ST	A7
CRYSTAL SHORE DR	A7
CUMBERLAND CT	B6
CYPRESS LN	A5
DAKOTA CT	B4
DANBURY DR	C4
DANCING WATER CT	D6
DARTMOUTH DR	B5
DAVID LN	C5
DEARBORN CIR	D6
DEERSKIN TRAIL	C6
DELAWARE TRAIL	C6
DEVON CT	B7
DODGE CT	D6
DOGWOOD LN	A5
DONEGAL CT	A7
DORIS AV	E1
DORY CIR-E	C8
DORY CIR-W	C8
DUBLIN CT	D7
EAGLEVIEW DR	E4
EASY ST	E2
EDGEBROOK CT	D5
EDINGTON CT	C7
EDINGTON DR	C7
EL PASO LN	D4
ELK TRAIL	E6
ERIE CT	C5
ESSELEN CT	B4
ESSEX DR	C4
ETHEL ST	B4
EVERGREEN DR	A5
EXECUTIVE DR	F1
FAIR OAKS RD	A6
FARM GLEN LN	B8
FAWN CT	D5
FEATHER CT	D6
FLAME CT	H2
FLAME DR	H2
FLINT TRAIL	D6
FOREST CT	B7
FOREST LN	B8
FOX CT	A5
FULLERTON AV	E4
GARY AV	**E1-E5**
GENEVA RD	**G1**
GEORGETOWN DR	A8
GLEN CT	B8
GLEN FLORAL DR	E5
GLEN LAKE DR	B8
GLOUSTER CIR	A8
GREENWAY TRAIL	E5
GUNDERSEN DR	F1
HAMPTON CT	C7
HAMPTON DR	C6
HARBOR PT	A8
HARWICH DR	A8
HEARTH LN	G2
HEATHER LN	E4
HEMLOCK LN	A5
HERITAGE DR	C8
HIAWATHA DR	D4
HICKORY LN	A5
HIGHRIDGE PASS	A6
HILLCREST DR	A6
HOPI CT	D6
HORSESHOE	B6
HUNTER DR	D7
HUNTINGTON CT	C7
HUNTINGTON DR	C7
HURON CT	D6
HYANNIS CIR	A7
IDAHO ST	D6
ILLINI DR	C4
INCA BL	C5
INDIANWOOD DR	D4
IOWA CT	D4
IRIS AV	A6
IRON HAWK CT	D5
IROQUOIS TRAIL	B5
JEFFERSON ST	B4
JUNIPER CT	D6
KALAMAZOO CT	D6
KAMIAH CT	C4
KANSAS ST	D6
KEHOE BL	E4
KELLY DR	B8
KERRY CT	D7
KILDARE CT	D7
KILKENNY CT	D7
KIMBERLY DR	F4
KINGSBRIDGE DR	C7
KLEIN CREEK CT	E6
KNOLLWOOD DR	B8
KUHN RD	C3
LACROSSE ST	D6
LAGUNA CT	D6
LAKESHORE DR	B7
LAKESIDE DR	A7
LAKEWOOD DR	B7
LANCE CT	A6
LANCE LN	A6
LAUREL CT	A5
LIES RD	B6
LIGHTNING TRAIL	A5
LILAC CT	A6
LILAC LN	A6
LILY LN	A6
LONGMEADOW DR	B6
MAGNOLIA WAY	A6
MAIN PL-S	F2
MAIN ST	F1
MALIBU CT	D6
MANTLE LN	G2
MAPLE RIDGE CT	A7
MARDON RD	A4
MAYFAIR DR	C7
MEADOW LN	G2
MEDFORD DR	B4
MERBACH DR	D7
MERCEDES DR	E5
MERRIMAC LN-E	C8
MERRIMAC LN-N	C8
MERRIMAC LN-S	C8
MERRIMAC LN-W	C8
MESA VERDE CT	C4
MILL CT	B7
MINNESOTA CIR	B4
MOCASSIN CT	D6
MOHAWK DR	E4
MOHICAN RD	C5
MONITOR DR	C8
MORTON RD	A4
MOUNTAIN GLEN WAY	A6
MUNSON DR	B4
MYSTIC CT	A8
NAPA ST	D6
NATOMA CIR	E4
NAVAJO CT	D6
NAVAJO ST	G3
NEBRASKA CIR	B4
NEKOMA CT	B4
NEW BRITTON RD	A6
NEW LONDON CT	A5
NEZ PERCE CT	C5
NIAGARA ST	D6
NORTH AV	**D4-G5**
NORTH AV	C3
OHIO CT	D6
OLD GARY AV	E7
OLD MEADOW CT	A6
OMAHA CT	C6
ONEIDA CT	B4
OSAGE CIR	B4
OSWEGO CT	B5
OSWEGO DR	B5
OTTAWA CT	C5
OVERLOOK LN	A6
PADDOCK DR	B6
PALOMINO	C6
PAPOOSE CT	C6
PARK HILL TRAIL	E3
PARKSIDE CT	C7
PARKSIDE DR	C7
PAWNEE DR	B4
PAXTON PL	C4
PEBBLE CREEK TR	E5
PENNSBORO CT	A8
PEORIA CT	B4
PETERSBURG CT	A8
PETERSON AV	C3
PLAINS CT	B4
PLYMOUTH CT	A7
POCAHONTAS TRAIL	D5
PONTIAC LN	B4
PORTSMOUTH CT	A8
POTOMAC CT	A8
PRAIRIE CT	B5
PRESIDENT ST	H1
PRINCETOWN CT	C6
PROVINCETOWN DR	C6
QUAIL RUN CT	E3
RAINTREE CT	A5
RANDY RD-E	F3
REGENCY LN	C7
RIDGE TR	A6
RIVER DR	B6
RED HILL TRAIL	E5
ROBIN DR	A7
ROCK VALLEY WAY	A6
ROCK PORT DR	A8
ROLLING OAKS DR	A6
ROSE AV	A6
ROYAL GLEN WAY	A6
ST CHARLES RD-W	D2
ST PAUL BL	F4
SAGINAW CT	C6
SAND CREEK DR	B4
SANDHURST CT	C7
SANDHURST LN	C7
SANTA FE CT	C5
SAUK CT	C4
SCHMALE RD-N	G4
SCHMALE RD-S	G1
SEABURY CIR	A8
SEMINOLE LN	D3
SENECA DR	B4
SEQUOIA CT	B4
SHAGBARK CT	A5
SHAWNEE DR	D3
SHEFFIELD ST	A6
SHELBURNE DR	C4
SHENANDOAH DR	B5
SHINING WATER DR	A5
SILVERLEAF BL	D4
SIOUX LN	D4
SOMMERSET CT	C7
SOMMERSET DR	C7
SORREL CT	B6
SPLIT TRAIL DR	B6
SPRINGBROOK CT	D5
SPRINGBROOK LN	D5
SPRINGVALE RD	A4
SPRING VALLEY DR	A7
SPUR CT	B6
STANFORD LN	B7
STARK DR	E8
STOCKBRIDGE DR	B5
STONEHENGE CT	A6
STONEWOOD CIR	D7
STUART DR	C5
SUMMIT PASS	A6
SUNDANCE CT	B4
SUNRISE CT	D5
SURREY DR	D3
SUSSEX RD	A6
TACOMA DR	B4
TAHOE CT	B4
TAMA CT	C5
TETON CIR	B4
TEXAS CT	B4
THORNHILL DR-E	G1
THUNDERBIRD TRAIL	C4
TIMBER RIDGE DR-S	H1
TIOGA CT	C6
TOMAHAWK CT	D4
TONTO CT	C5
TOPEKA CT	B4
TRAILSIDE CT	D8
TREMONT CT	B5
TRINITY CT	B7
TRINITY DR	B7
TUBEWAY DR	D2
UTE LN	C5
VALE RD	B4
VALLEY VIEW TRAIL	B5
VILLAGE CT	E4
VILLAGE DR	E4
VIOLET ST	A6
WABASH ST	C6
WALNUT CIR	A7
WALNUT CT	A7
WAMPUM CT	C6
WARWICK CT	B7
WARWICK DR	C7
WATERFORD CT	D7
WEST ST	F1
WESTGATE DR	D2
WEYFORD CT	D7
WILLIAMSTOWN DR	B6
WILLOW WOOD DR	G2
WINDMERE LN	C4
WINDSOR PARK DR	D3
WOODCREST CT	D5
WOODHILL DR	B7
YELLOWSTONE ST	C6
YARDLEY DR	C7
YORKSHIRE LN	A5
YUMA LN	E3

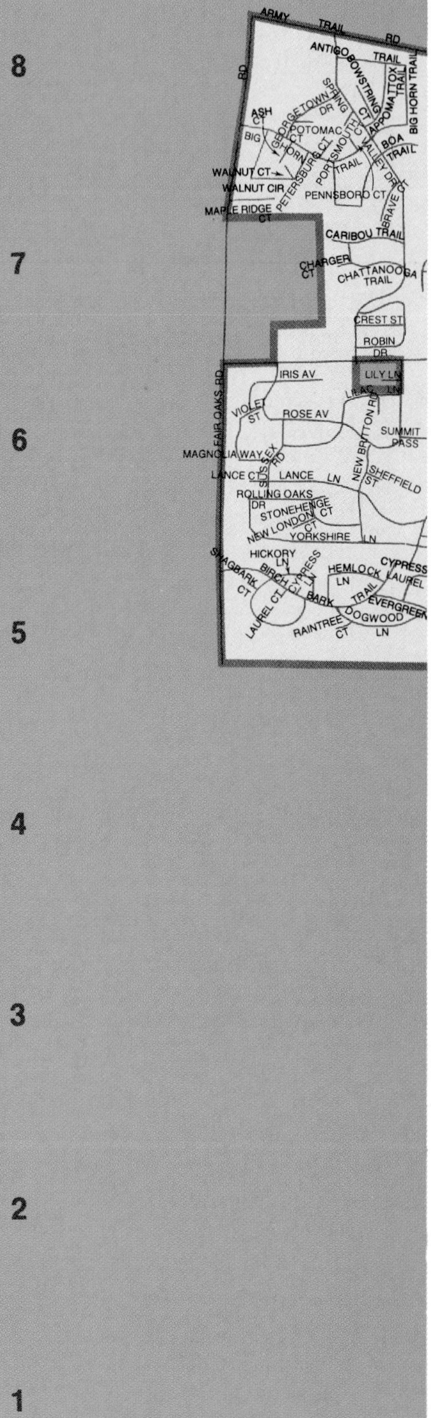

© DonTech Chicago, Il. 1992

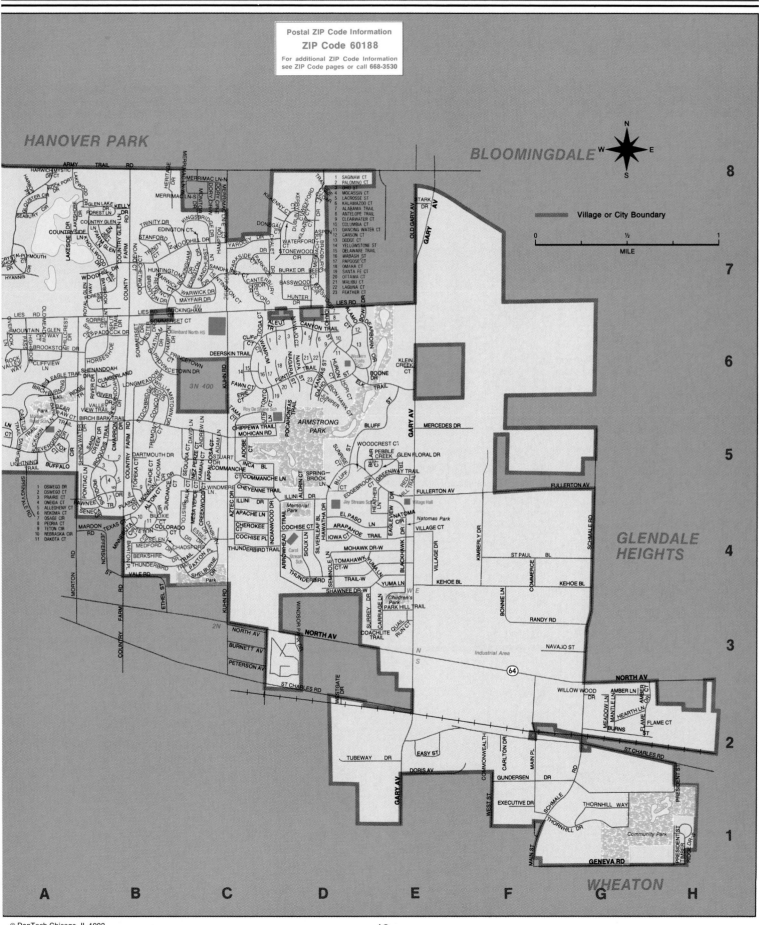

© DonTech Chicago, Il. 1992

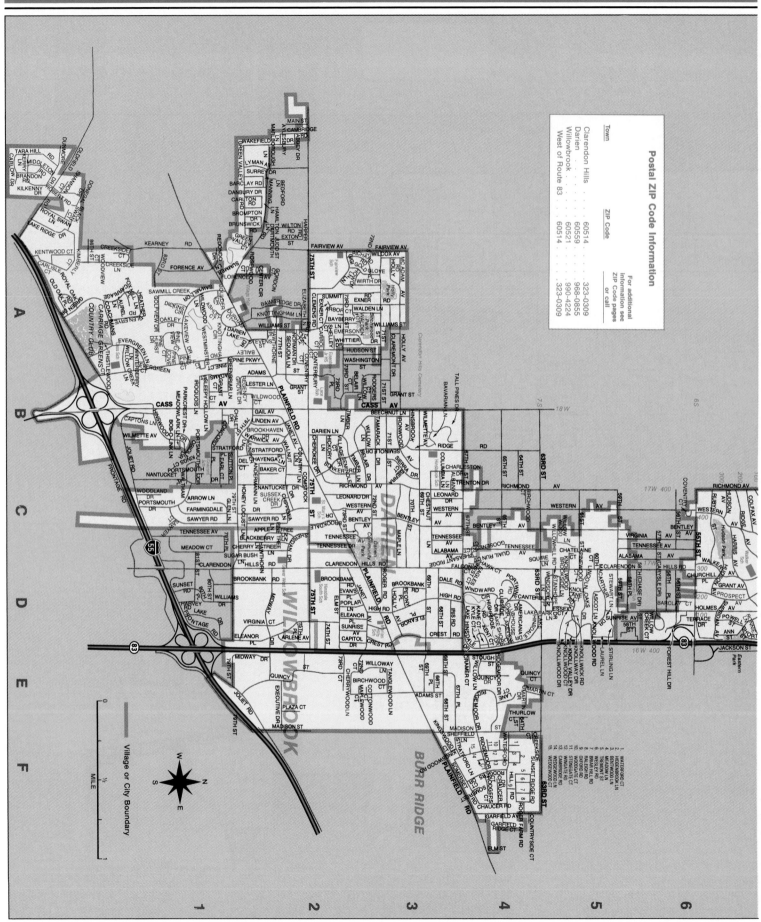

© DonTech Chicago, Il. 1992

Clarendon Hills

Street	Grid
ALGONQUIN RD	C7
ANN ST	C7
ARTHUR AV	C7
BARCLAY CT	D6
BLACKHAWK	B8
BLODGETT AV	D7
BONNIE LN	D7
BURLINGTON AV	D7
BYRD CT	D7
CHESTNUT AV	D7
CHICAGO AV	**D8**
CHURCHILL PL	D6
CLARENDON HILLS RD	D6
COE RD	D4
COLFAX AV	D7
COLUMBINE DR	C8
COVENTRY CT	C7
EASTERN AV	D7
FAIRVIEW CT	D7
FOREST HILL DR	C7
GILBERT AV	C7
GOLF AV	D6
GRANT AV	C7
HAMILL AV	D7
HARRIS AV	D7
HIAWATHA DR	D7
HICKORY ST	D8
HOLMES AV-S	D8
HUDSON AV	D6
INDIAN DR	C7
IROQUOIS DR	C7
JACKSON ST-N	E8
JACKSON ST-S	E8
JANE CT	D7
JANE RD	D7
JOLIET CT	D7
LARKSPUR LN	C8
MAPLE ST	D8
MCINTOSH AV	D7
MIDDAUGH RD	D7
MOHAWK DR	C7
NAPERVILLE RD	C7
NORFOLK AV	C7
OGDEN AV	**C8**
OXFORD AV	C7
PARK AV	C7
POWELL ST	D7
PROSPECT AV-N	D7
PROSPECT AV-S	D7
RAILROAD AV	D6
RICHMOND AV-N	C6
RICHMOND AV-S	C7
ROSE PL	D7
ROUTE 83	**E6**
RUBY ST	D6
SHERIDAN AV	D6
SHORT ST	D6
STONEGATE RD	C8
TERRACE DR	C8
TRAUBE AV	C8
TUTTLE AV	C8
WALKER AV	D6
WALNUT ST	D8
WAVERLY AV	D7
WESTERN AV	D6
WILLOW WOOD LN	C5
WILLOW CREEK CT	C5
WOODSTOCK AV	C7
55TH ST	**D6**
67TH ST	C4

Darien

Street	Grid
ABBEY DR	A2
ADAMS ST	B1
ALABAMA AV	A2
ALBANY LN	C3
ANDERMANN LN	C1
ARBOR CT	A2
ARROW LN	C1
ASHLEY CT	D4
AYLESBURY LN	C7
BAILEY RD	A1
BAKER CT	A2
BAMBRIDGE DR	A2
BARCLAY RD	A2
BAVARIAN LN	B3
BAYBERRY LN	B3
BEDFORD LN	A1
BEECHNUT LN	B3
BELAIR CT	B3
BELAIR DR	B3
BENTLEY AV	C3
BOB-O-LINK LN	C3
BOULDER DR	A1
BRANDON RD	A1
BRITTANY CT	A2
BROMPTON DR	A2
BROOKBANK RD	D2
BROOKDALE DR	B1
BROOKHAVEN DR	B1
BRUNSWICK RD	C3
BUNKER RD	C3
CAMBRIDGE RD	A2
CANTERBURY CT	A2
CAPITOL DR	A2
CAPTONS LN	E3
CARLISLE CT	A1
CARLTON RD	A2
CARLOW DR	A2
CARRIAGE GREEN DR	**C8**
CARROL CT	C7
CASS AV	**B1**
CENTER CIR	A1
CHALET DR	B1
CHARLESTON DR	C3
CHEROKEE DR	B2
CHESTNUT LN	B1
CHIPPEWA LN	C2
CLARENDON HILLS RD	A3
CLEMENS RD	A2
COACHMANS RD	C3
COLUMBIA LN	A1
COMSTOCK LN	C3
CONCORD PL	B1
COUNTRY CT	B2
COVENTRY CT	C7
CREEKSIDE LN	E3
CREST RD	E3
DALE RD	D3
DANBURY DR	B1
DARIEN LN	A2
DARIEN LAKE DR	B2
DARTMOUTH LN	A2
DEL CT	A2
DICKENS CIR	A1
DONEGAL DR	A1
DUNMORE DR	A1
DURHAM CT	A1
EAGLES NEST CT	A1
ELEANOR PL	A1
ELIZABETH LN	A1
ELM ST	D2
EMERSON DR	A1
EVANS PL	A2
EVERGREEN CT	A1
EVERGREEN LN	A1
EXNER CT	A1
EXNER RD	A1
FAIRVIEW AV	A2
FALCON CT	A2
FARMINGDALE DR	C1
FLORENCE AV	A1
FOX HILL PL	A1
GAIL AV	A1
GIGI LN	A3
GLEN ERVE RD	A1
GLEN LN	A1
GOLD GLOVE PL	A3
GOLFVIEW DR	A3
GOOSENECK CT	A1
GORDON CT	C4
GRANT CT	B1
GRANT RD	B1
GREEN VALLEY CT	A2
GREEN VALLEY RD	A2
GREENBRIAR LN	A3
GREENWAY DR	B1
HAMILTON LN	A1
HAWK CT	C4
HAWTHORNE PL	A2
HAYENGA LN	A2
HEATHER LN	A2
HICKORY LN	E3
HIGH RD	A1
HINSBROOK AV	B3
HINSWOOD DR	B3
HOLLY AV	A3-D3
HONEY LOCUST LN	C1
HOWDY LN	A3
HUDSON ST	A1
IRIS RD	D3
IRONWOOD LN	A1
IROQUOIS LN	B1
JANET AV	A1
JOLIET RD	C1
JULIET AV	A1
JUNIPER LN	A1
KEARNEY RD	A1
KENTWOOD CT	A3
KERRY LN	A1
KILKENNY DR	A1
KIMBERLY CT	C3
KNOTTINGHAM CIR	B1
KNOTTINGHAM LN	B1
LAKE DR	D1
LAKEVIEW DR	A1
LAUREL LN	A1
LEONARD DR	A1
LESTER LN	B1
LINDEN AV	B1
LYMAN AV	A2
MANNING RD	A2
MAPLE LN	A2
MARLBOROUGH LN	A2
MC ADAM RD	A3
MEADOWLARK LN	B1
MIDDLETOWN RD	B1
NANTUCKET RD	C2
NORMAN DR	A1
OAKLEY DR	A1
OLD OAK PL	A1
ORIOLE DR	A1
PARKCREST DR	D3
PEONY PL	B1
PINE CT	B1
PINE BLUFF CT	B1
PINE COVE CT	A1
PINE HURST DR	A1
PINE VIEW CT	A1
PINE PKWY	A2
PLAINFIELD RD	**B2**
PLEASANT RIDGE CT	C1
POPLAR LN	A1
PORTSMOUTH DR	A1
QUAIL RUN CT	C4
REDONDO DR	A1
REGENCY GROVE DR	B1
RICHARD RD	A1
RICHMOND AV	C2
RIDGE RD	B3
ROBERT RD	C4
RODGERS CT	B1
ROSEWOOD CT	A1
ROUTE 83	A1
ROYAL OAK RD	A1
SAWMILL CREEK	A1
SAWMILL DR	A1
SAWYER CT	C1
SAWYER RD	C1
SEMINOLE DR	B2
SEQUOIA LN	B2
SHANNON CT	A1
SHELLEY CT	B3
SIERRA CT	C3
SIERRA DR	B1
SLEEPY HOLLOW CT	B1
SLEEPY HOLLOW LN	B1
STEVENS CT	A1
STRATFORD PL	B2
SUMMIT RD	A1
SUNRISE AV	B1
SUNRISE CT	E2
SURREY DR	A1
SUSSEX CREEK DR	C2
TALL PINES DR	A1
TAMARACK DR	A1
TARA HILL RD	A1
TENNESSEE AV	A1
THISTLEWOOD CT	D2
TIMBER LN	A1
TRENTON DR	C3
VILLAGE CT	A2
WAKEFIELD DR	A2
WALDEN CT	A1
WALDEN LN	A1
WALNUT LN	A2
WARWICK AV	B1

Willowbrook

Street	Grid
ADAMS ST	A3-C3
ALABAMA AV	C6
AMERICANA DR	C2
APPLE TREE LN	C2
ARLENE AV	C2
ASCOT LN	D5
BENTLEY AV	C1
BENTWOOD LN	C1
BIRCHWOOD CT	E3
BLACKBERRY LN	B2
BRIARHILL RD	D1
BROOKBANK RD	D1
BROOKSIDE LN	C3
CAMBRIDGE RD	C3
CANTERBURY LN	D4
CHATELAINE CT	E4
CHAUCER CT	C2
CHAUCER RD	D2
CHERRY TREE LN	C1
CHERRYWOOD LN	B1
CLARENDON HILLS RD	D4
CLUBHOUSE DR	C2
CLUBSIDE DR	A2
COTTONWOOD CT	B3
CRAMER CT	C2
CREEKSIDE CT	E4
ELEANOR PL	E2
ELM ST-S	C3
ESSEX CT	C3
EXECUTIVE DR	A2
GARFIELD AV	A2
GARFIELD AV-S	A2
GARFIELD RIDGE CT	C1
HAWTHORN LN	A2
HIDDENBROOK LN	B2
HIGHRIDGE RD	B1
HILL RD	C3
HONEY LOCUST LN	C1
KANE CT	C1
KENT CT	D3
KINGSWOOD CT	F3
KINGSWOOD RD	F3
KNOLL LANE CT	D5
KNOLL VALLEY DR	D5
KNOLLWAY DR	D5
KNOLLWOOD CT	D5
KNOLLWOOD DR	D5
KNOLLWOOD RD	D5
KYLE CT	E4
LAKE HINSDALE DR	D4
LAKE PARK LN	D4
LAKE SHORE DR	D4
LAKEVIEW CT	E4
LANE CT	E4
LAUREL LN	D5
LINCOLN OAKS DR	D5
MACARTHUR DR	D5
MADISON ST	E4
MAPLEWOOD CT	E4
MARTIN DR	C6
MEADOW LN	F4
MIDWAY DR	D2
OXFORD RD	C1
PINE TREE LN	C2
PINEWOOD CT	C2
PLAINFIELD RD	**E3**
PLAZA CT	E4
PORTWINE RD	D4
QUINCY DR	E4
RALEIGH RD	E4
RIDGEMOOR CT	E4
RIDGEMOOR DR-W	F4
RODGERS CT	F4
RODGERS DR	F4
ROUTE 83	**E2**
SHEFFIELD LN	F4
SHERIDAN DR	F4
SOMERSET CT	F4
SOMERSET RD	F4
STANHOPE DR	D5
STANHOPE RD	D5
STEWART DR	D5
STIRLING LN	C5
STONEGATE CT	C5
STOUGH ST	F4
STRATFORD LN	D1
SUGAR BUSH LN	D1
SUNSET RIDGE RD	E3
TANGLEWOOD LN	E3
TENNESSEE AV	A2
TENNESSEE DR	D2
TREMONT RD	D2
VIRGINIA AV	C6
VIRGINIA CT	C6
WATERFORD CT	F4
WATERFORD DR	F4
WEDGEWOOD CT	F4
WEDGEWOOD LN	F4
WESLEY RD	F4
WESTERN AV	C5
WILLOW LN	E4
WILLOWHILL RD	D5
WASHINGTON ST	B2
WESTERN AV	C3
WESTMINSTER CT	B1
WHITTIER DR	A2
WILCOX AV	C3
WILDWOOD CT	B1
WILDWOOD LN	B1
WILLIAMS ST	A2
WILLOW LN	B3
WILMETTE AV	A2
WINTERBERRY LN	C1
WIRTH DR	A3
WOODVIEW CT	C1
67TH ST	B1
68TH ST	B1
69TH ST	D3
70TH ST	D3
70TH PL	D3
71ST ST	D3
71ST PL	D3
72ND ST	D3
73RD ST	D3
74TH ST	A1
75TH ST	A1
77TH ST	A1
79TH ST-W	A1
83RD ST	C2
86TH ST	A1

Unincorporated Area

Street	Grid
ADAMS ST	D6
BARCLAY CT	C4
BIRCHWOOD RD	A1
BLACK SWAN CT	B1
EARL CT	B1
EXTON ST	D2
FRONTAGE RD	E2
FRONTAGE RD-N	E2
HARPER RD	B1
HARVEY RD	B1
JOLIET RD	B1
JUDD ST	B1
KINGS CT	B1
LAKE RIDGE DR	B1
LAKE RIDGE DR	B1
MAIN ST	B1
NANTUCKET DR	C4
OLDFIELD RD	D6
PORTSMOUTH CT	C4
QUINCY CT	B1
QUINCY ST	B1
ROYAL SWAN LN	A2
SQUIRE LN	C4
STRATFORD PL	D6
SUNRISE AV	B1
SUTTON PL	B1
THURLOW CT	B1
WALTHAM PL	B1
WILLIAMS DR	A2
WILTON RD	A2
56TH PL	D6
57TH ST (CARYSLE DR)	D6
58TH ST (CHASE DR)	D6
61ST ST	C5
63RD ST	**C4**
64TH ST	B4
79TH ST	D1
79TH PL	D1
80TH PL	D1
80TH ST-W	D1
81ST ST	C1
WILLOWAY LN	D6
WINDSOR LN	D5
WINDWARD CIR	D5
WINGATE RD	F4
WOODGATE CT	F4
58TH PL	D5
59TH CT	D5
60TH CT	E3
63RD CT	**D4**
67TH CT	E3
67TH ST	E4
68TH ST	E3
68TH PL	E3
69TH ST	E3
72ND CT	E2
73RD CT	E2
75TH PL	E2
75TH ST-W	**D2**
79TH ST-W	**D1**

© DonTech Chicago, Il. 1992

Countryside

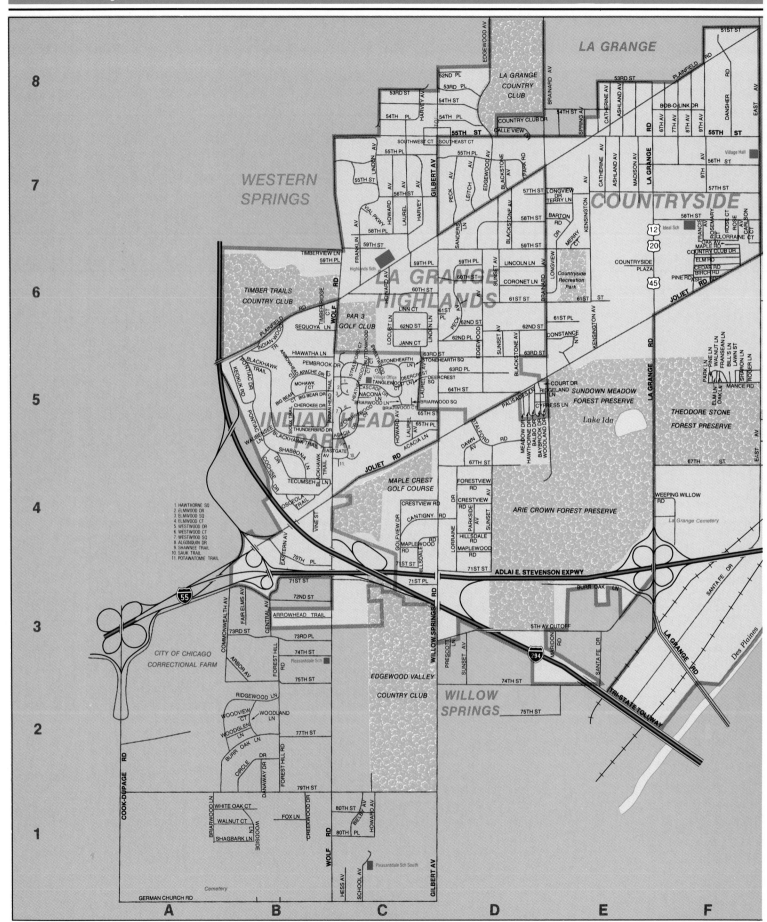

© DonTech Chicago, Il. 1992

Postal ZIP Code Information

Town	ZIP Code	For additional information see following pages or call
Countryside	60525	352-3611
Hodgkins	60525	352-3611
Indian Head Park	60525	352-3611
La Grange Highlands	60525	352-3611

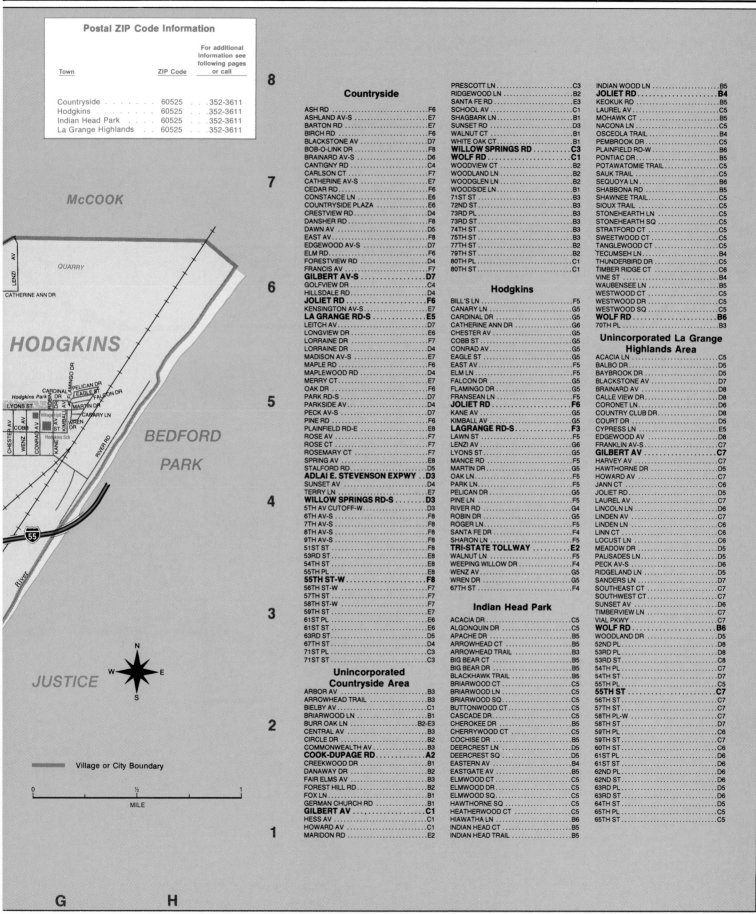

Countryside

ASH RD	F6
ASHLAND AV-S	E7
BARTON RD	E7
BIRCH RD	F6
BLACKSTONE AV	D7
BOB-O-LINK DR	F8
BRAINARD AV-S	D6
CANTIGNY RD	C4
CARLSON CT	F7
CATHERINE AV-S	E7
CEDAR RD	F6
CONSTANCE LN	E6
COUNTRYSIDE PLAZA	E6
CRESTVIEW RD	D4
DANSHER RD	F8
DAWN AV	D5
EAST AV	F8
EDGEWOOD AV-S	D7
ELM RD	F6
FORESTVIEW RD	D4
FRANCIS AV	F7
GILBERT AV-S	**D7**
GOLFVIEW DR	C4
HILLSDALE RD	D4
JOLIET RD	**F6**
KENSINGTON AV-S	E7
LA GRANGE RD-S	**E5**
LEITCH AV	D7
LONGVIEW DR	E6
LORRAINE DR	F7
LORRAINE DR	D4
MADISON AV-S	E7
MAPLE RD	F6
MAPLEWOOD RD	D4
MERRY CT	E7
OAK DR	F6
PARK RD-S	D7
PARKSIDE AV	D4
PECK AV-S	D7
PINE RD	F6
PLAINFIELD RD-E	E8
ROSE AV	F7
ROSE CT	F7
ROSEMARY CT	F7
SPRING AV	E8
STALFORD RD	D5
ADLAI E. STEVENSON EXPWY	**D3**
SUNSET AV	D4
TERRY LN	E7
WILLOW SPRINGS RD-S	**D3**
5TH AV CUTOFF-W	D3
6TH AV-S	F8
7TH AV-S	F8
8TH AV-S	F8
9TH AV-S	F8
51ST ST	F8
53RD ST	E8
54TH ST	E8
55TH PL	E8
55TH ST-W	**F8**
56TH ST-W	F7
57TH ST	F7
58TH ST-W	F7
59TH ST	E7
61ST PL	E6
61ST ST	E6
63RD ST	D5
67TH ST	D4
71ST PL	C3
71ST ST	C3

Unincorporated Countryside Area

ARBOR AV	B3
ARROWHEAD TRAIL	B3
BIELBY AV	C1
BRIARWOOD LN	B1
BURR OAK LN	B2-E3
CENTRAL AV	B3
CIRCLE DR	B2
COMMONWEALTH AV	B3
COOK-DUPAGE RD	**A2**
CREEKWOOD DR	B1
DANAWAY DR	B2
FAIR ELMS AV	B3
FOREST HILL RD	B2
FOX LN	B1
GERMAN CHURCH RD	B1
GILBERT AV	**C1**
HESS AV	C1
HOWARD AV	C1
MARIDON RD	E2

PRESCOTT LN	C3
RIDGEWOOD LN	B2
SANTA FE RD	E3
SCHOOL AV	C1
SHAGBARK LN	B1
SUNSET RD	D3
WALNUT CT	B1
WHITE OAK CT	B1
WILLOW SPRINGS RD	**C3**
WOLF RD	**C1**
WOODVIEW CT	B2
WOODLAND LN	B2
WOODGLEN LN	B2
WOODSIDE LN	B1
71ST ST	B3
72ND ST	B3
73RD PL	B3
73RD ST	B3
74TH ST	B3
75TH ST	B3
77TH ST	B2
79TH ST	B2
80TH PL	C1
80TH ST	C1

Hodgkins

BILL'S LN	F5
CANARY LN	G5
CARDINAL DR	G5
CATHERINE ANN DR	G6
CHESTER AV	G5
COBB ST	G5
CONRAD AV	G5
EAGLE ST	G5
EAST AV	F5
ELM LN	F5
FALCON DR	G5
FLAMINGO DR	G5
FRANSEAN LN	F5
JOLIET RD	**F6**
KANE AV	G5
KIMBALL AV	G5
LAGRANGE RD-S	**F3**
LAWN ST	F5
LENZI AV	G6
LYONS ST	G5
MANCE RD	G5
MARTIN DR	G5
OAK LN	F5
PARK LN	F5
PELICAN DR	G5
PINE LN	F5
RIVER RD	G4
ROBIN DR	G5
ROGER LN	F5
SANTA FE DR	F4
SHARON LN	F5
TRI-STATE TOLLWAY	**E2**
WALNUT LN	F5
WEEPING WILLOW DR	F4
WENZ AV	G5
WREN DR	G5
67TH ST	F4

Indian Head Park

ACACIA DR	C5
ALGONQUIN DR	C5
APACHE DR	B5
ARROWHEAD CT	B5
ARROWHEAD TRAIL	B3
BIG BEAR CT	B5
BIG BEAR DR	B5
BLACKHAWK TRAIL	C5
BRIARWOOD CT	C5
BRIARWOOD LN	C5
BRIARWOOD SQ	C5
BUTTONWOOD CT	C5
CASCADE DR	C5
CHEROKEE DR	B5
CHERRYWOOD CT	C5
COCHISE DR	B5
DEERCREST DR	D5
DEERCREST SQ	D5
EASTERN AV	B4
EASTGATE AV	B5
ELMWOOD CT	C5
ELMWOOD DR	C5
ELMWOOD SQ	C5
HAWTHORNE AV	C5
HEATHERWOOD CT	C5
HIAWATHA LN	B6
INDIAN HEAD CT	B5
INDIAN HEAD TRAIL	B5

INDIAN WOOD LN	B5
JOLIET RD	**B4**
KEOKUK RD	B5
LAUREL AV	C5
MOHAWK CT	B5
NACONA LN	C5
OSCEOLA TRAIL	B4
PEMBROOK DR	C5
PLAINFIELD RD-W	B6
PONTIAC DR	B5
POTAWATOMIE TRAIL	C5
SAUK TRAIL	C5
SEQUOYA LN	B6
SHABBONA RD	B5
SHAWNEE TRAIL	C5
SIOUX TRAIL	C5
STONEHEARTH LN	C5
STONEHEARTH SQ	C5
STRATFORD CT	C5
SWEETWOOD CT	C5
TANGLEWOOD CT	C5
TECUMSEH LN	B4
THUNDERBIRD DR	C5
TIMBER RIDGE CT	C6
VINE ST	B4
WAUBENSEE LN	B5
WESTWOOD CT	C5
WESTWOOD DR	C5
WESTWOOD SQ	C5
WOLF RD	**B6**
70TH PL	B3

Unincorporated La Grange Highlands Area

ACACIA LN	C5
BALBO DR	D5
BAYBROOK DR	D5
BLACKSTONE AV	D7
BRAINARD AV	D8
CALLE VIEW DR	D8
CORONET LN	D6
COUNTRY CLUB DR	D8
COURT DR	D5
CYPRESS LN	E5
EDGEWOOD AV	D8
FRANKLIN AV-S	C7
GILBERT AV	**C7**
HARVEY AV	C7
HAWTHORNE DR	C7
HOWARD AV	C7
JANN CT	C6
JOLIET RD	D5
LAUREL AV	C7
LINCOLN LN	D6
LINDEN AV	C7
LINDEN LN	C6
LINN CT	C6
LOCUST LN	C6
MEADOW DR	D5
PALISADES LN	D5
PECK AV-S	D6
RIDGELAND LN	D5
SANDERS LN	D7
SOUTHEAST CT	C7
SOUTHWEST CT	C7
SUNSET AV	D6
TIMBERVIEW LN	C7
VIAL PKWY	C7
WOLF RD	**B6**
WOODLAND DR	D5
52ND PL	D8
53RD PL	D8
53RD ST	C8
54TH PL	C7
54TH ST	D7
55TH PL	C5
55TH ST	**C7**
56TH ST	C7
57TH ST	C7
58TH PL-W	C7
58TH ST	D7
59TH PL	C6
59TH ST	C7
60TH ST	C6
61ST PL	D6
61ST ST	D6
62ND PL	D6
62ND ST	D6
63RD PL	D5
63RD ST	D6
64TH ST	D5
65TH PL	C5
65TH ST	C5

McCOOK

QUARRY

CATHERINE ANN DR

LENZI AV

HODGKINS

HODGKINS

Hodgkins Park

PELICAN DR
FLAMINGO DR
CARDINAL DR
EAGLE ST
FALCON DR
MARTIN DR
KIMBALL AV
ROBIN DR
CANARY LN
WREN DR
LYONS ST
CHESTER AV
COBB
WENZ AV
CONRAD AV
KANE AV
Village Hall
Hodgkins Sch

RIVER RD

BEDFORD PARK

River

JUSTICE

N W E S

I-55

Village or City Boundary

0 ½ 1
MILE

G   H

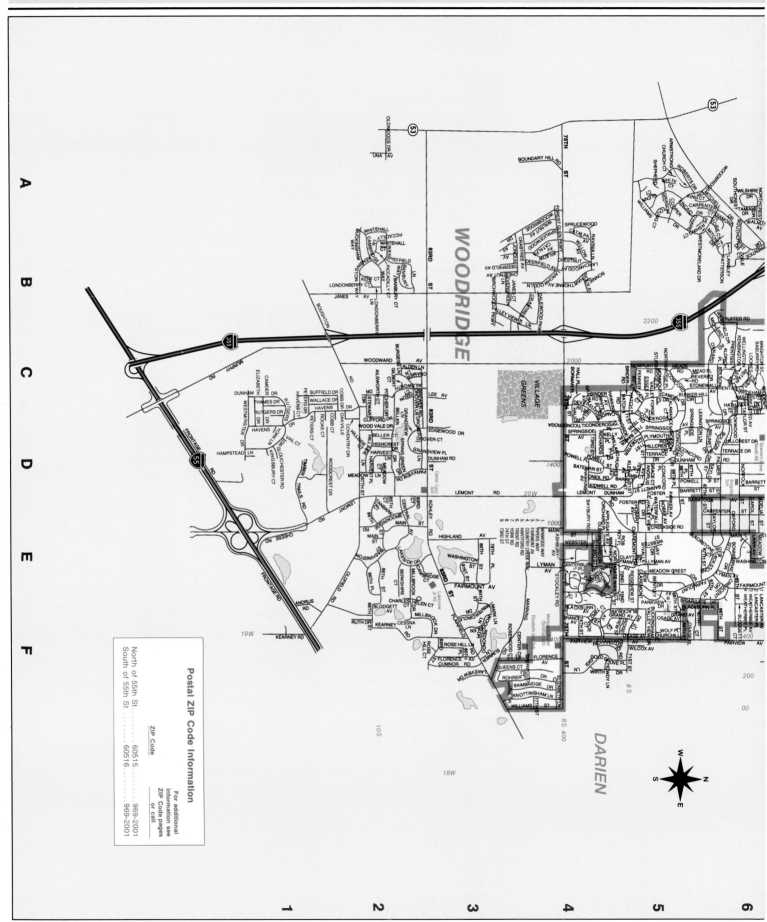

© DonTech Chicago, Il. 1992

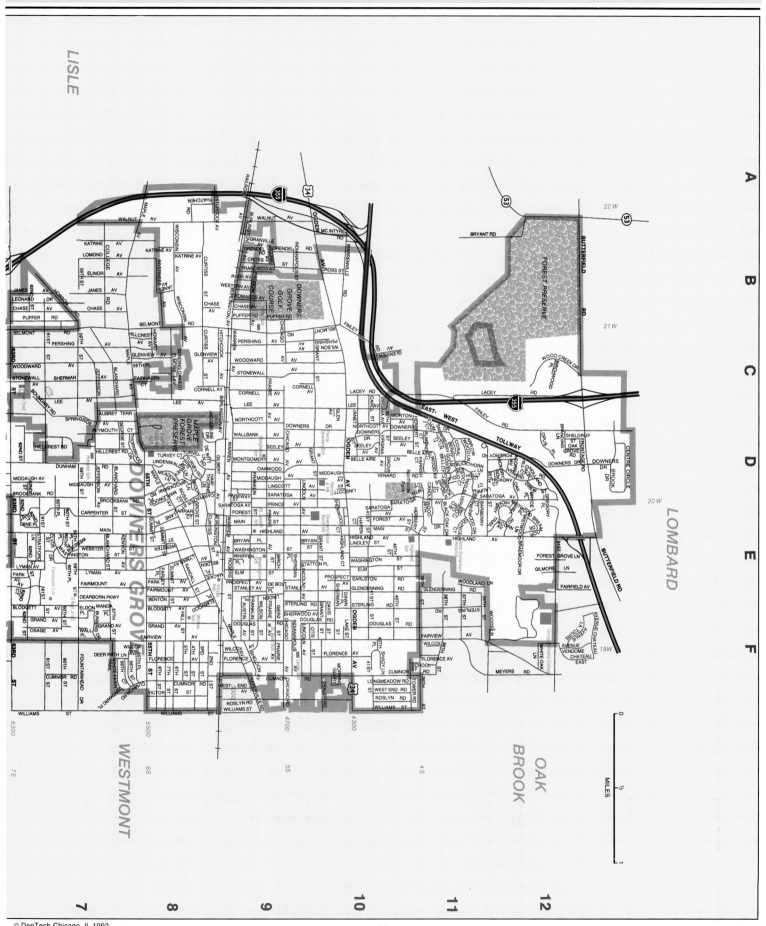

© DonTech Chicago, Il. 1992

Downers Grove

ACORN AV ... D12
ADELIA ST ... D6
ALAMANCE CT ... C5
ALDRICH PL ... C6
ALMOND CT ... D11
ANDRUS AV ... D5
APPLEGATE AV ... E4
ARROW WOOD LN ... D11
ASHBURY AV ... E4
AUBREY TERR ... C7
AUSTIN AV ... F9
BABURRY RD ... C6
BAIMBRIDGE DR ... F4
BAKER PL ... D4
BARBERRY CT ... D11
BARNESWOOD DR ... D11
BARRET ... D5
BARRETT ST ... D6
BATEMAN ST ... C4
BATES PL ... C6
BAYBURY RD ... E4
BELDEN AV ... E8
BELLE AIRE CT ... D11
BELLE AIRE LN ... D10
BELMONT RD ... B9
BENDING OAKS CT ... C8
BENTLEY ... E5
BENTON AV ... E8
BINDER RD ... C5
BIRCH ST ... E9
BIRCHWOOD PL ... C12
BLACKBURN AV ... E4
BLACKBURN CT ... E4
BLACK OAK DR ... D11
BLACKSTONE CT ... E6
BLACKSTONE DR ... E6
BLANCHARD ... C7
BLANCHARD ST ... E7
BLODGETT AV ... F8
BOLSON DR ... E6
BONNIE BRAE DR ... E6
BORMAN PL ... C4
BRAEMOOR DR ... E12
BRANDING LN ... D12
BREASTED AV ... C6
BRIARGATE DR ... E5
BRIGHTON ST ... C6
BRODGETT CT ... E6
BROOK DR ... D12
BROOK LN ... D8
BROOKBANK RD ... D7
BROOKSIDE LN ... D11
BROOKWOOD ST ... C6
BRUNETTE DR ... D6
BRYAN PL ... E9
BRYAN ST ... E9
BRYANT RD ... B12
BRYCE PL ... D12
BUCKINGHAM ... E5
BUCKTHORN LN ... D11
BUNKER HILL CIR ... C5
BUNNING DR ... F7
BURLINGTON AV ... E9
BUTTERFIELD RD ... D12
CAMDEN CT ... C5
CAMDEN DR ... C5
CAMDEN RD ... C4
CANDLEWOOD CT ... D11
CANDLEWOOD DR ... D11
CANTERBURY PL ... E4
CAROL ST ... D6
CAROL ST-NORTH ... C10
CARPENTER ST ... D6-D8
CENTRE CIR ... D12
CHASE AV ... B9
CHICAGO AV ... D9
CHICAGO RD ... F9
CHURCHILL PL ... F5
CLAREMONT CT ... E5
CLAREMONT DR ... E5
CLAYTON CT ... E5
CLYDE DR ... E7
CONCORD CT ... D5
CONCORD DR ... C5, D5
CONCORD PL ... D5
CORAL BERRY LN ... D11
CORNELL AV ... C9
COUNTRY CREEK WAY ... E4
CREEKSIDE RD ... E5
CREEKWOOD CT ... D11
CRESCENT DR ... E6
CROSS ST ... B10
CUMNOR RD ... F8-F11
CURTISS ST ... B8
DAVIS ST ... E10
DAWN PL ... E10
DEARBORN PKWY ... E7
DE BOLT PL ... E9
DEER PATH LN ... F7
DEVEREUX RD ... C4
DE WITT LN ... D8
DEXTER RD ... D5
DICKSON DR ... D5
DOUGLAS RD ... F9
DOWNERS DR ... D9-D11
DREW ST ... D12
DROVE AV ... D10
DUCHESS CT ... D11
DUNHAM DR ... C1, D5
EARLSTON RD ... E10
EAST-WEST TOLLWAY ... C11
EDWARDS AV ... B9
ELDON PL ... E7
ELIZABETH LN ... F4
ELM ST ... E10
ELMORE AV ... C8
ELMWOOD PL ... E8
ESSEX PL ... C5
FAIRMOUNT AV ... E5-E8
FAIRVIEW AV ... F8
FARLEY PL ... E8
FARRAR CT ... D8
FINLEY RD ... C11
FLORENCE AV ... F3-F11
FOREST AV ... D9, E10
FOSTER PL ... D5
FOSTER RD ... D5
FRANCISCO AV ... B9
FRANKLIN ST ... E9
FRONTAGE RD ... D12
GEORGE ST ... D7
GIERZ ST ... F9
GILBERT AV ... D8
GLEN AV ... C10
GLENDENNING RD ... E10
GLENVIEW AV ... C8
GOLDEN BELL CT ... D11
GRACE CT ... D5
GRAHM AV ... C4
GRAND AV ... F4-F8
GRAND CT ... F4
GRANDVILLE AV ... B9
GRANT ST ... D9
GREGORY PL ... D12
GROVE ST ... D8
HADDOW AV ... B9
HALL AV ... C4
HALL ST ... C4
HARMARC PL ... F7
HARTFORD RD ... E4
HATCH PL ... C5
HATCH ST ... C5
HATHAWAY LN ... C6
HAVEN CT ... E10
HAWKINS AV ... C4
HAWTHORNE LN ... D8
HERBERT ST ... D11
HICKORY CT ... D12
HICKORY RD ... D12
HICKORY TR ... D12
HIGHLAND AV ... E9-E11
HIGHLAND CT ... E10
HILL ST ... F8
HILLCREST DR ... D6
HILLCREST RD ... D6-D7
HITCHCOCK AV ... C8
HOBART AV ... E5
HOLLAND PL ... D12
HOLLY CT ... D11
HUGHES AV ... D5
INDIANAPOLIS AV ... F9
INVERNESS AV ... B8
JACQUELINE DR ... D8
JANES AV ... B8
JANET ST ... C10
JAY DR ... E5
JEFFERSON ... C7
JEFFERSON AV ... D7
KATRINE AV ... B7
KELLY PL ... D4
KENSINGTON ... C6
KENYON AV ... E7
KIDWELL RD ... D4
KLEIN AV ... D5
KNOTTINGHAM LN ... F4
LACEY RD ... C11
LAKE ST ... F10
LAMB CT ... D5
LANCASTER AV ... E6
LANCASTER PL ... E6
LANE PL ... E7-E8
LAUREL CT ... D11
LEE AV ... C10
LEMONT RD ... D4
LEXINGTON LN ... D5
LINCOLN AV ... E9
LINDEN PL ... E9
LINDENWALD LN ... D8
LINDLEY ST ... E8
LINSCOTT AV ... D9
LONGMEADOW RD ... F10
LOOMES ST ... C6
LYMAN AV ... E5-E8
MACKIE PL ... E8
MAIN ST ... E4-E11
MANNING RD ... F3
MAPLE AV ... E8
MAPLEWOOD PL ... D8
MARIE DR ... F3
MEAD PL ... C5
MEADE RD ... C5
MEADOW LN (SOUTH) ... D8
MEADOW CREST DR ... E5
MEADOW LAWN AV ... E6
MIDDAUGH AV ... D7-D10
MIDHURST RD ... C6
MISTWOOD LN ... E12
MISTWOOD PL ... D12
MONMOUTH PL ... C5
MONTGOMERY AV ... D9
MORTON AV ... C10
NASH ST ... C6
NEWPORT RD ... C5
NORFOLK ST ... D6
NORTHBRIDGE PL ... C5
NORTHCOTT AV ... C9-C10
NORTHGATE WAY ... E4
OAK GROVE RD ... D12
OAK HILL CT ... D12
OAK HILL RD ... D12
OAKWOOD AV ... D9
OGDEN AV ... D10
OLD ORCHARD DR ... E4
O'NEILL RD ... D4
OPUS PL ... D12
ORCHARD PL ... E4
OSAGE AV ... F5-F7
OTIS ST ... F9
OXFORD ST ... E6
OXNARD DR ... C6
PALMER ST ... D6
PARK AV ... E7-E8
PARKER AV ... D5
PARKVIEW DR ... E5
PARKWAY ST ... D9
PARRISH CT ... D11
PENNER AV ... C5
PERSHING AV ... C9
PIPERS WAY ... F4
PLUM CT ... D11
PLYMOUTH CT ... D7
PLYMOUTH RD ... D5
POMEROY RD ... D12
POWELL PL ... D4
POWELL ST ... D4
PRAIRIE AV ... C9
PRENTISS CT ... C6
PRENTISS DR ... C6
PRIDEHAM ST ... C6
PRINCE AV ... D9
PROSPECT AV ... E9
PUFFER RD ... B6-B7
QUEENS CT ... F3
QUINCE CT ... E11
RAILROAD AV ... A9
RANDALL ST ... E8
RED BUD CT ... D11
RED SILVER CT ... D11
REVERE RD ... C5
RICHARDS ... D4
RIDGEVIEW ST ... E5
ROBEY AV ... E5
ROB ROY PL ... E5
ROE CT ... F4
ROGERS ST ... E9
ROHRER DR ... F3-F4
ROSE AV ... B9
ROSLYN RD ... F10
ROSS CT ... D8
ROUTE 53 ... A12
SARATOGA AV ... D6-D11
SAYLOR ST ... D6
SCHELDRUP ST ... D17
SCHOOL ST ... F11
SEELEY AV ... D9
SELIG PL ... C4
SHADY LN ... F10
SHELDON AV ... F9
SHERIDAN PL ... E9
SHERMAN ST ... E10
SHERWOOD AV ... F9
SHERWOOD CT ... F4
SNOWBERRY CT ... D11
SNOWBERRY LN ... D11
SPRINGSIDE AV ... D7
SPRINGSIDE PL ... D5
STAIR ST ... C6
STANLEY AV ... E9
STATTON PL ... E9
STERLING RD ... E10
STONEWALL AV ... C5
STRATFORD LN ... E7
STOCKLEY RD ... E4
STURBRIDGE PL ... C5
SUMMIT ST ... E8
TAYLOR ST ... C6
TERRACE DR ... D6
THATCHER RD ... A8
THORNWOOD DR ... D8
TICONDEROGA PL ... D4
TICONDEROGA RD ... D4
TOWER RD ... F11
TRAUBE RD ... F10
TRENT RD ... E4
TURVEY CT ... D8
TURVEY LN ... D8
TURVEY RD ... D8
VALLEY FORGE CT ... C5
VALLEY VIEW DR ... E5
VENARD RD ... D10
VICTOR ST ... F8
VIRGINIA AV ... D10
WALLBANK AV ... D9
WALNUT AV ... A8
WANDA PL ... E7
WARREN AV ... C9-E9
WARRENVILLE RD ... B10
WASHINGTON ST ... E7-E9
WATERFALL PL ... E5
WEATHERBEE AV ... E6
WEATHERBEE PL ... E6
WEBSTER PL ... E8
WEBSTER ST ... E7
WELLINGTON ... C6
WELLS ST ... C6
WEST END RD ... F10
WESTERN AV ... B9
WESTFIELD DR ... B6
WHIFFEN PL ... E9
WHITE FAWN TRAIL ... F7
WHITE PL ... C4
WIDDEN ST ... C6
WILCOX AV ... F8
WILLARD PL ... D4
WILLIAMS ST ... F4-F10
WILSON AV ... C10
WILSON ST ... F9
WINWOOD WAY ... E4
WISCONSIN AV ... B8
WOOD AV ... D11
WOOD CREEK DR ... C12
WOODS LN ... F11
WOODWARD AV-S ... C9
YORK RD ... E4
2ND ST ... A8
3RD ST ... A8
4TH ST ... A8
5TH ST ... A8
6TH ST ... A8
7TH ST ... A8
8TH ST ... A8
31ST ST ... E12
35TH ST ... D12
36TH ST ... E12
39TH CT ... D10
39TH ST ... F11
40TH PL ... F10
40TH ST ... E10
41ST ST ... E10
55TH PL ... F8
55TH ST ... D8
56TH CT ... F8
56TH ST ... F8
57TH ST ... E8
59TH ST ... E7
59TH PL ... E7
60TH PL ... D7
60TH ST ... F7
61ST ST ... D11
62ND CT ... D11
62ND PL ... D7
62ND ST ... E7
63RD ST ... C7-F7
65TH ST ... E6
67TH PL ... D5
67TH ST ... E5
68TH CT ... E5
68TH PL-W ... D5
68TH ST-W ... D5
70TH PL ... D5
71ST CT ... D5
71ST ST ... D5
72ND CT ... E5
72ND ST ... E4
73RD ST-W ... E4
74TH ST ... E4
75TH ST-W ... F4
77TH ST ... F4

Unincorporated Area

ACORN AV ... E12
AILSWORTH CT ... C2
AILSWORTH DR ... C2
ALDEN LN ... C2
ANDRUS RD ... J1
ARMSTRONG ... A5
AVENUE CHATEAU ... F12
AVENUE LA TOURS ... F12
AVENUE VENDOME ... F12
BANBURY WAY ... B2
BELLER CT ... D2
BELLER DR ... D2
BERKSHIRE CT ... E2
BIRCHWOOD PKWY ... B3
BLACKBURN PL ... B5
BONNIE ... B4
BOUGHTON RD ... B1
BOUNDARY RD ... C7
BOUNDARY HILL RD ... A4
BREWER RD ... D3
BROOKRIDGE RD ... E2
BUCKINGHAM WAY ... B2
BURGESS PL ... C2
CAMBRIDGE CT ... E2
CAMBRIDGE WAY ... B2
CAMDER RD ... C1
CARPENTER CT ... A5
CATALPA AV ... B4
CENTER CIR ... F4
CENTRAL AV ... D2
CESSNA LN ... E2
CHARLES CT ... E2
CHATEAU EAST ... F12
CHEESE RD ... E1
CHESTNUT ... B4
CHESTNUT AV ... B4
CHURCH CT ... A5
CLIFFORD DR ... A5
COBB CT ... D2
COBB DR ... C2
COLLEGE RD ... B7
COOPER ... A5
COVENTRY DR ... D2
CRABTREE AV ... B4
CRAMER LN ... C2
CROSS ST ... B9
DALEWOOD PKWY ... B4
DEERFIELD AV ... B4
DIAMOND CT ... A4
DIXON CT ... C2
DRENDEL RD ... B9
DROVER CT ... D2
DROVER LN ... D2
DU PAGE DR ... A5
EDGEWOOD DR ... D3
ELINOR AV ... A6
ELIZABETH DR ... C1
EVERGREEN LN ... B3
FAIRFIELD AV ... E12
FAIRHAVEN CT ... C8
FOREST GLEN PKWY ... A4
FOREST GROVE LN ... F12
FOUNTAINHEAD DR ... F7
FRONTAGE RD ... D1-E1
GIGI LN ... F4
GILBERT CT ... C2
GILMORE LN ... E12
GLENN CT ... A5
GLOUCHESTER RD ... D1
GOLD GROVE PL ... F4
GRANDVIEW LN ... D2
GRANDVIEW PL ... D2
GRISSOM ... A5
HAMPSTEAD LN ... D1
HARVEST LN ... D1
HARVEST PL ... D2
HAWTHORNE AV ... B4
HAVENS CT ... C1
HAVENS DR ... C2
HELEN CT ... E3
HIGHCREST DR ... D2
HIGHLAND AV ... E3
HILLCREST AV ... C8
HILLSIDE CT ... D2
HILLSIDE LN ... D2
HOBSON RD ... B7
HOWARD AV ... C8
HOWDY LN ... F4
JANES CT ... B3
JONQUIL ... B3
KEARNEY RD ... F2
KENSINGTON WAY ... B2
KENT CT ... B2
KINCAID DR ... B2
KING CT ... A5
KINGSBURY CT ... D1
KOHLEY RD ... D3
LAKESIDE DR ... E2
LAKEVIEW DR ... F3
LANGLEY ... B6
LARCHWOOD AV ... B4
LARCHWOOD LN ... B4
LEONARD DR ... B7
LOMOND AV ... B7
LONDONBERRY CT ... B2
LONDONBERRY LN ... B2
MAIN ST ... E2
MARK LN ... E3
MC INTYRE RD ... B10
MEADOW CT ... D2
MEADOW LN ... D2
MEYERS RD ... F12
MILLBROOK DR ... E2
MITCHELL DR ... A6
MORNING GLORY ... F10
MURPHY RD ... C1
NAPERVILLE RD ... F9
NORTHCREST DR ... A6
OARVILLE ... D2
OGILIVIE CT ... E2
O'HARE ... A5
OLDFIELD RD ... E2
OLDWOODS DR ... A2
OSAGE AV ... F5
OSAGE PL ... F5
PARKVIEW DR ... D2
PATTERSON ... B6
PERSHING CT ... A5
PETERS CT ... D1
PETERS DR ... C1
PICCADILLY CT ... B2
PICCADILLY LN ... B2
PITCHER DR ... C2
PLAINFIELD RD ... F3
PRAIRIE AV ... B9
PRENTICE DR ... B6
RAVINIA LN ... B4
REDONDO DR ... F3
RICHARD RD ... F4
ROBERTS DR ... A5
ROOKE CT ... D1
ROSE HILL CT ... F3
ROSE HILL LN ... F3
ROSEWOOD CT ... F3
ROSLYN RD ... F9
RUTGERS DR ... D1
RUTH DR ... F2
SHEFFIELD LN ... B2
SHEPHERD ... A5
SHERMAN AV ... C7
SIOUX AV ... B4
SOUTHCREST DR ... B6
SPRING GREEN DR ... D2
SPRUCEWOOD AV ... A4-B3
STEWART DR ... C2
SUFFIELD DR ... C1
SUMMER LN ... F3
TAMIAMI DR ... A6
TANBARK CT ... D2
THAMES DR ... C1
TIMBER TRAILS RD ... D1
TOWER CT ... E4
UNA AV ... B6
VAIL CT ... D1
VALLEY VIEW LN ... B3
WALLACE DR ... C1
WALNUT AV ... A4
WASHINGTON ST ... E2
WEST END AV ... F9
WESTMINSTER DR ... C1
WESTMORELAND DR ... B5
WHITE CT ... A5
WHITE OAK LN ... F12
WHITEHALL WAY ... B2
WILCOX ... F11
WILLIAMS DR ... A5
WILLIAMS ST ... F9
WILLOW AV ... B4
WILSHIRE DR ... A6
WINTER CIRCLE DR ... E3
WINTHROP CT ... E4
WINTHROP WAY ... E4
WIRTH DR ... F4
WOLF PL ... F5
WOODBRIDGE DR ... A4
WOODCREST DR ... D1
WOODGLEN LN ... F3
WOODLAND LN ... E11
WOOD VALE DR ... D2
YORK CT ... A6
YORK LN ... D1
YOUNG CT ... A5
31ST ST ... E12
37TH ST ... E11
38TH ST ... E11
66TH ST ... F6
67TH CT ... F5
79TH PL ... E3
80TH PL ... F3
80TH ST ... E3
81ST ST ... E3
83RD CT ... D2
83RD ST ... D3
85TH CT ... D2
86TH PL ... E2
86TH ST ... E2
87TH ST ... D2

© DonTech Chicago, Il. 1992

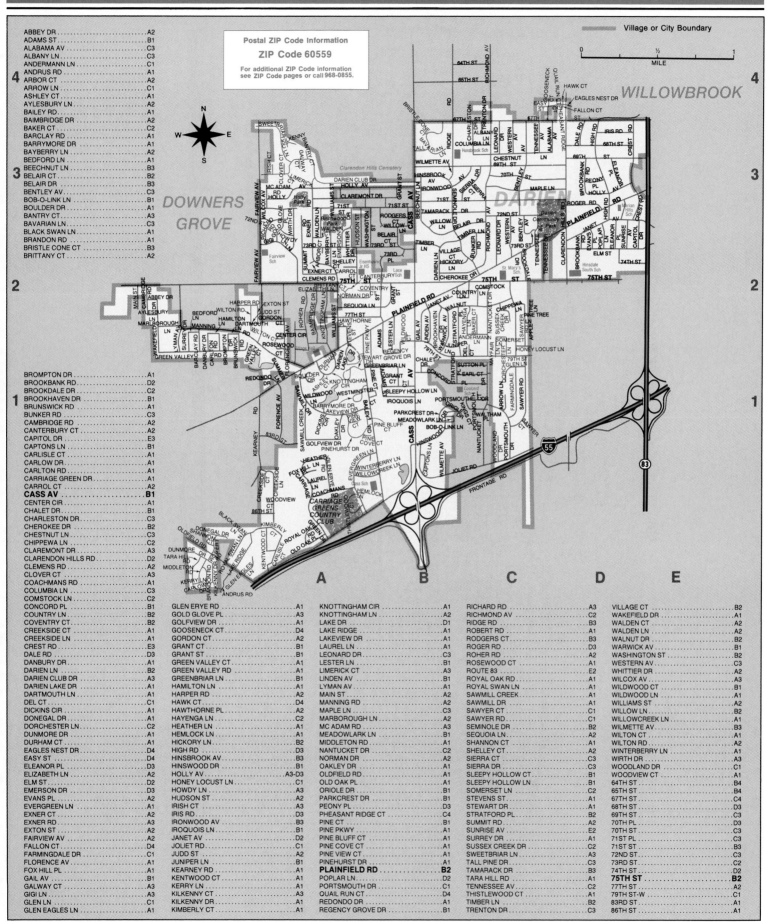

Postal ZIP Code Information
ZIP Code 60559

For additional ZIP Code information
see ZIP Code pages or call 968-0855.

Village or City Boundary

WILLOWBROOK

DOWNERS GROVE

DARIEN

© DonTech Chicago, Il. 1992

51

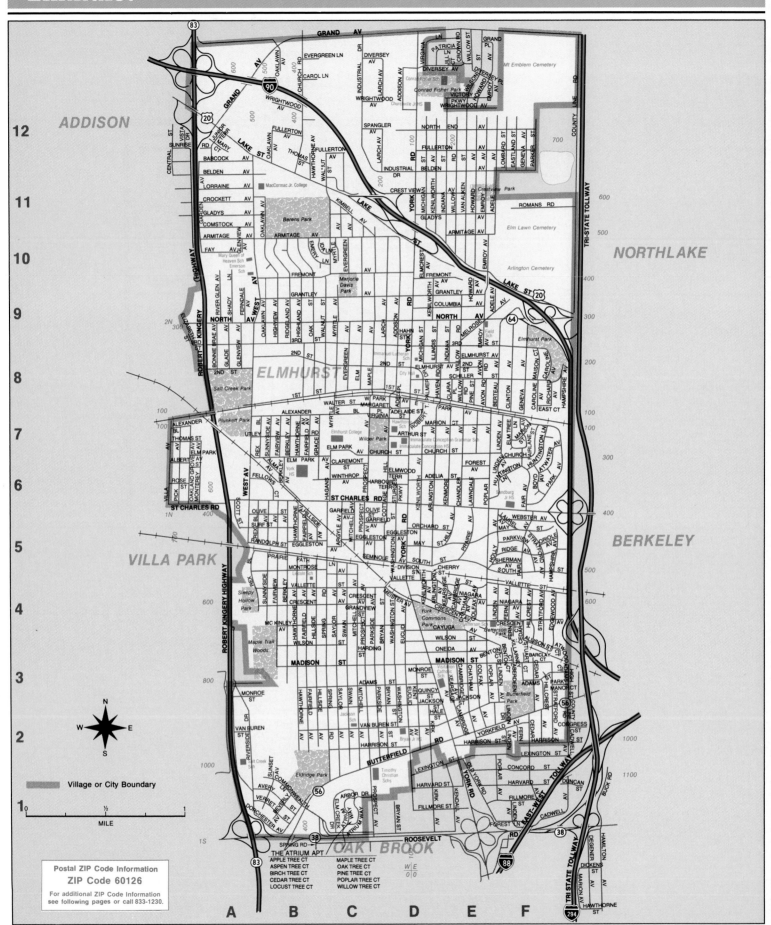

ADDISON

NORTHLAKE

BERKELEY

ELMHURST

VILLA PARK

OAK BROOK

Village or City Boundary

MILE

Postal ZIP Code Information

ZIP Code 60126

For additional ZIP Code Information
see following pages or call 833-1230.

THE ATRIUM APT
APPLE TREE CT   MAPLE TREE CT
ASPEN TREE CT   OAK TREE CT
BIRCH TREE CT   PINE TREE CT
CEDAR TREE CT   POPLAR TREE CT
LOCUST TREE CT   WILLOW TREE CT

© DonTech Chicago, Il. 1992

Elmhurst

ABERDEEN CT	F3
ADAMS CT	F3
ADAMS ST	C3
ADDISON AV-N	D9-D12
ADELAIDE ST	D7
ADELE AV	E9
ADELIA ST	D6
ADELL PL	D7
ALBERT ST	A6
ALEXANDER BL	B7
ALLISON ST	F3
ALMA AV	B6
APPLE TREE CT	C1
ARBOR DR	C1
ARGYLE AV	C5
ARLINGTON AV	D5
ARMITAGE AV	B10
ARTHUR ST	D7
ASPEN TREE CT	C1
ATRIUM WAY	C1
ATWATER AV	F6
ATWOOD CT	F3
AVERY ST	B1
AVON RD	E8
BABCOCK AV	A11
BARCLAY CT	F3
BELDEN AV	D11
BENTON ST	F3
BENTON CT	F3
BERKLEY AV	B4
BERTEAU AV	E8
BEVERLY AV	A1
BIRCH TREE CT	C1
BONNIE BRAE AV	A8
BOYD AV	F6
BRYAN ST	D2
BUTTERFIELD RD	**D2**
CADWELL AV	F2
CAMBRIDGE AV	E2
CAROL LN	B12
CAROLINE AV	F7
CAYUGA AV	D4
CEDAR AV	F3
CEDAR TREE CT	C1
CHANDLER AV	E6
CHATHAM AV	E2
CHERRY ST	E5
CHURCH RD	B11
CHURCH ST	C7
CLARA PL	E8
CLAREMONT ST	C7
CLINTON AV	F8
COLFAX AV	E2
COLUMBIA AV	D9
COMMONWEALTH LN	B1
COMSTOCK AV	A10
COTTAGE HILL AV	D5
COUNTY LINE RD	F2
CRESCENT AV	C4
CREST VIEW AV	B11
CROCKETT AV	A11
DIVERSEY AV	D12
DIVISION ST	D5
DORCHESTER AV	B1
EAST CT	F8
EASTLAND ST	F11
EDGEWOOD AV	F4
EGGLESTON AV	B5
ELIZABETH ST	A8
ELM AV	C8
ELMCREST AV	D10
ELMHURST AV	D8
ELM CREEK DR	C1
ELM PARK AV	B7
ELM TREE LN	F7
ELMWOOD TERR	D6
EMERY LN	C10
EMROY AV	E8
EUCLID AV	D2
EVERGREEN AV	C6
EVERGREEN LN	C12
FAIR AV	F5
FAIRFIELD AV	C4
FAIRLANE AV	F7
FAIRVIEW AV	B4
FAY AV	A10
FELLOWS CT	B6
FERN AV	F4
FERN CT	F4
FERNDALE AV	A9
FOREST AV	E6
FOREST LN	F1
FREMONT AV	C10
FULLERTON AV	D11
GARDEN AV	A10
GARFIELD AV	C6
GENEVA AV	F7-F12
GLADE AV	A8
GLADYS AV	A10
GLENVIEW AV	A8
GRACE AV-S	C6
GRAND AV	**C12**
GRANDVIEW ST	C4
GRANTLEY AV	B9
HAGANS AV	C6
HAHN ST	D9
HALE ST	E2
HAMPSHIRE AV	F5-F8
HARBOUR TERR	D6
HARDING ST	C4
HARRISON ST	E2
HAVEN RD	E8
HAWTHORNE AV	B4
HIGH ST	F3
HIGHLAND AV	B8
HIGHVIEW AV	B9
HILL AV	E5
HILLCREST AV	F3
HILLSIDE AV	C4
HOLLY AV	F5
HOWARD AV	E9
HUNTINGTON LN	F6
IDA LN	C10
ILLINOIS ST	D8
INDIANA ST	E8
INDUSTRIAL DR	C12
JACKSON ST	D3
KEARSAGE AV	E3
KENILWORTH AV	D6-D11
KENMORE AV	E6
KENT AV	D2
KILLARNEY CT	F3
KIMBELL AV	C10
KIRK AV	E1
LAKE ST	**D10**
LARCH AV	C12
LAUREL AV	F6
LAWNDALE AV	E6
LINDEN AV	E2-E7
LINDEN DR	
LOCUST TREE CT	C1
LOMBARD ST	E11
LORRAINE AV	A11
MADISON ST	**E3**
MAISON CT	F8
MAPLE AV	C8
MAPLE TREE CT	C1
MARGARET PL	C7
MARION ST	D7
MARY CT	A11
MAY ST	D5
MC KINLEY AV	B4
MEISTER AV	D4
MELROSE AV	E9
MICHIGAN ST	D8-D11
MITCHELL AV	D2-D5
MONROE ST	A3-D3
MONTEREY AV	A6
MONTROSE AV	B5
MYRTLE AV	C8
NIAGARA AV	E4
NORTH AV	**D9**
NORTH END AV	D12
OAK ST	B9
OAK TREE CT	C1
OAKLAND GROVE AV	A8
OAKLAWN AV	B9-B11
OLIVE ST	B6
ONEIDA AV	D4
ORCHARD ST	D5
ORIOLE AV	F5
PARK AV	F6
PARK AV	C7
PARKER ST	F12
PARK MANOR CT	F3
PARKSIDE AV	D3
PARKVIEW AV	F5
PICK AV	A6
PINE ST	E8
PINE TREE CT	C1
POPLAR AV	F3
POPLAR TREE CT	C1
PRAIRIE AV	E5
PRAIRIE PATH LN	B5
PROSPECT AV	C4
QUINCY ST	D3
RANDOLPH ST	B5
REX BL	B4
RICHARD	F7
RIDGE AV	F5
RIDGELAND AV	B9
RIVER GLEN AV	A8
RIVERSIDE DR	A2
ROMANS RD	F11
ROSE ST-S	A6
ROBERT KINGERY EXPWY	**A9**
ROBERT T. PALMER DR	D7
ST CHARLES RD	**C6**
SAYLOR AV	C2
SCHILLER ST	D8
SCOTT ST	A6
SEMINOLE AV	C5
SHADY LN	A9
SHERMAN AV	F5
SOUTH ST	D5
SPRING RD	B1-C2
STRATFORD AV	F4
STUART CT	F3
STURGES PKWY	D6
SUNNYSIDE AV	B4
SUNRISE RD	A12
SUNSET AV	B1
SURF ST	B5
SWAIN AV	C2
THOMAS ST	A7
THOMAS ST	B12
TRI-STATE TOLLWAY	**F1**
UTLEY RD	B7
VALLETTE ST	D5
VAN AUKEN ST	E11
VAN BUREN ST	C2
VERRET ST	B1
VILLA AV	A6
VIRGINIA LN	D12
VIRGINIA ST	D7
WALNUT ST	C9
WALTER ST	C7
WASHINGTON ST	D2
WEBSTER AV	F6
WEST AV	**B7**
WILLOW RD	E8
WILLOW TREE CT	C1
WILSON ST	E12
WILSON ST	B4
WINTHROP AV	C6
WRIGHTWOOD AV-E	D12
YORK RD	**D5**
YORKFIELD AV	E2
1ST ST	D8
2ND ST	C8
3RD ST-E	D8

Unincorporated Elmhurst Area

BUCK RD	F1
CENTRAL ST	A11
CONCORD ST	E2
CONGRESS ST	F2
CROWN RD	D12
DEGENER AV	F1
DIVERSEY PL	F12
DUNCAN ST	F1
EAST-WEST TOLLWAY	**F1**
FILLMORE ST	F1
GRAND PL	F12
HAMILTON AV	F1
HARVARD ST	D1
JILL CT	D12
KENDALL AV	E2
LEXINGTON ST	D2
OLD YORK RD	D1
PATRICIA LN	D12
ROOSEVELT RD	**D1**
VICTORY PKWY	E12
VISTA DR	A12
WILLOW ST	F12

© DonTech Chicago, Il. 1992

Elmwood Park

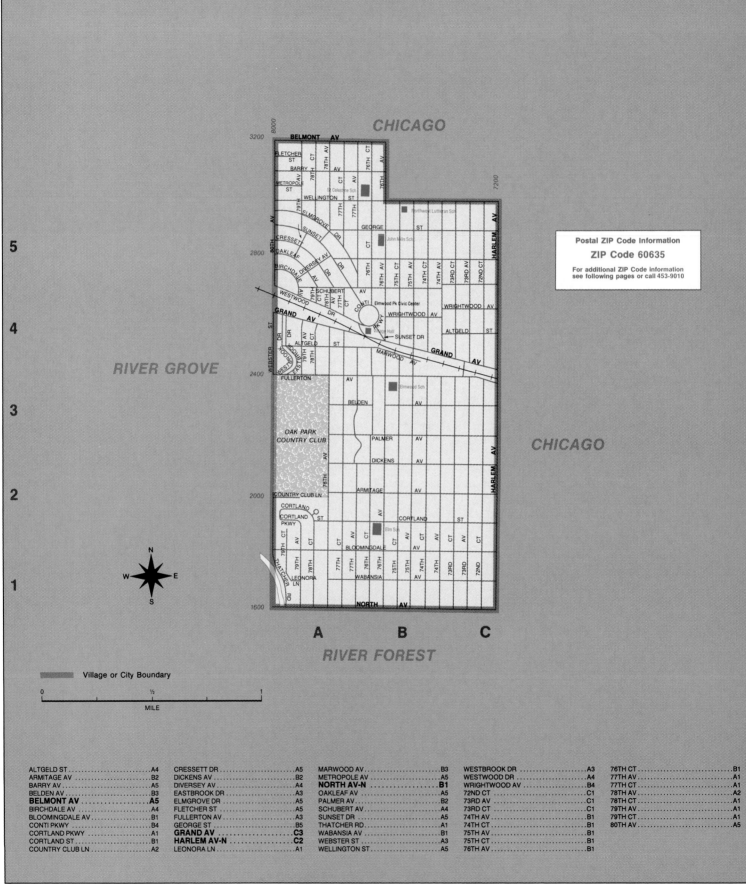

Village or City Boundary

Postal ZIP Code Information

ZIP Code 60635

For additional ZIP Code information
see following pages or call 453-9010

© DonTech Chicago, Il. 1992

Forest Park

ADAMS ST B5	DUNLOP AV B3	HARVARD ST C4	POLK ST B4	WILCOX ST B5
BELOIT AV C3	**EISENHOWER EXPWY** **B4**	INDUSTRIAL DR-W B1	RANDOLPH ST C6	YORK ST B4
BELVIDERE AV C6	ELGIN AV C3	JACKSON BL B5	ROCKFORD AV C6	YUBA ST B3
BERGMAN CT C6	FERDINAND AV B4	LATHROP AV B4	**ROOSEVELT RD** **B3**	13TH ST C3
BROWN AV C6	FILLMORE ST C3	LEHMER ST C4	TAYLOR ST B3	14TH ST C2
BURKHARDT CT C5	FRANKLIN ST C6	LEXINGTON ST C4	THOMAS AV C3	15TH ST C2
CERMAK RD **B1**	GREENBURG RD B1	LINCOLN CT C6	TROOST AV B3	16TH ST C2
CIRCLE AV C5	HANNAH AV C4	**MADISON ST** **B5**	VAN BUREN ST-W B5	
DES PLAINES AV B4	**HARLEM AV-S** **C2**	MARENGO AV C3	WARREN ST C5	
DIXON ST C6	HARRISON ST B4	MONROE ST B5	WASHINGTON ST C5	

Village or City Boundary

0   ¼   ½
MILE

Postal ZIP Code Information

ZIP Code 60130

For additional ZIP Code information
see following pages or call 366-0015

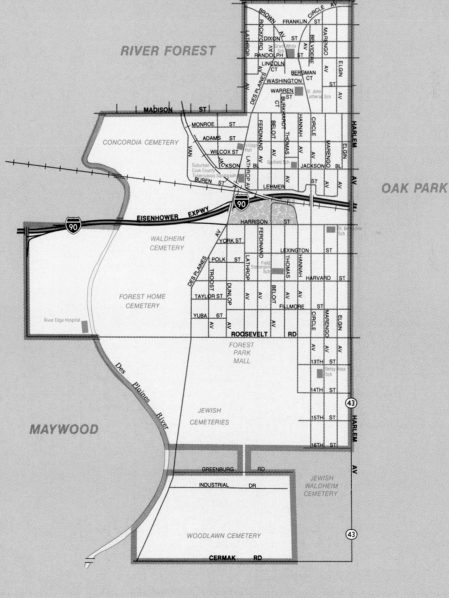

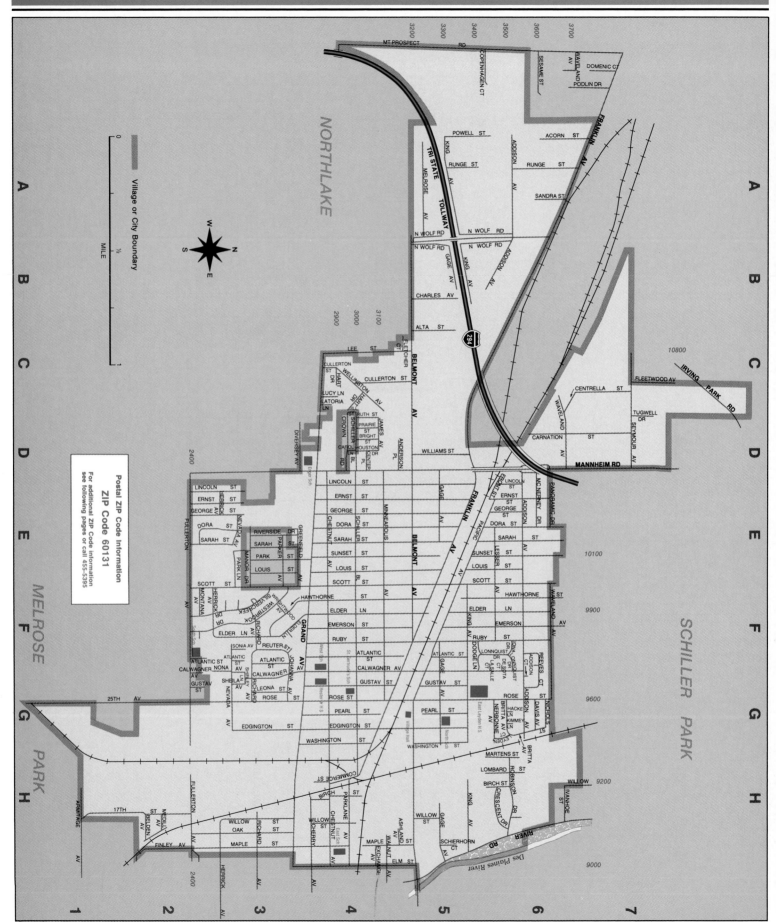

© DonTech Chicago, Il. 1992

ACORN ST A6	DAVIS AV G6	HERRICK AV F2	MELROSE AV A5	RUNGE ST A5
ADDISON CT G6	DE SOTA CT F6	HOUSTON DR D4	MINNEAPOLIS AV E4	RUTH ST D4
ADDISON AV A6	DIVERSEY AV D3	IONA DR F6	MONTANA AV F2	SANDRA ST A6
ALTA ST-N C5	DODGE LN F5	**IRVING PARK RD** **C7**	MT PROSPECT RD A5	SARAH ST E2
ANDERSON PL D4	DOMENIC CT A6	JAMES AV D4	NERBONNE AV F5	SCHIERHORN CT H5
ARMITAGE AV H1	DORA ST E2	JILL ST D4	NEVADA AV E3	SCHILLER BL D4
ASHLAND AV H4	EDGINGTON ST G3	JOHANNA AV F3	NICHOLS ST G6	SCOTT ST F2
ATLANTIC ST F2	ELDER LN F3	KIMMEY CT G6	NONA AV F3	SESAME ST A6
BELDEN AV H2	ELM ST H4	KING AV A5	OAK ST H3	SEYMOUR AV D7
BELMONT AV **C5**	EMERSON ST F4	LA SALLE CT F5	PANORAMIC DR E6	SHEILA AV G3
BIRCH ST H4	ERNST ST E4	LATORIA LN C4	PARK LN E3	SHIRLEY LN G3
BRIGHT ST D4	EXCHANGE AV H4	LEE ST C4	PARKER AV E3	SILVERCREEK DR F3
BRITTA AV G6	FINLEY AV H2	LEONA ST G3	PARKLANE AV H4	SONIA AV F3
CALWAGNER AV G2	FLEETWOOD AV C7	LESSER AV E5	PEARL ST G4	SUNSET ST E4
CARNATION ST D6	FLETCHER CT C5	LEYDEN CT G6	PODLIN DR A6	TUGWELL DR D7
CAROL LN D4	**FRANKLIN AV** **E5**	LINCOLN ST D2	POWELL ST A5	WALNUT AV H4
CENTER PL D4	FRONT ST D6	LOMBARD ST H5	PRAIRIE ST D4	WASHINGTON ST G4
CENTRELLA ST C7	FULLERTON AV E2	LONNQUIST DR F5	REEVES CT F6	WAVELAND AV D6
CHARLES AV B5	GAGE AV E5	LOUIS ST E3	REUTER ST F3	WELLINGTON AV C4
CHERRY ST H3	GEORGE ST E2	LUCY LN C4	RICHARD AV F3	WESTBROOK DR F3
CHESTNUT AV E4	**GRAND AV** **F3**	**MANNHEIM RD** **D6**	RICHARD ST H3	WILLIAMS ST D5
COMMERCE ST H4	GREENFIELD AV E3	MANOR DR E3	**RIVER RD** **H6**	WILLOW ST H3
COPENHAGEN CT A5	GUSTAV ST G2	MAPLE ST H3	RIVERSIDE DR E3	WOLF RD B5
CRESCENT DR H5	HACKE LN G6	MARTENS ST H5	ROBINSON DR H6	WRIGHTWOOD AV F3
CROWN RD D4	HART DR C4	MC NERNEY DR E6	ROSE ST G3	17TH ST H1
CULLERTON ST C4	HAWTHORNE ST F4	MEDILL AV H2	RUBY ST F4	25TH AV G1

© DonTech Chicago, Il. 1992

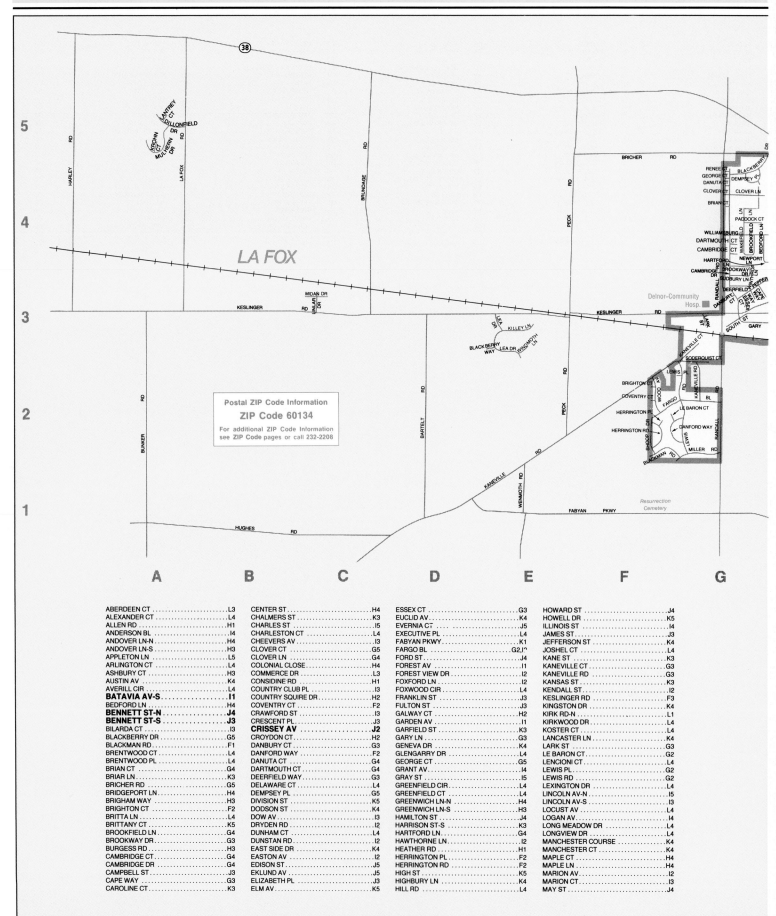

Postal ZIP Code Information
ZIP Code 60134
For additional ZIP Code Information
see ZIP Code pages or call 232-2208

© DonTech Chicago, Il. 1992

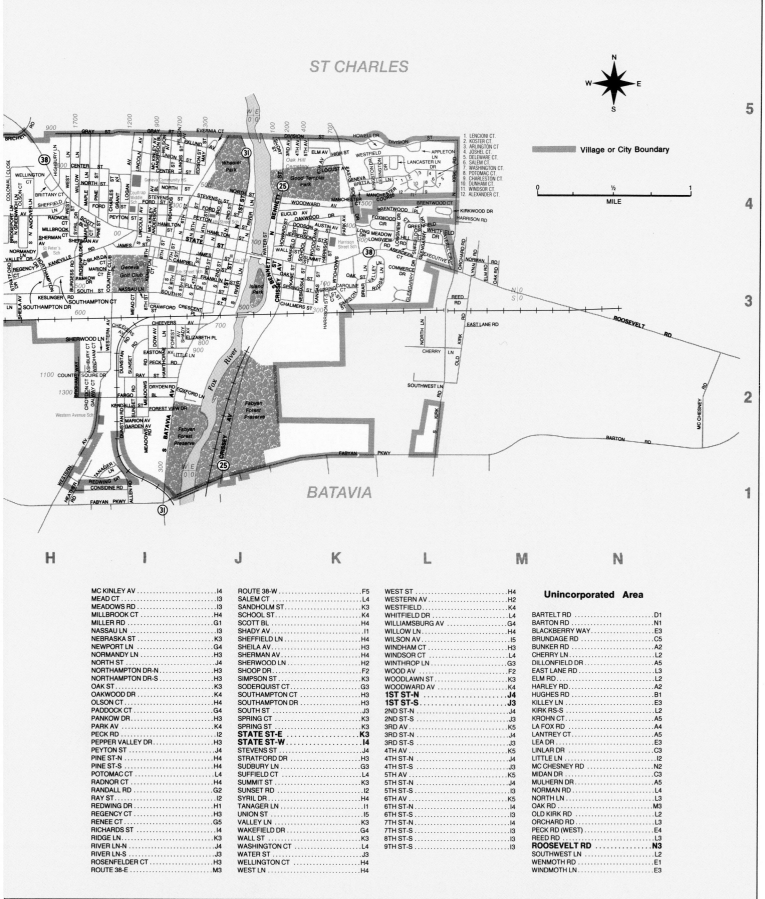

© DonTech Chicago, Il. 1992

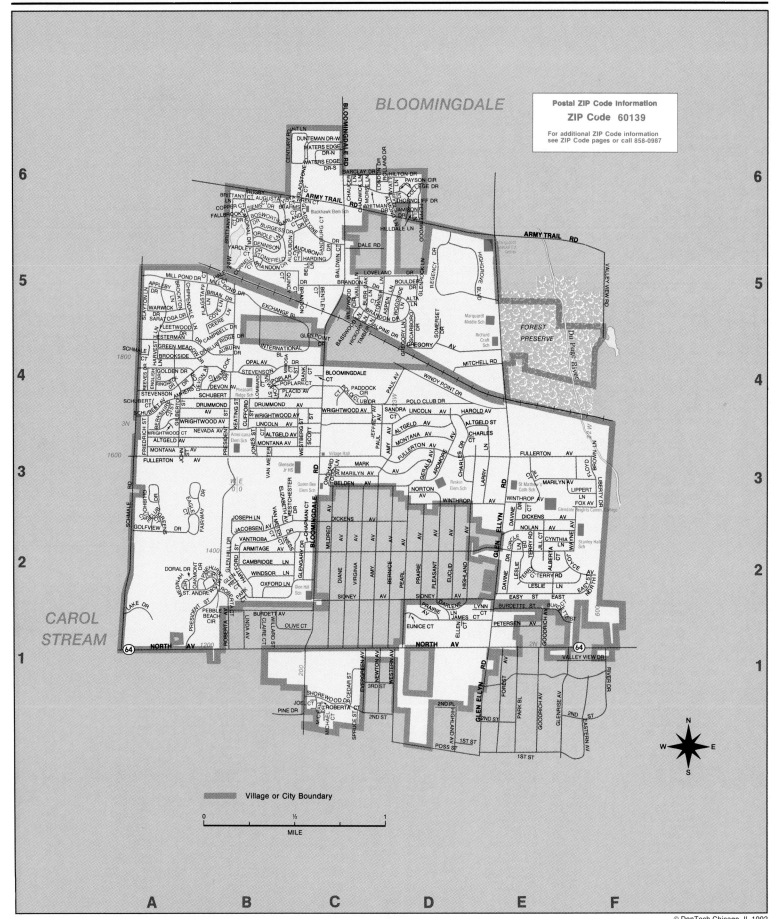

BLOOMINGDALE

Postal ZIP Code Information
ZIP Code 60139
For additional ZIP Code information
see ZIP Code pages or call 858-0987

CAROL
STREAM

Village or City Boundary

0   ½   1
MILE

N
W   E
S

© DonTech Chicago, Il. 1992

© DonTech Chicago, Il. 1992

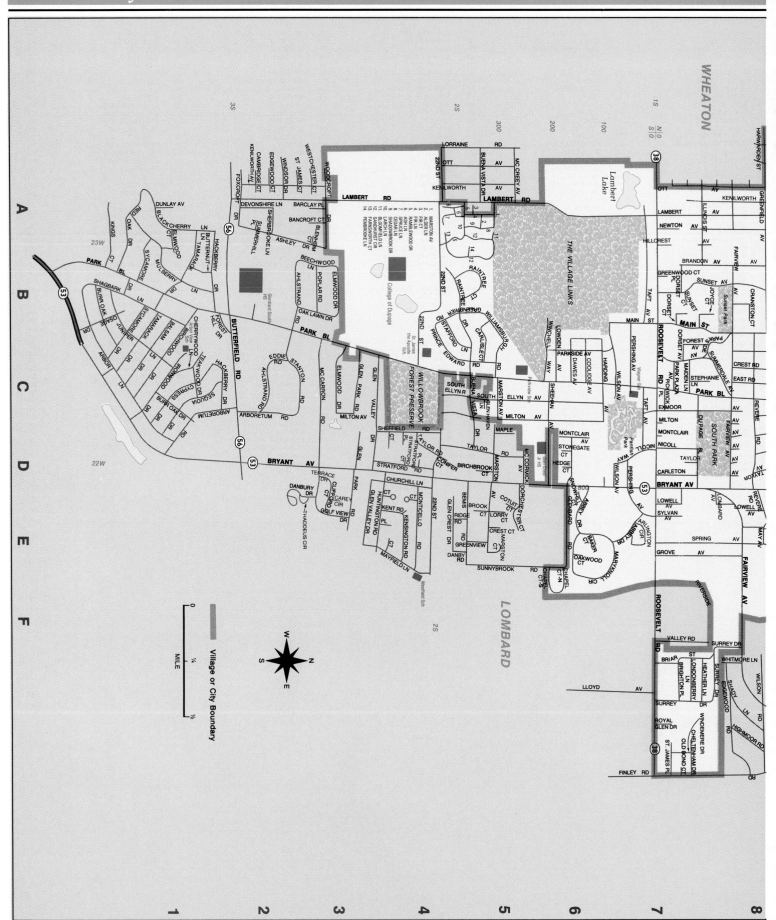

© DonTech Chicago, Il. 1992

Postal ZIP Code Information

Town	ZIP Code
Glen Ellyn	60137
Post Office Boxes	60138
Unincorporated Area	60137
Glendale Heights	60139

For additional information see ZIP Code pages or call

469-0252
469-0252
469-0252
858-0987

© DonTech Chicago, Il. 1992

Glen Ellyn Street Guide

Glen Ellyn

ABBEY DR ... D7
ABBOTSFORD CT ... F8
ALDER LN ... A5
ANNANDALE AV ... C10
ANTHONY ST ... A10
APPIAN WAY ... C9
APOLLO AV ... D11
ARBOR CT ... B8
ARLINGTON AV ... B8
ARLINGTON CIR ... D7
ASH LN ... A4
BAKER CT ... E6
BLOOMFIELD LN ... B5
BRANDON AV ... B9
BREMER CT ... C9
BRIAR ST ... F7
BHIGHTON PL ... F7
BRYANT AV ... D8
BUENA VISTA DR ... A5-C5
CARLETON AV ... D7-D10
CARLISLE CT ... B5
CAROLYN DR ... C12
CEDAR LN ... A5
CENTER ST ... A10
CHAPEL CT-N ... E6
CHAPEL CT-S ... E5
CHELTENHAM DR ... F7
CHESTERFIELD AV ... A9
CHIDESTER AV ... D12
CLIFTON AV ... E11
COLCORD PL ... E11
COOLIDGE AV ... C6
COTTAGE AV ... A10-B10
CRANSTON CT ... B8
CRESCENT BL ... E11
CRESCENT CT ... C10
CRESCENT DR ... D12
CREST RD ... C8
CUMNOR AV ... E8-E11
DALE AV ... F8
DAVIS TERR ... A11
DAWES AV ... B6
DAWN AV ... A10
DEER PATH RD ... C10
DELL AV ... E7
DORSET AV ... C7
DORSET CT ... B7
DORSET PL ... B7
DUANE ST ... C10
DUANE TERR ... D10
DU PAGE BL ... D7
EAST RD ... C8
EASTERN AV ... D12
EDGEWOOD DR ... D11
ELLYN CT ... C10
ELLYNWOOD DR ... E11
ELM ST ... B12
EMERSON AV ... C13
ESSEX CT ... C11
ESSEX RD ... C11
EUCLID AV ... B11-B16
EVERGREEN AV ... A10-A14
EXMOOR AV ... C8
FAIRVIEW AV ... C8
FARNSWORTH CT ... B4
FINLEY RD ... F7
FIR CT ... A5
FIR LN ... A5
FLORENCE AV ... F8
FOREST AV ... B7-C14-C10
GENEVA RD ... A12
GLEN ELLYN PL ... C11
GLEN HAVEN LN ... C5
GLEN OAK AV ... E9
GLEN PARK RD ... D3
GLENBARD RD ... F6
GLENWOOD AV ... B9
GOODRICH AV ... C14
GRAND AV ... D12
GRANDVIEW AV ... E7
GREAT WESTERN AV ... D13
GREENBRIER RD ... B4
GREENFIELD AV ... A8
GREENWOOD CT ... B7
GROVE AV ... E7
HARDING AV ... C6
HARVEY AV ... C6
HAWTHORNE BL ... B11
HEATHER LN ... F7
HEDGE CT ... D6
HICKORY RD ... D11
HIGH RD ... C8
HIGHLAND AV ... B11-B16
HIGHVIEW AV ... D9
HILL AV ... C9
HILLCREST AV ... A7
HILLSIDE AV ... D10
ILLINOIS ST ... A7
INDIAN RD ... F9
JOYCE CT ... B7
KENILWORTH AV-N ... A13
KENILWORTH AV-S ... A2
KENILWORTH CT ... A11
LAKE RD ... C11
LAKEVIEW TERR ... C9
LAMBERT AV ... A7
LAMBERT RD-N ... A3
LARCH LN-S ... A5
LAWRENCE AV ... A9
LEE ST ... D11
LENOX RD ... C12
LINCOLN AV ... D12
LINDEN ST ... B11
LOMBARD AV ... E8
LONDONBERRY LN ... F7
LONGFELLOW AV ... E10
LORRAINE ST ... A8
LOWDEN AV ... C6
LOWELL AV ... D7-E10
MAIDEN LN ... C7
MAIN ST-N ... C12
MAIN ST-S ... B7-C14
MAPLE ST ... B11
MARION AV ... A11
MARSTON AV ... A5-D5
MARYKNOLL CIR ... E6
MAY AV ... E9
MELROSE AV ... B9
MEMORY CT ... F9
MEREDITH PL ... D12
MERTON AV ... D8
MIDWAY PK ... E11
MILLER CT ... B9
MILTON AV-N ... C7
MILTON AV-S ... C3
MONTCLAIR AV ... C9
MUIRWOOD DR ... C12
NEWTON AV ... A7-A14
NICOLL AV ... D7
NICOLL WAY ... D7
NORTH ELLYN AV ... C10
OAK ST ... B12
OAKWOOD CT ... E6
OLD BOND CT ... F7
OTT AV ... A4-A7
OXFORD RD ... F8
PARK BL-N ... C13
PARK BL-S ... B1-C14
PARK PLAZA AV ... C7
PARK ROW ... C10
PARKSIDE AV-N ... B8
PARKSIDE AV-S ... C6
PEMBROKE LN ... B4
PENNSYLVANIA AV ... B10
PERSHING AV ... A7-F7
PHILLIPS AV ... B9
PICKWICK PL ... C7
PLEASANT AV ... B11-B16
PLUM TREE RD ... D11
PRAIRIE AV ... B11-B16
PRINCE EDWARD RD ... B4
PROSPECT AV ... B9
RAINTREE CT ... B5
RAINTREE DR ... B4
RAMBLEWOOD DR ... A4
REGENT ST ... B8
REVERE RD ... D8
RIDGEWOOD AV ... A9
RIFORD RD ... D11
RIVERSIDE AV ... F7
ROGER RD ... E11
ROOSEVELT RD ... C7
ROSLYN RD ... E9
ROUTE 53 ... B1-F8
ROYAL GLEN DR ... F7
ST. CHARLES RD ... A13-D12
ST. JAMES PL ... F7
ST. MORITZ DR ... A10
SANDHURST CIR ... B4
SAWYER AV ... A9
SCOTT AV ... F8
SHADOWBROOK DR ... A4
SHADY LN ... F9
SHEEHAN AV ... C6
SHEFFIELD LN ... A10
SMITH ST ... E9
SNOWHILL CT ... D6
SOUTH ELLYN AV ... C5
SOUTH ELLYN RD ... C4
SPAULDING ST ... C10
SPRING AV ... E8
SPRUCE LN ... A4
STAFFORD LN ... B4
STEPHANIE LN ... C7
STONEGATE CT ... D6
STUART AV ... C10
SUMMERDALE AV ... C8
SUNSET AV ... B8
SUNSET CT ... B7
SURREY DR ... F8
SYLVAN AV ... E7
TAFT AV ... B7
TAYLOR AV ... D7-D10
TRAVER AV ... A8
TURNER AV ... B9-D9
VALLEY AV ... E8
VALLEY RD ... F7
VAN DAMIN AV ... D9
VINE ST ... A9
WALNUT ST ... E10
WAVERLY RD ... F9
WESTERN AV ... B10-B14
WHITTIER AV ... E10
WILLIAMSBURGH RD ... B5
WILLIS ST ... D10
WILSON AV ... A6-D6
WINCHELL WAY ... C6
WINDEMERE DR ... F7
WINDSOR AV ... A9
WINGATE RD ... D8
WOODCROFT DR ... A3
WOODLAND DR ... E11
WOODSTOCK AV ... E9
22ND ST ... C4

Unincorporated Glen Ellyn Area

ACORN AV ... F10
AHLSTRAND RD ... B2
AMY AV ... A15
ARBOR LN ... C1
ARBORETUM RD ... C2
ARMITAGE AV ... B16
ARNOLD AV ... A13
ASHLEY DR ... A2
BALSAM DR ... B1
BANCROFT CT ... A3
BARCLAY PL ... A3
BEECHWOOD LN ... B3
BELDEN AV ... A16
BEMIS RD ... E4
BERNICE AV ... A15
BIRCHBROOK CT ... D5
BIRCHWOOD DR ... C1
BLACKCHERRY LN ... A1
BLENHEIM CT ... A3
BLOOMINGDALE RD ... A15
BROOKS CT ... E5
BURDETTE AV ... C15
BURR OAK DR ... B1
BUSCH RD ... D14
BUTTERFIELD RD ... C2
BUTTERNUT LN ... B1
CAMBRIDGE CT ... A2
CAREY CIR ... D3
CHERRY LN ... B13
CHERRYWOOD LN ... C1
CHURCHILL LN ... D4
CLIFFORD CT ... D3
CLIFTON AV ... F11
CONIFER CT ... D4
COTUIT CT ... E5
CREST CT ... E5
CYPRESS DR ... C1
DANBURY DR ... D2
DANBY RD ... E4
DAWN AV ... A13
DEVONSHIRE LN ... A2
DIANE AV ... A15
DICKENS AV ... A16
DORCHESTER CT ... E5
DUNLAY AV ... A1
EAST AV ... F11
EASTERN AV ... D14
EDDIE RD ... C2
EDGEWOOD CT ... A2
EDGEWOOD RD ... F8
ELMWOOD CT ... A1
ELMWOOD DR ... B3
EMERSON AV ... C13
EUCLID AV ... B16
FAIRWAY ST ... F10
FOREST HILL DR ... B2
FOXCROFT DR ... A2
GLEN CREST DR ... E4
GLEN ELLYN RD ... C16
GLEN VALLEY DR ... D3
GLENRISE AV ... D14
GOLF AV ... F10
GOLF VIEW DR ... E3
GREAT WESTERN AV ... A13
GREENVIEW ... E5
HACKBERRY DR ... B1
HARWARDEN ST ... A8
HIGHMOOR RD ... F8
HUNTINGTON CT ... D3
HUNTINGTON PL ... E3
HUNTINGTON RD ... E3
IRONWOOD DR ... C1
JUNIPER LN ... B1
KENSINGTON RD ... E4
KENT RD ... E4
KINGS CT ... A1
LAWLER AV ... F6
LLOYD AV ... F6
LORRY CT ... E5
MAPLE LN ... C5
MARSTON CT ... E5
MAYFIELD CT ... E3
MAYFIELD LN ... E4
MC CARRON RD ... C3
MC CORMICK AV ... D5
MC CREEY AV ... A5
MILDRED AV ... A13-A16
MONTICELLO CT ... D4
MONTICELLO RD ... E4
MULBERRY LN ... B1
NORTH AV ... B15
OAK LAWN DR ... B3
OSAGE DR ... B1
PEARL AV ... B15
PETERSON AV ... C15
PINE DR ... A14
POPLAR RD ... B3
POSS ST ... B13
RAILROAD ST ... B13
RED OAK DR ... A1
RIDGE RD ... E4
RIVER DR ... D14
SADDLEWOOD DR ... E11
ST. JAMES CT ... A2
SEQUOIA DR ... C1
SHADY LN ... F8
SHAGBARK LN ... B2
SHEFFIELD CT ... D3
SHEFFIELD PL ... D4
SHEFFIELD RD ... C4
SHERBROOKE LN ... A2
SIDNEY AV ... B15
STACY AV ... B13
STACY CT ... C12
STANTON RD ... C2
STRATFORD CT ... D4
STRATFORD PL ... D4
STRATFORD RD ... D4
SUMMERHILL PL ... A2
SUNNYBROOK RD ... E5
SWIFT RD ... E13
SYCAMORE DR ... B1
TAMARACK DR ... B1
TAYLOR RD ... D4
TEAKWOOD DR ... C1
TERRACE DR ... D3
THADDEUS CIR ... E2
TRAILS END ... A13
VALLEY VIEW DR ... D14
VIRGINIA AV ... A15
WALNUT RD ... F11
WESTCHESTER CT ... A3
WHITMORE LN ... F8
WILSON RD ... F8
WINDSOR DR ... A2
WINTHROP AV ... B16
1ST ST ... C13
2ND PL ... B14
2ND ST ... A14-C14
3RD ST ... A14

© DonTech Chicago, Il. 1992

The Ultimate Business Reference Tools

Increase Sales, Speed Service, Reduce Costs

The Street Address Telephone Directory provides you with all the names and numbers of potential customers in your immediate sales area to help you direct your sales message with pin-point accuracy. It can help you contact your service people and quickly validate customers locations.

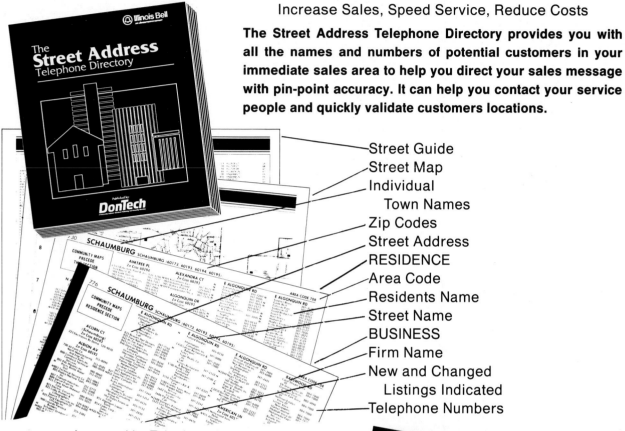

- Street Guide
- Street Map
- Individual Town Names
- Zip Codes
- Street Address
- RESIDENCE
- Area Code
- Residents Name
- Street Name
- BUSINESS
- Firm Name
- New and Changed Listings Indicated
- Telephone Numbers

Arranged by Telephone Number

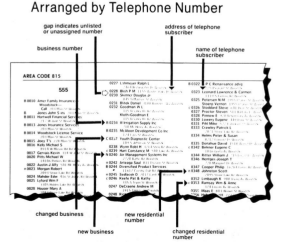

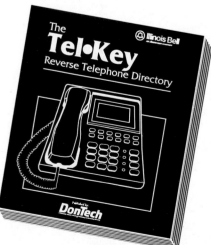

For details and further information call DonTech at **708-449-7500**

© DonTech Chicago, Il. 1992

65

Harwood Heights

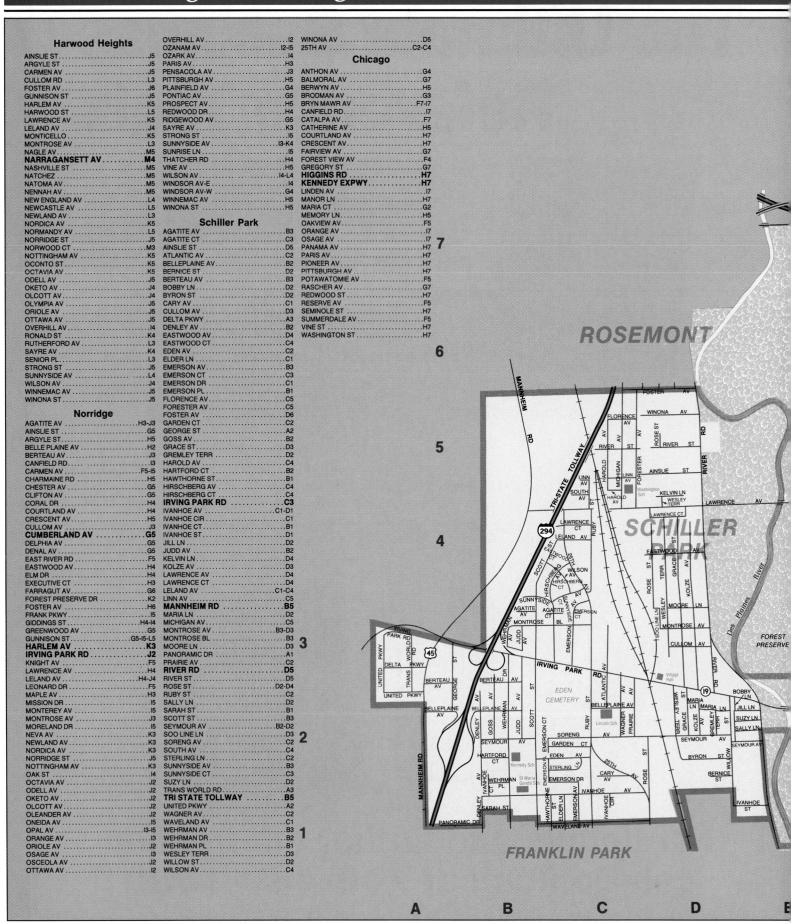

© DonTech Chicago, II. 1992

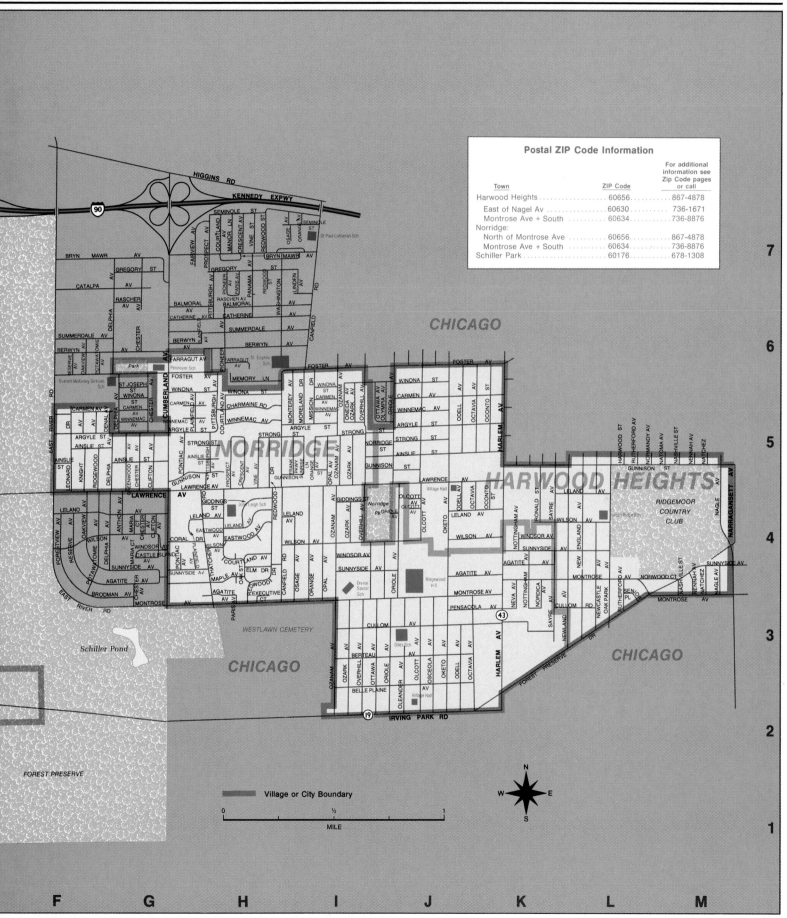

Postal ZIP Code Information

Town	ZIP Code	For additional information see Zip Code pages or call
Harwood Heights	60656	867-4878
East of Nagel Av	60630	736-1671
Montrose Ave + South	60634	736-8876
Norridge:		
North of Montrose Ave	60656	867-4878
Montrose Ave + South	60634	736-8876
Schiller Park	60176	678-1308

Village or City Boundary

MILE

© DonTech Chicago, Il. 1992

Hinsdale

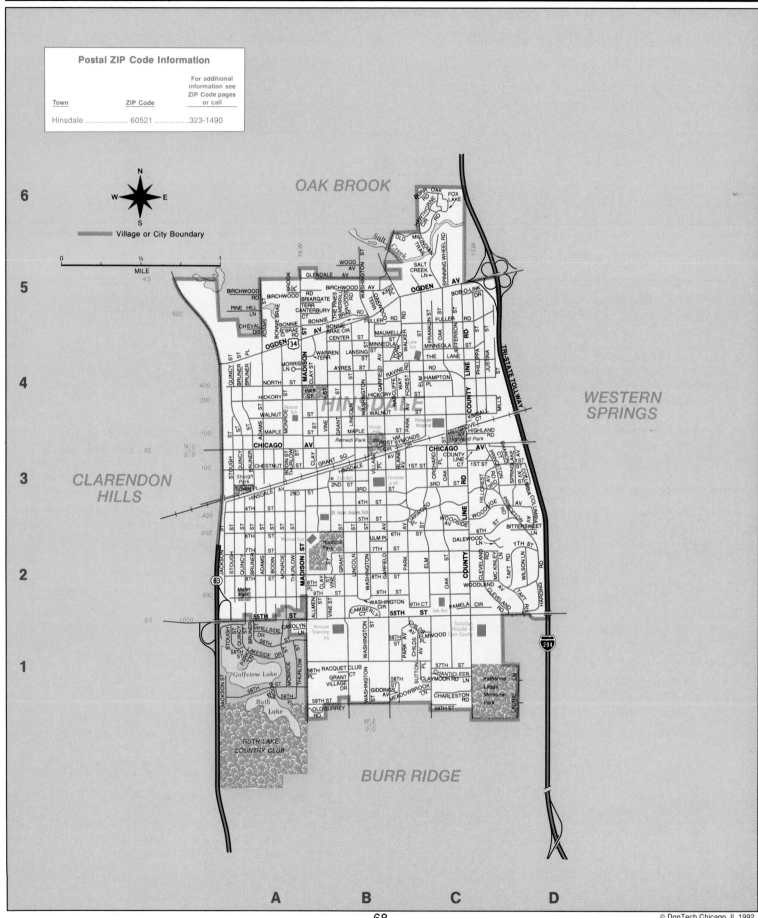

Postal ZIP Code Information

Town	ZIP Code	For additional information see ZIP Code pages or call
Hinsdale	60521	323-1490

OAK BROOK

WESTERN SPRINGS

CLARENDON HILLS

HINSDALE

BURR RIDGE

Village or City Boundary

6
5
4
3
2
1

A   B   C   D

© DonTech Chicago, Il. 1992

© DonTech Chicago, Il. 1992

Street Guide

ACERRA DR E4	DARMSTADT RD A6	HAWTHORNE AV B7	MAPLE AV-S D4	SPEECHLEY BL-N C7
ADAMS ST B6	DICKENS AV C3	HIGH RIDGE PKWY-S C1	MAPLE LN-N D7	SUNNYSIDE DR B7
ASHBEL AV-N B5	DIVISION ST E4	HIGH RIDGE RD-N C7	MAY ST E4	TAFT AV-N A6
AUGUSTINE AV B5	EAST AV-S E4	HILLSIDE AV-N B5-B7	MELROSE AV-N D7	TERRACE LN C1
BELLWOOD AV-N E7	EAST END AV-N B7	HOWARD AV-N B5	MORRIS AV-N C7	**TRI-STATE TOLLWAY A2**
BROADVIEW AV-N D7	EDGEWATER ST D4	HYDE PARK AV-N E7	MUELLER DR E6	VAN BUREN ST B5
BUCK RD A4	**EISENHOWER EXPWY E5**	IDLEWILD LN D6	OAK AV-S E4	VANNA CT-N D6
BUCKTHORN LN-N D7	ELECTRIC AV B7	IROQUOIS RD-N C7	OAK RIDGE AV-S D4	WARREN AV B7-E7
BUTTERFIELD RD B6	ELM ST-N B5	IRVING AV-N B5-B7	ORCHARD ST-S D4	**WASHINGTON BL B7-E7**
CANTERBURY ST C2	ENGLEWOOD AV-N E7	JACKSON BL C6	RAILROAD AV-N B6	WESTWOOD DR-S C1
CENTER ST-S E4	FENCL LN C4	LA VERNE AV-N B5	RAILROAD AV-S D5	**WOLF RD-N C6**
CERMAK RD B1	FENWOOD LN D6	LEE BL-N C7	RANDOLPH CT B7	**WOLF RD-S C2**
CHARLES ST C2	FOREST AV-N D6	LIND AV-N B5	RANDOLPH ST C7	50TH AV-N D7
CLAYTON RD-E D6	FOREST AV-S D6	LITT DR E7	RAYMOND DR E6	51ST AV-N D7
CLAYTON RD-N C7	FRONTAGE DR C5	LOCUST AV B7	RIDGE AV A7	
CRAIG DR D6	GENEVA AV-N E7	MADISON ST B6-D6	RODHE AV-N C7	
CYPRESS CT B7	GRANVILLE AV-N E7	**MANNHEIM RD-N E6**	**ROOSEVELT RD B4-E4**	
CYPRESS DR B7	HARRISON ST B5	**MANNHEIM RD-S E4**	ST PAUL CT B7	

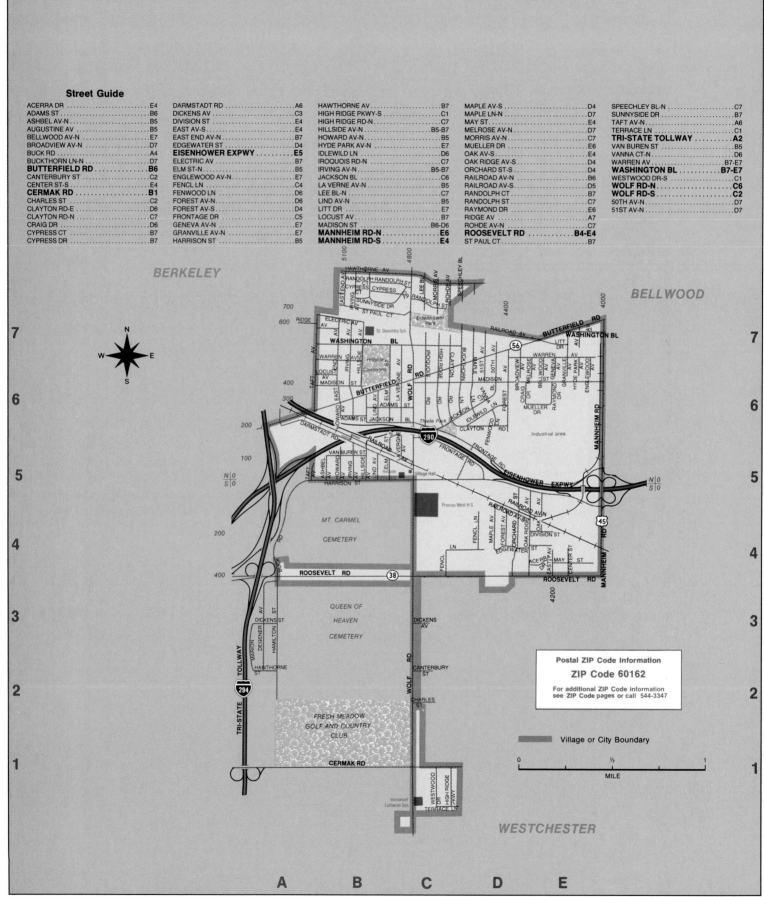

Postal ZIP Code Information
ZIP Code 60162
For additional ZIP Code information see ZIP Code pages or call 544-3347

Village or City Boundary

© DonTech Chicago, Il. 1992

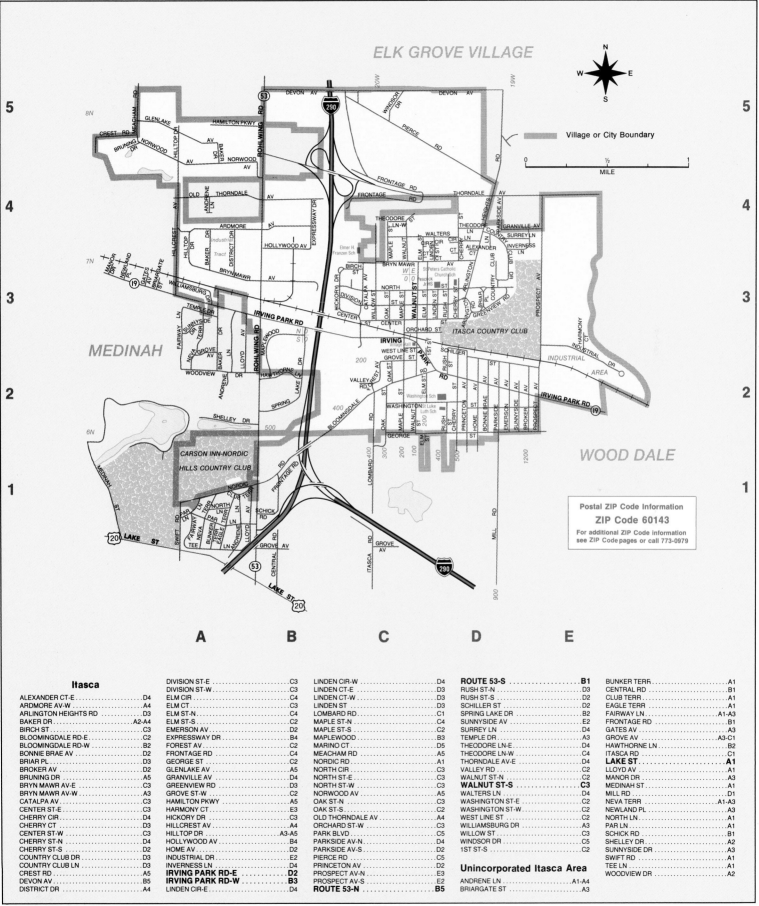

© DonTech Chicago, Il. 1992

LaGrange

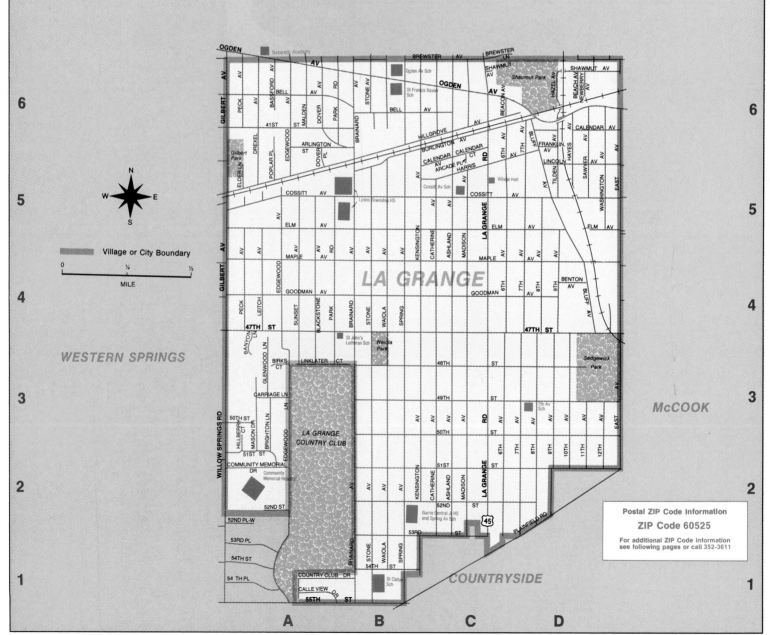

© DonTech Chicago, Il. 1992

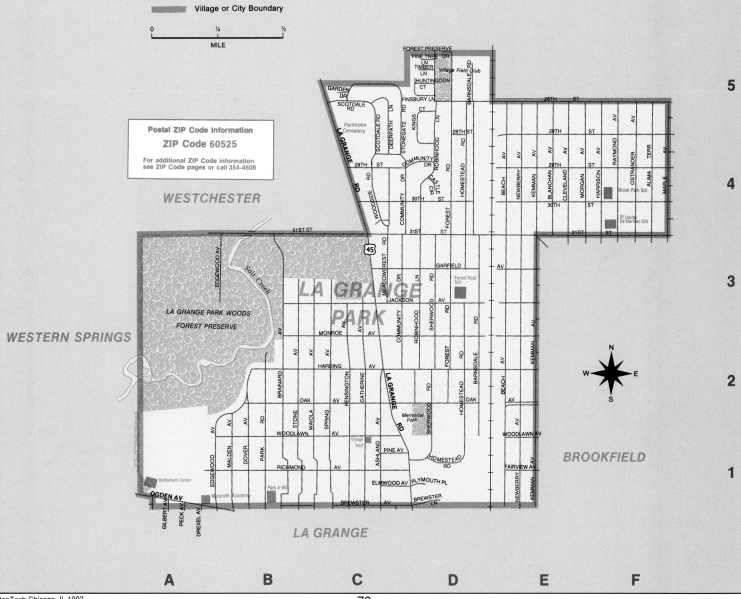

Postal ZIP Code Information

ZIP Code 60525

For additional ZIP Code information see ZIP Code pages or call 354-4606

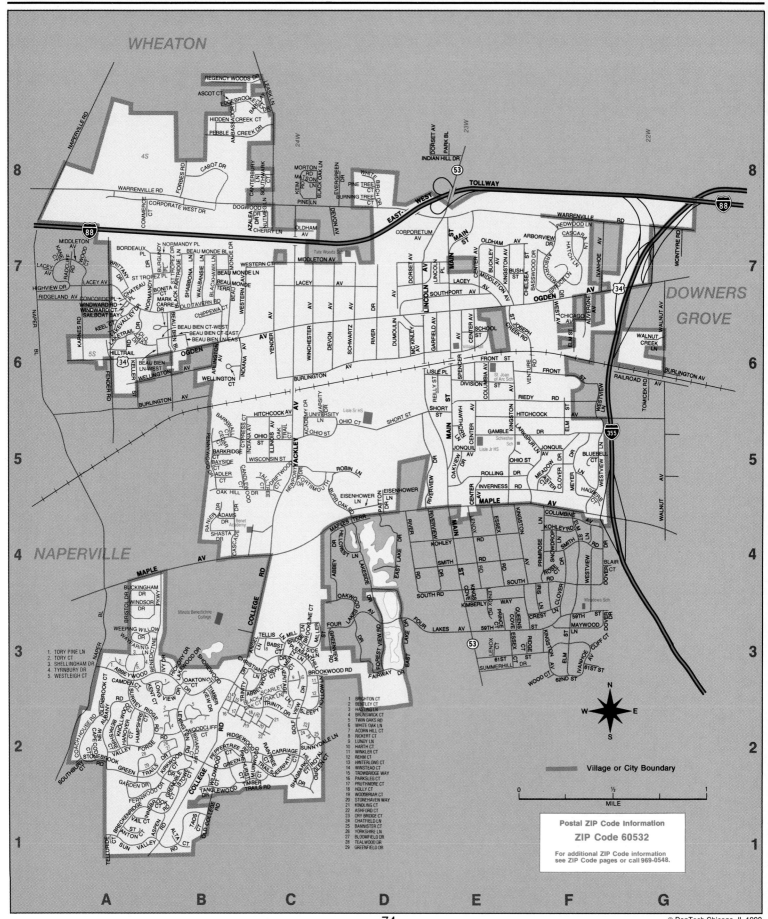

WHEATON

NAPERVILLE

DOWNERS GROVE

1. TORY PINE LN
2. TORY CT
3. SHELLINGHAM DR
4. TYRNBURY DR
5. WESTLEIGH CT

1. BRIGHTON CT
2. BENTLEY CT
3. HASTING LN
4. BRUNSWICK CT
5. TWIN OAKS RD
6. WHITE OAK LN
7. ACORN HILL CT
8. RICKERT CT
9. LUNDY LN
10. HARTH CT
11. WINKLER CT
12. REHM CT
13. HINTERLONG CT
14. WINSTEAD CT
15. TROWBRIDGE WAY
16. PARKSLEG CT
17. PRUTHMORE CT
18. HOLLY CT
19. WOODBRIAR CT
20. STONEHAVEN WAY
21. KINDLING CT
22. ASHFORD CT
23. DRY BRIDGE CT
24. CHATFIELD LN
25. BANNISTER CT
26. YORKSHIRE LN
27. BLOOMFIELD DR
28. TEALWOOD CT
29. GREENFIELD DR

—— Village or City Boundary

0   ½   1
MILE

N
W   E
S

Postal ZIP Code Information
ZIP Code 60532

For additional ZIP Code information
see ZIP Code pages or call 969-0548.

© DonTech Chicago, Il. 1992

© DonTech Chicago, Il. 1992

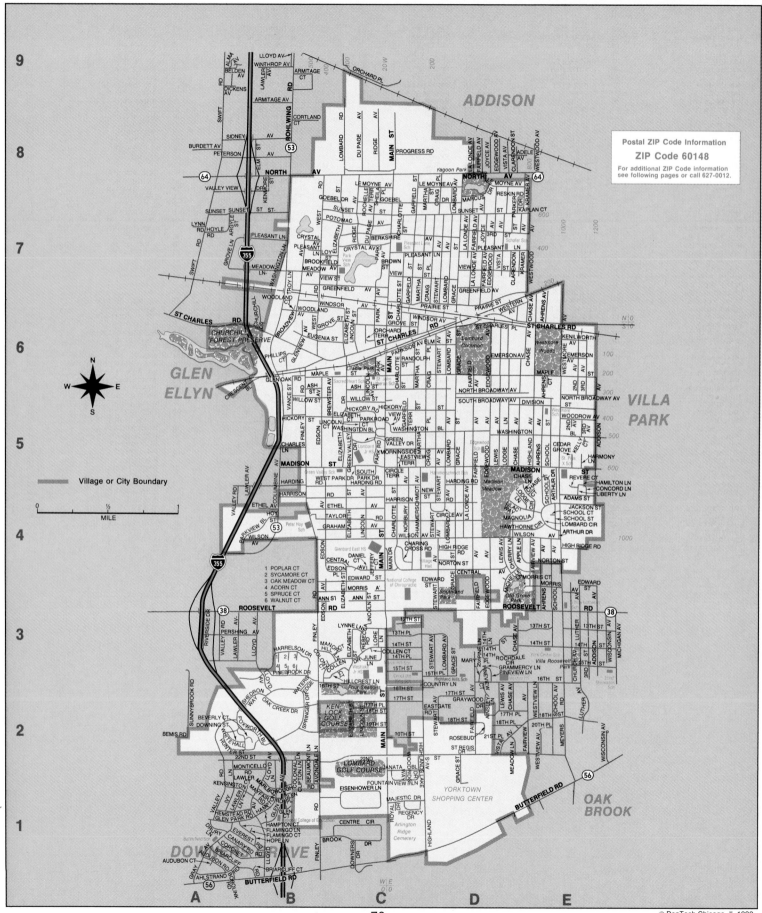

© DonTech Chicago, Il. 1992

Lombard

Street	Grid
ACORN CT	B2
ADAMS ST-E	E5
ADDISON AV-S	E5
AHRENS AV-N	E6
AHRENS AV-S	E5
AHRENS CT	E6
AINSLEY LN	D2
ANN ST-W	C3
APPLE LN	E4
ARTHUR DR	E5
ASH ST-E	C6
ASH ST-W	B6
BEMIS RD	A2
BERKSHIRE AV-E	D7
BERKSHIRE AV-W	C7
BEVERLY CT	B2
BREWSTER AV-S	B5
BRADLEY LN	D4
BROADVIEW AV-N	B7
BROOKFIELD AV	B7
BROWN ST	C7
BUTTERFIELD RD-E	**D1**
CEDAR GROVE	E5
CENTRAL AV-E	D4
CENTRAL AV-W	C4
CHARING CROSS RD	C4
CHARLES LN	B5
CHARLOTTE ST-N	C7
CHARLOTTE ST-S	C4
CHASE AV-N	E6
CHASE AV-S	D5
CHASE CT	E5
CHASE LN	E4
CHERRY LN	D4
CIRCLE AV-E	D4
CIRCLE TERR	C5
CLARENDON ST-N	C7
COLLEN CT	C3
COLLEN DR	C3
COLONY CT	B3
COLUMBINE AV-N	B7
COLUMBINE AV-S	B5
CONCORD LN	E5
CRAIG PL-N	C7
CRAIG PL-S	C5
CRYSTAL AV-W	C7
DANIEL CT	C4
DIVISION ST-E	E5
DOWNING ST	B2
DU PAGE AV	C7
EASTVIEW TERR	C5
EDGEWOOD AV-N	D7
EDGEWOOD AV-S	D4
EDSON AV-S	B5
EDSON PL	B4
EDWARD ST-E	D6
EDWARD ST-W	C4
EISENHOWER LN	C1
ELIZABETH CT	C5
ELIZABETH DR-S	C5
ELIZABETH ST-N	C7
ELIZABETH ST-S	C4
ELM ST-E	D6
EMERSON AV-E	D6
ETHEL AV-W	C4
EUGENIA ST	B6
FAIRFIELD AV-N	D7
FAIRFIELD AV-S	E4
FINLEY RD-S	B3
FOUNTAIN VIEW LN	C3
FOXWORTH BL	B2

Street	Grid
GARFIELD ST-N	C8
GARFIELD ST-S	C7
GARFIELD TERR	C5
GLEN OAK RD	B6
GLENVIEW AV-N	B6
GLENVIEW AV-S	B6
GOEBEL DR-E	D8
GOEBEL DR-W	C8
GRACE ST-N	D7
GRACE ST-S	D2
GRAHAM AV-W	C4
GRAMMERCY LN	D3
GREENFIELD AV-E	D7
GREENFIELD AV-W	B7
GREENFIELD ST-E	D7
GREEN VALLEY DR	C5
GROVE ST-E	C6
GROVE ST-W	C6
HAMILTON LN	E5
HAMMERSCHMIDT AV	C4
HARDING RD-E	D5
HARDING RD-W	B5
HARMONY LN	E5
HARRELSON DR	B3
HARRISON RD-E	D4
HARRISON RD-W	B4
HAWTHORNE AV	E4
HICKORY RD-W	C5
HICKORY ST-E	C5
HICKORY ST-W	B5
HIGHLAND AV-E	E6
HIGHLAND AV-S	E5
HIGHLANDS LAKE DR	C2
HIGH RIDGE RD	E4
HILLCREST CT	C3
HILLCREST LN	C3
HOY ST	A4
HUNTER ST	A2
JACKSON ST-E	E4
JANATA BL-E	C2
JEFFERY CT	C4
JOYCE AV-N	D7
JUNE LN	C3
KAPLAN CT	D7
KELLY CT	E5
KENILWORTH AV	E6
KRAMER AV-N	D7
LA LONDE AV-N	D7
LA LONDE AV-S	D4
LE MOYNE AV-E	D8
LE MOYNE AV-W	C8
LEWIS AV-S	D4
LIBERTY LN	E5
LILAC WAY	D4
LINCOLN AV-N	C6
LINCOLN AV-S	C4
LINCOLN CT	C5
LINCOLN ST	C3-C6
LLOYD AV	B3
LODGE LN-S	D4
LOMBARD AV-N	D7
LOMBARD AV-S	D3
LOMBARD CIR	E4
LOMBARD RD	C8
LORE LN	C3
LOY ST	B7
LYNNE LN	C3
MADISON ST-E	**E5**
MADISON ST-W	**B5**
MAGNOLIA CIR	E4
MAIN DR	C4
MAIN ST-N	**C8**
MAIN ST-S	**C4**
MAJESTIC DR	C1

Street	Grid
MANOR HILL CT	B3
MANOR HILL LN	B3
MAPLE ST-E	E6
MAPLE ST-W	B6
MARCUS DR	D8
MARION AV	D5
MARTHA ST-N	C7
MARTHA ST-S	C5
MARY'S LN	D3
MEADOW AV-W	B7
MICHELLE LN	D4
MORNINGSIDE AV-E	C5
MORRIS AV-E	E4
MORRIS AV-W	C3
MORRIS CT	E4
NEW ST	C5
NORBURY AV-S	C4
NORTH AV-E	**D8**
NORTH AV-W	**B8**
NORTH BROADWAY AV-E	D6
NORTON ST	E4
OAK CREEK DR	B2
OAK MEADOW CT	B3
ORCHARD PL	C6
ORCHARD TERR	C6
PARK AV-N	C7
PARK AV-S	C6
PARK RD	C5
PARKER DR	D8
PARK ROAD CT	C5
PARKSIDE AV-E	D6
PARKSIDE AV-W	C6
PARKVIEW BL	B4
PHILLIPS CT-W	B6
PINEBROOK DR	B2
PINEVIEW LN	D3
PLEASANT LN-E	D7
PLEASANT LN-W	B7
POPLAR CT	B3
POTOMAC AV-W	C7
PRAIRIE ST-E	D6
PRAIRIE ST-W	C6
PROGRESS RD	C8
RANDOLPH ST	C6
REBECCA RD	C3
REGENCY DR	C1
RESKIN RD	D8
REVERE CT	E5
RIDGE AV-N	C7
ROCHELLE TERR	C8
ROHLWING RD	**B8**
ROOSEVELT RD-W	**B3**
ROOSEVELT RD-E	**E3**
ROSEBUD	D2
ROYAL DR	C1
ST CHARLES PL-E	D6
ST CHARLES RD-E	**E6**
ST CHARLES RD-W	**A6**
ST REGIS DR	D2
SCHOOL CT	E4
SCHOOL ST-S	E5
SCHOOL ST-E	E5
SHEDRON WAY	A2
SHEILA PL	C8
SOUTH BROADWAY AV-E	D6
SOUTH PARK DR	C5
SPRINGER DR	B2
SPRUCE CT	B2
STEWART AV-N	D7
STEWART AV-S	D3
SUNNYBROOK RD	A2
SUNSET ST-E	D7
SUNSET ST-W	C7
SYCAMORE CT	B3

Street	Grid
TAYLOR RD-E	D4
TAYLOR RD-W	C4
TROY LN-N	B7
VANCE ST-S	B5
VIEW AV	C5
VIEW ST-E	D7
VIEW ST-W	B7
VISTA AV-N	D7
WALNUT CT	B2
WASHINGTON BL-E	D5
WASHINGTON BL-W	C5
WASHINGTON LN	B7
WATERS EDGE	B2
WEST RD	B7
WESTERN AV	D6
WESTMORE AV-N	E7
WESTMORE AV-S	E5
WEST PARK DR	C5
WESTWOOD AV-N	E7
WHITEHALL	A2
WILLOW ST-E	C5
WILLOW ST-W	B5
WILSON AV-E	D4
WILSON AV-W	B4
WINDSOR AV-E	C6
WINDSOR AV-W	B6
WOODLAND AV	B6
WOODLAND CT	B6
WOODRIDGE WAY	C2
WOODROW AV	E5
2ND AV-S	E5
3RD AV-S	E5
3RD ST	D7
17TH PL	C2
16TH ST	C3
18TH ST	C2
19TH ST	C2
22ND ST-E	D2
22ND ST-W	C2

Unincorporated Area

Street	Grid
ADELE AV	D8
AHLSTRAND RD	A1
ALMA AV	A9
ARGYLE ST	A7
ARMITAGE AV	B9
ARMITAGE CT	B9
AUDUBON CT	A1
AUDUBON RD	A1
AVONDALE LN	B2
BEAUMONT LN	B2
BELDEN AV	A9
BOBOLINK RD	A1
BRIARCLIFF CT	B1
BRIARCLIFF RD	A1
BROOK DR	C1
BURDETT AV	A8
BUTTERFIELD RD-W	**B1**
CANARY RD	A1
CENTRE CIR	C1
CHURCH AV	E3
CHURCHILL DR	B6
CLIFTON LN	B2
COLONIAL LN	B2
CORONET RD	A1
CORTLAND AV	B8
COUNTRY LN	D2
CRESCENT BL	B6
DICKENS AV	A9
DOWNERS DR	C1
DRURY LN	A1
EASTGATE RD	D2
ELM ST-N	B8

Street	Grid
EVEREST RD	A1
FAIRVIEW AV	D8-E2
FLAMINGO CT	B1
FLAMINGO LN	B1
FULLERTON AV	B9
GLEN AV	B1
GLEN CT	B1
GLEN PL	B1
GLENBARD RD	A3
GLEN PARK RD	A1
GRAY AV	A1
GRAYWOOD DR	D2
GROVE LN	A7
HAMPTON CT	B1
HAMPTON LN	B1
HELEN AV	A9
HEMSTEAD RD	A1
HOPE LN	B1
HOYLE RD	A7
IVY LN	A1
KENMORE ST	B8
KENSINGTON RD	B1
LAWLER AV-N	B9
LAWLER AV-S	B3
LAWLER CT	A1
LAWLER LN	A1
LLOYD AV-N	B9
LLOYD AV-S	B1
LUTHER AV	E2
LYNN RD	A7
MAGNOLIA AV	B9
MARLBOROUGH RD	B1
MAYFAIR RD	B1
MEADOW LN-S	D2
MEADOW LN-W	B7
MEYERS RD-S	E2
MICHIGAN AV	E3
MONTICELLO RD	B2
PERSHING AV	A3
PETERSON AV	B8
PINE LN	D3
PINEVIEW CT	D2
RIVERSIDE DR	A3
ROCHDALE CIR	D3
SCHOOL AV	E2
SIDNEY AV	B8
SWIFT RD	A8
VALLEY RD	A1-A4
VALLEY VIEW DR	A8
VISTA AV-S	D2
WESTVIEW AV	E2
WESTVIEW LN	E2
WINTHROP AV	B9
WISCONSIN AV	E3
3RD ST	E3
13TH PL-E	C3
13TH ST-E	E3
14TH LN	D3
14TH PL-E	C3
14TH ST-E	D3
15TH PL-E	D3
15TH ST-E	C3
16TH ST-E	D3
17TH PL-E	D2
17TH ST-E	D2
18TH PL-E	D2
18TH ST-E	D2
20TH PL-E	E2
20TH ST-E	C2
21ST PL-E	D2

© DonTech Chicago, Il. 1992

Lyons

ABBOTT TERR	D4
AMELIA AV	E4
ANNA AV	C5
BARRYPOINT RD	D5
CENTER AV	E4
CHRISTIE AV	D4
CIRCLE DR-N	C5
CLYDE AV	D4
COLLINS AV	E5
CRACOW AV	C4
CUSTER AV	C4
ELM AV	E4
FERN AV	C5
FISHERMAN'S TERR	E4

GAGE AV	E4
HAAS AV	F5
HARLEM AV	**F4**
HAWTHORNE AV	D4
JOLIET AV	D4
JOLIET RD	**E4**
KONRAD AV	C5
LAWNDALE AV	D4
LELAND AV	D5
LINCOLN DR	C4
MAPLE AV	E5
OAK AV	E4
OAKWOOD AV	E5
PATRICIA DR	C5
PLAINFIELD RD	C4
POWELL ST	F5

PRESCOTT AV	E5
PULASKI AV	C4
RIVERSIDE AV	C4
ROSE AV	C5
SALISBURY AV	D5
SOUTHVIEW AV	C5
WARSAW AV	C4
WHITE AV	D5
WINCHESTER AV	D5
1ST AV	**C3**
39TH ST	**E5**
40TH ST	C5
41ST CT	E5
41ST PL	E5
42ND CT	D4
42ND PL	E5

42ND ST	D5
43RD PL	D4
43RD ST	D4
44TH CT	D4
44TH PL	C4
44TH ST	C4
45TH CT	D4
45TH PL	E4
45TH ST	C4
46TH ST	D4
47TH ST	**D3**

McCook

CLYDE TERR	D3
EAST AV	A2
EGANDALE ST	C3

GLENCOE AV	C3
GRAND AV	D3
JOLIET AV	D3
JOLIET RD	**A1**
KANE AV	A1
LAWNDALE AV	D3
RIVERSIDE AV	C3
WINCHESTER AV	D3
1ST AV	**C3**
47TH ST-S	**E3**
49TH PL	C3
50TH ST	C3
53RD ST	C2
56TH ST	A1

Postal ZIP Code Information

For additional information see following pages or call

Town	ZIP Code	
Lyons	60534	442-5400
McCook	60525	352-3611
N. of Salt Creek	60513	485-0572

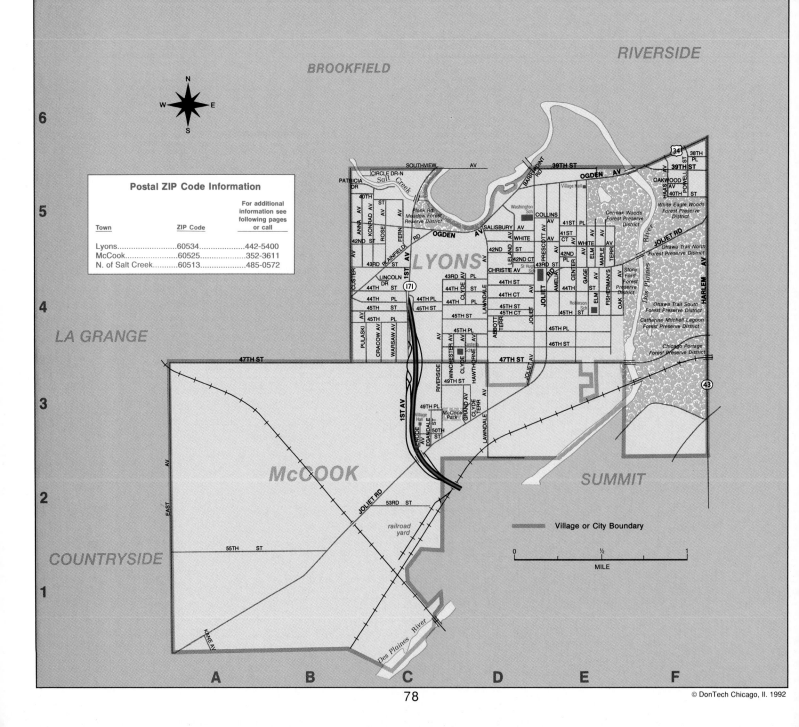

© DonTech Chicago, Il. 1992

Maywood

ADAMS ST	B2
AUGUSTA ST	D7
BATAAN DR	A2-D2
CHICAGO AV	D6
CONGRESS ST	D2
EISENHOWER EXPWY	**E2**
ERIE ST	D6
FILLMORE ST	D1
GREEN ST	D3
GREENWOOD AV	E3
HARRISON ST	B2-D2
HARVARD AV	A1-D1
HURON ST	D6
IOWA ST	D6
LAKE ST	**D5**

LEGION ST	D3
LEXINGTON ST	A2-D2
MADISON ST	**B3-E3**
MAIN ST	D5
MAPLE ST	D5
MAYBROOK DR	E2
MAYWOOD DR-N	B3
MAYWOOD DR-S	B3
NICHOLS LN	D7
OAK ST	B5-D5
OHIO ST	D5
ORCHARD AV	E3
PINE ST	D4
QUINCY ST	D2
RAILROAD ST	B5
RANDOLPH ST	B4
RICE ST	D6

ROOSEVELT RD	**E1**
ST CHARLES RD	**B5**
SCHOOL ST	D3
SUPERIOR ST	D6
VAN BUREN ST	B2-D2
WALNUT ST	D4
WALTON ST	D7
WARREN AV	B4
WASHINGTON BL	**B4-E4**
1ST AV-N	**D6**
1ST AV-S	**D1-D4**
2ND AV-N	D6
2ND AV-S	D1-D4
3RD AV-N	D6
3RD AV-S	D1-D4
4TH AV-N	D6

4TH AV-S	D1-D4
5TH AV-N	**D6**
5TH AV-S	**D1-D4**
6TH AV-N	D6
6TH AV-S	D1-D4
7TH AV-N	D6
7TH AV-S	D1-D4
8TH AV-N	C6
8TH AV-S	C1-C4
9TH AV-N	C7
9TH AV-S	C1-C4
10TH AV-S	C1-C4
11TH AV-S	C1-C4
12TH AV-S	C1-C4
13TH AV-N	B1-B4
13TH AV-S	B1-B4
14TH AV-S	B4
15TH AV-S	B4

16TH AV-S	B4
17TH AV-S	**B4**
18TH AV-S	B4
19TH AV-S	A4
20TH AV-S	A4
21ST AV-S	A4
22ND AV-S	A2
23RD AV-S	A2
24TH AV-S	A2
25TH AV-S	**A2**

Hines

CROSSMAN CIR	D1
HINES ST	D1
ROOSEVELT RD	E1
1ST AV-S	E1

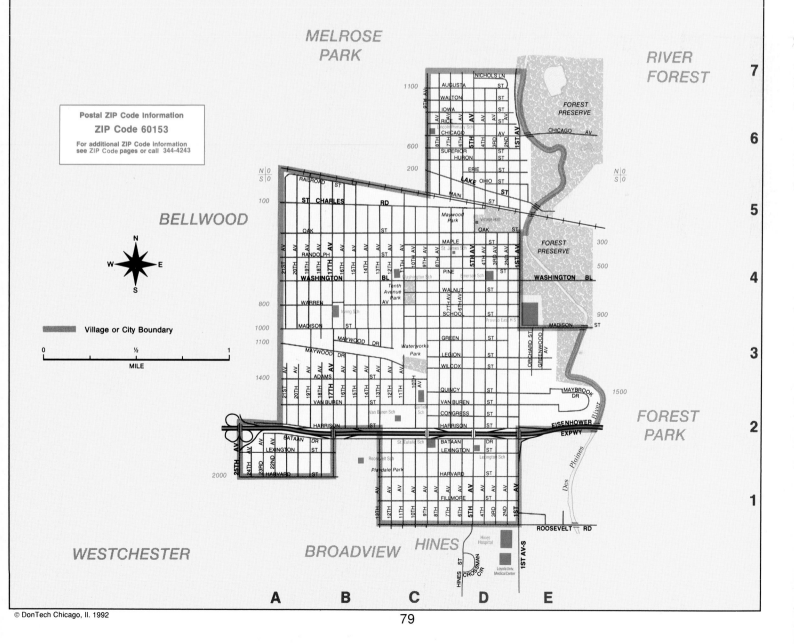

Postal ZIP Code Information
ZIP Code 60153
For additional ZIP Code information
see ZIP Code pages or call 344-4243

Village or City Boundary

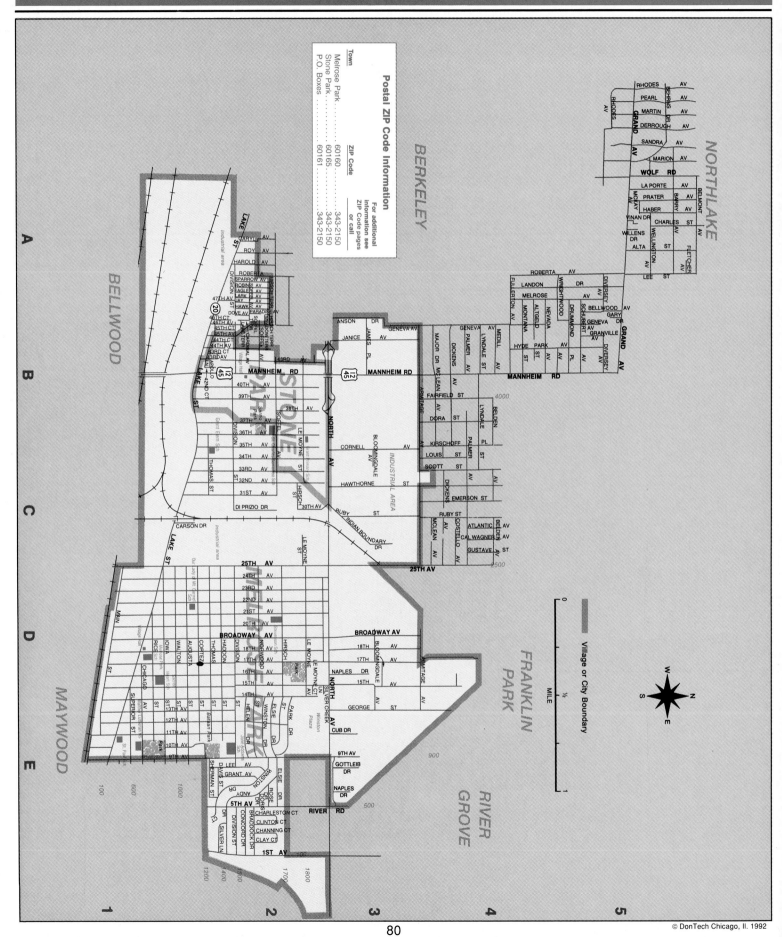

© DonTech Chicago, Il. 1992

Melrose Park

Street	Grid
ANDY DR	E2
ANSON DR	B3
ARMITAGE AV-W	B3
AUGUSTA ST	D2
BLOOMINGDALE AV	C3
BRADDOCK DR	E2
BROADWAY AV-N	**D2**
CARDINAL AV	B2
CARSON DR	C1
CARYL ST	A2
CHANNING CT	E2
CHARLESTON CT	E2
CHICAGO AV	D1
CLAY CT	E2
CLINTON CT	E2
CONCORD DR	E2
CORNELL AV	C3
CORTEZ ST	D2
CUB DR	E3
DAVIS ST	E2
DI PRIZIO DR	C2
DIVISION ST	A2
DORIS DR	E2
DOVE AV	B2
EAGLE AV	A2
ELSIE DR	E2
GENEVA AV	B3
GEORGE ST	E3
GOTTLIEB DR	E3
GRANT AV	E2
HADDON ST	D2
HAROLD AV	A2
HAWK AV	B2
HAWTHORNE ST	C3
HELEN DR	E2
HIRSCH ST	C2
HIRSCH TERR	A2
INDIAN BOUNDARY DR	C3
IOWA ST	D1
JAMES PL	B3
JANICE AV	B3
JAY AV	A2
LAKE ST-W	**C1**
LAKE TERR	B2
LARK AV	A2
LEE AV	E2
LE MOYNE CT	D2
LE MOYNE ST	D2
MAIN ST	D1
MANNHEIM RD	**B3**
MEADOW TERR	B2
NAPLES DR	D3
NORTH AV-W	**D3**
NORWOOD ST	D2
PARADISE AV	B2
PARK DR	E2
RICE ST	D1
ROBERTA AV	A2
ROBIN AV-N	A2
ROSE DR	E2
ROY AV	A2
RUBY ST	C3
SHERMAN ST	E2
SILVER LN	E2
SILVER CREEK LN	D3
SOFFEL AV	A2
SOFFEL TERR	B2
SPARROW AV	A2
SUPERIOR ST	E1
THOMAS ST	C2
WALTON ST	D1
WINSTON CT	E2
WINSTON DR	E2
1ST AV	**E2**
5TH AV	**E2**
9TH AV	E1
10TH AV	E1
11TH AV	E1
12TH AV	E1
13TH AV	E1
14TH AV	D2
14TH CT	D2
15TH AV	D2
16TH AV	D2
17TH AV	D2
18TH AV	D2
20TH AV	D2
21ST AV	D2
22ND AV	D2
23RD AV	D2
24TH AV	D2
25TH AV	**C2**
30TH AV	C2
31ST AV	C2
32ND AV	C2
33RD AV	C2
34TH AV	C2
35TH AV	C2
36TH AV	B2
37TH AV	B2
45TH AV	B2
45TH CT	B2
46TH AV	B2
46TH CT	B2
47TH AV	A2

Stone Park

Street	Grid
APOLLO LN	B2
DIVISION ST	B2
LAKE ST	**B2**
LAKE TERR	B2
LE MOYNE ST	C2

Street	Grid
MANNHEIM RD	**B2**
NORTH AV-W	**B3**
SOFFEL AV	B2
32ND AV	C2
33RD AV	C2
34TH AV	C2
35TH AV	C2
36TH AV	B2
37TH AV	B2
38TH AV	B2
39TH AV	B2
40TH AV	B2
42ND CT	B2
43RD AV	B2
43RD CT	B2
44TH AV	B2
44TH CT	B2
45TH AV	B2

Unincorporated Area

Street	Grid
ALTA ST	A5
ALTGELD ST	B4
ATLANTIC AV	C4
BARRY AV	A5
BEHRNS DR	A5
BELDEN AV	B4
BELLWOOD AV	B5
BELMONT AV	A5
CAL WAGNER AV	C4
CHARLES ST	A5
COSTELLO AV	C4
DERROUGH AV	A5
DICKENS AV	B4
DIVERSEY AV	A5
DORA ST	B4
DRUMMOND PL	B5
EMERSON ST	C4

Street	Grid
FAIRFIELD ST	B4
FLETCHER AV	A5
FULLERTON AV	B4
GARY DR	B5
GRAND AV	**A5**
GRANVILLE AV	B5
GUSTAVE ST	C4
HABER AV	A5
HYDE PARK AV	B4
KIRSCHOFF PL	C3
LA PORTE AV	A5
LANDON DR	A4
LEE ST	A5
LOUIS ST	C4
LYNDALE ST	B4
MAJOR DR	B4
MARION AV	A5
MARTIN AV	A5
MCKAY AV	A5
MCLEAN AV	C4
MEDILL AV	B4
MELROSE AV	A4
MONTANA ST	B4
NEVADA AV	B4
PALMER AV	B4
PEARL AV	A5
PRATER AV	A5
RHODES AV	A5
RIVER RD	**E3**
ROBERTA AV	A4
SANDRA AV	A5
SCHUBERT AV	B5
SCOTT ST	C4
VINAN DR	A5
WELLINGTON AV	A5
WILLENS DR	A5
WOLF RD	**A5**
WRIGHTWOOD AV	A5

© DonTech Chicago, Il. 1992

© DonTech Chicago, Il. 1992

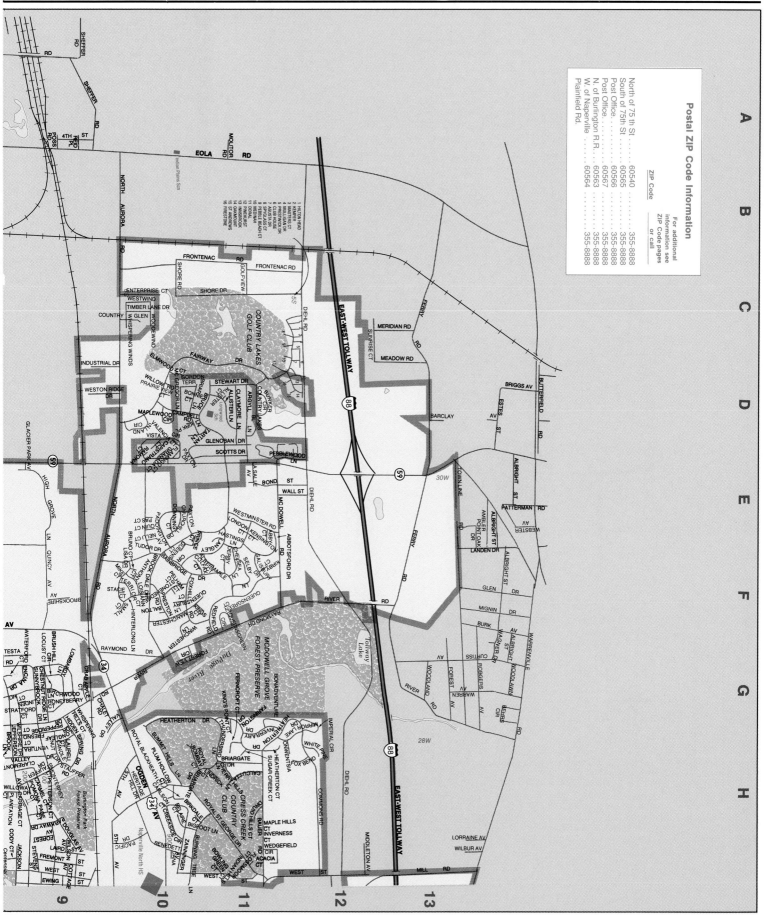

Postal ZIP Code Information

For additional information see ZIP Code pages or call

	ZIP Code	
North of 75 th St	60540	355-8888
South of 75th St	60565	355-8888
Post Office	60566	355-8888
Post Office	60567	355-8888
N. of Burlington R.R.	60563	355-8888
W. of Naperville	60563	355-8888
Plainfield Rd.	60564	355-8888

1 HILTON HEAD
2 KEMPER
3 MASTERS CT
4 MULLIGAN DR
5 PRESTWICK DR
6 CLUB HOUSE
7 AUGUSTA DR
8 SPYGLASS CT
9 PEBBLE BEACH CT
10 MEDINAH
11 DORAL
12 PINEHURST
13 INNSBROOK
14 OAKMONT
15 ST ANDREWS
16 FIRESTONE

© DonTech Chicago, Il. 1992

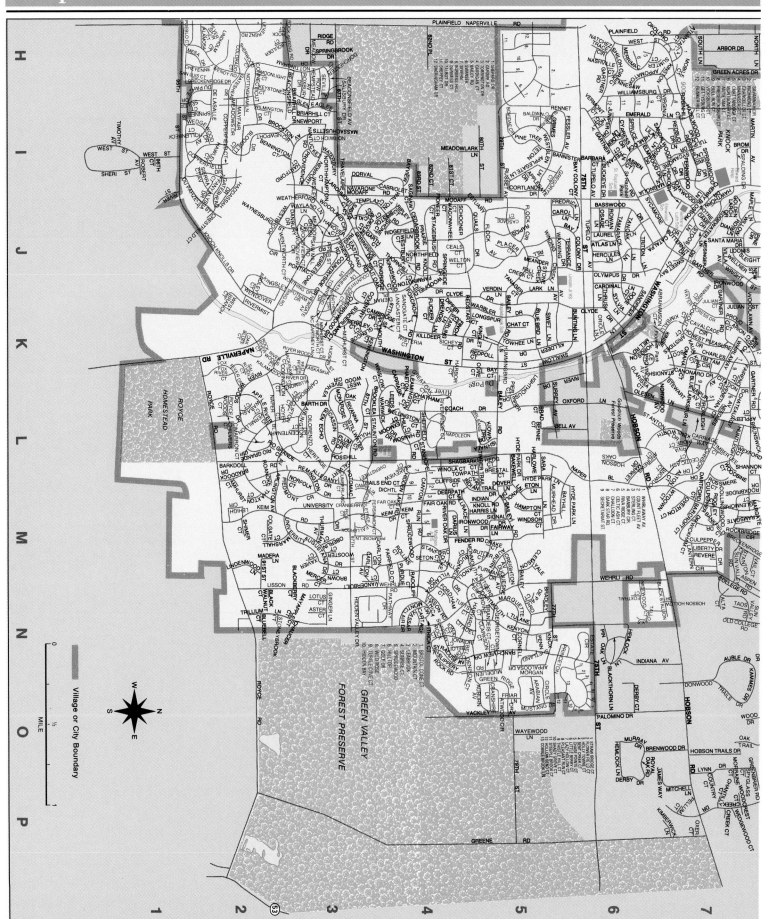

© DonTech Chicago, Il. 1992

© DonTech Chicago, Il. 1992

© DonTech Chicago, Il. 1992

© DonTech Chicago, Il. 1992

Street	Grid
PRESTON RD	F10
PRESTWICK DR	C12
PRIMROSE LN	M3
PRINCE CT	E10
PRINCETON CR	N5
PROSPECT CT	H6
PROUD CLARION CT	K7
PROVIDENCE CT	I3
PUEBLO CT	H1
PURDUE AV	M4
PUTNAM DR	K3
QUAIL HOLLOW	K9
QUAILS DR	J5
QUEENS CT	E10
QUEENSBURY CT	F10
QUEENSGREEN CIR	F11
QUEENSGREEN CT	F11
QUIN CT	E10
QUINCY AV	F9
RADCLIFF CT	M4
RADCLIFF RD	L11
RAINTREE	G7, N8
RAMM DR	B3
RAMONA CT	D10
RAMSGATE	M7
RANCHVIEW DR	N5
RAPIDAN CT	L8
RAPIDS	J5
RANIER DR	N10
RAYMOND DR	G10, F11
REBECCA CT	F1
RED RIVER CT	K3
REDBUD DR	I7
REDFIELD RD	F11
REDPOLL CT	J5
REDSTART RD	K4
REHM CT	O9
REID PL	A9
REMINGTON DR	L3
RENNET	H5
REVERE	M7
RHOADES DR	H6
RICE CT	M3
RICHARD DR	F1
RICHARD RD	L8
RICHMOND CT	H7
RICKERT	N9
RICKERT DR	G6
RIDGE RD	H3
RIDGEFIELD LN	J4
RIDGELAND AV	L12
RIDGEVIEW LN	N10
RIDGLEY CT	M7
RILL	J5
RING RD	J3
RIO GRANDE CIR	L2
RIO GRANDE CT	L2
RIPLEY CT	J4
RIVA RIDGE CT	L7
RIVANNA CT	L3
RIVER BEND RD	H8
RIVER BLUFF CIR	H8
RIVER DR	G8, K3, K6
RIVER FRONT CIR	H8
RIVER OAK DR	M4
RIVER RIDGE CT	I4
RIVER RD	G6, G13
RIVER ST	I1
RIVER WOODS CT	K2
RIVER WOODS DR	K2
RIVERLEA CIR	K3
RIVERMIST	K2
RIVERVIEW RD	I8
ROANOKE CT	L2
ROBERT AV	J1
ROBINHILL CT	H7
ROBINHILL DR	I7
ROCK CT	H2
ROCK RIVER CT	K2
ROCK SPRING RD	H3
ROCKBRIDGE CIR	M7
ROCKBRIDGE DR	M7
RODGERS AV	G13
ROLLING GROVE CT	G7
ROLLING MEADOWS DR	H2
ROLLINS CT	M4
ROSE LN	I6
ROSE WOOD	K11
ROSEHILL	L3
ROSSMERE CT	L7
ROUTE 59	D6, D13
ROWAN CT	J6
ROXBURY DR	H3
ROYAL ST	H11
ROYAL BLACK HEATH CT	H10
ROYAL BOMBAY CT	H10
ROYAL GLEN CT	O8
ROYAL OAK RD	O6, O8
ROYCE RD	L2, O2
ROYCE WOODS CT	L2
RUSSET AV	I5
RUTGERS CT	M5
SABER CT	J3
SAGINAW CT	J4
ST. ANDREWS CT	D11
ST. CROIX AV	G3
ST. TROPEZ DR	M12
SALEM AV	L10
SALISBURY DR	F11, H3
SALT RIVER CT	K2
SAMSTAG CT	L11
SAN LUIS CT	H2
SANCTUARY LN	F6
SANDALWOOD DR	I6
SANDGATE CT	K4
SANDPIPER LN	K6
SANTA MARIA DR	J7
SARA LN	L5
SARANELL AV	G6
SAVANNAH CIR	H7
SAW MILL RD	J3
SAXON LN	G1
SCHOGER RD	B3
SCHOOL ST	J9
SCHOONER CT	J4
SCOTT CT	K7
SCOTTS DR	D11
SEABROOK CT	N10
SECRETARIAT ST	K7
SEILER DR	H1
SELBY LN	F11
SEQUOIA ST	H7
SETAUKET AV	L10
SETON HALL	M4
SEVERN	H5
SEVILLE ROW	H3
SHABBONA LN	M12
SHADY GROVE CT	M8, O6
SHAGBARK	O8
SHAGBARK CT	L4
SHANNON CT	L7
SHASTA DR	N10
SHAW AV	G1
SHEFFER RD	A9
SHEFFIELD RD	L4
SHELL LAKE DR	F2
SHENANDOAH LN	K11
SHEPARD DR	H5
SHEPPEY CT	H5
SHERI ST	I1
SHERINGHAM DR	H5
SHERMAN AV	K11
SHERWOOD DR	H2
SHETLAND	N5
SHILOH CIR	H6
SHIMER CT	M2
SHIRE CT	G1
SHOME CT	J4
SHORE DR	C11
SHORE RD	C10
SHUMAN BL	I12
SICHEY CT	K4
SIERRA AV	I2
SIERRA CT	I2
SIERRA LN	M10
SIGNAL DR	M5
SILVER CREEK CT	C4
SILVER MAPLE CT	J11
SILVER SPUR CT	H2
SIOUX CT	J11
SIR BARTON CT	K7
SKYLANE DR	E4
SLEEPY HOLLOW LN	O8
SLEIGHT ST	J7, J9
SLIPPERY ROCK CT	N4
SLIPPERY ROCK RD	N4
SMALL CT	F10
SMOKEY CT	J12
SNOWDON CT	L7
SOMERSET CT	M10
SOUTH LN	H7
SOUTH RD	C6
SPALDING DR	I7
SPENCER CT	G1
SPINDLETREE AV	M3
SPINNER CT	I2
SPLIT OAK RD	J3
SPRING AV	I9
SPRING BAY	N10
SPRING GARDEN	K11
SPRING HILL CIR	K10, L10
SPRING LAKE DR	F2
SPRINGBROOK DR	H3
SPRINGDALE CT	G2, M10
SPRINGSIDE DR	J3
SPRINGWOOD DR	I7
SPRUCE DR	I6
SPRUCEWOOD CT	M4
SPYGLASS CT	C11
SPYGLASS CT	P7
STACIE CT	F10
STAFFELDT DR	E1
STAFFORD LN	K8
STAGEBRUSH RD	J4
STANDISH CT	K7
STANFORD	M4
STANHOPE CT	L4
STANTON CT	M7
STANTON DR	L6
STARLING CT	M10
STARLING LN	J4
STARLITE CT	H2
STAUFFER DR	H9
STAUFFER RD	H9
STAUNTON RD	L3
STEARMAN CT	E4
STEEPLE RUN DR	M10
STEEPLEBROOK CT	O6
STERLING CT	L8
STEVENS ST	H9
STEWART	K7
STEWART DR	D11
STILLWATER CT	L3
STONE CREEK	J5
STONEGATE RD	G8
STONEHEDGE CT	F10
STONEYBROOK CT	N2
STOOS LN	J7
STRATFORD CT	G9
STRAWBRIDGE CT	N6
SUFFOLK ST	J11
SUGAR CREEK CT	H11
SUMMERSET CT	I5
SUMMIT DR	L12
SUMMIT HILLS LN	H10
SUMTER CT	H6
SUN VALLEY RD	M7, N8
SUNDERLAND CT	K3
SUNNYBROOK DR	G9
SUNRISE CT	C12, M4
SUNSET DR	I8
SURREY AV	J5
SURREY RIDGE RD	M8
SUSSEX AV	B8
SUSSEX CT	L9
SUSSEX RD	L9
SWALLOW ST	J5
SWANSEA	H5
SWEET BAY CT	J7
SWIFT LN	J5
SYCAMORE DR	I7
SYLVAN CIR	K8
SYLVIA LN	K6
SYRACUSE AV	N4
TALBOT DR	H5
TALLOAKS CT	N6
TALL TREE	N10
TAMARACK DR	J6
TANAGER CT	J5
TANGLEWOOD LN	J11
TANGLEWOODS LN	N8
TANOAK LN	J6
TAOS	N7
TARTAN LN	D10
TEAKWOOD CT	G7
TEAL WOOD	M8
TELLIS LN	N9
TEMPLAZ RD	J3
TENNYSON LN	H6
TERRANCE DR	J6
TERRI CIR	F10
TESTA DR	G9
TETON CT	I5
THAXTON CT	M2
THISTLE HILL CT	O6
THORNAPPLE RD	H7
THORNHILL CT	J4
THORNWOOD DR	I8
THRUSH LN	K6
THUNDERBIRD LN	G11
THURMAN AV	M3
TICONDEROGA LN	J11
TIFFANY CT	I2
TIM TAM CIR	K7
TIMBER LANE DR	C10
TIMBER LEE CT	L7
TIMBER TRAIL DR	L5, N8
TIMBERLAINE CT	K9
TIMBERVIEW DR	N9
TIMOTHY AV	I1
TORRINGTON DR	H5
TORRY PINE LN	M9
TOWHEE LN	J5
TOWN LINE RD	E13
TOWNSEND DR	K3
TOWPATH CT	L4
TRADE ST	D6
TRAILS END CT	L3
TRAVELAIRE AV	I3
TREFOIL CT	J11
TRILLIUM LN	N2
TRINITY DR	N8
TRITON LN	J6
TUDOR DR	E10
TUFTS CT	N4
TULANE DR	N5
TULIP LN	I7
TUPELO AV	I6
TURNBRIDGE RD	M8
TURTLE COVE CT	L4
TUTHILL RD	L11
TWIN OAKS LN	N8
UNIVERSITY DR	M3
VALENCIA CT	D10
VALLEY DR	G10
VALLEY FORGE RD	M8
VAIL CT	M8
VAN BUREN AV	I9, J9
VANDERBUILT CT	N3
VASSAR	N4
VAUGHAN RD	A7
VENETIAN CT	L7
VENTURA CT	H9
VERDIN LN	J5
VERMILLION CT	L2
VERMONT CT	H6
VEST AV	K10
VESTA AV	K11
VICKSBURG CT	H6
VICTORIA CT	I8
VILLA AV	J7
VILLAGE GREEN RD	H8
VILLANOVA DR	M4
VIRGINIA CT	J7
VISTA CIR	D10
WABASH CT	L2
WAGNER DR	F1, G13
WAGONWHEEL CT	J4
WAKEFIELD CT	K10
WALL ST	E11
WALTER LN	F1
WALTON CT	J4
WARBLER DR	J5

Street	Grid
WARRANVILLE RD	**M13**
WARREN AV	G13
WARRENVILLE RD	G13
WARWICK DR	L4
WASHINGTON ST	**K4, K6**
	J10, J12
WATERBURY CT	I3
WATER ST	I8
WATER CRESS DR	K7
WATERFORD CT	G9
WATERSIDE CT	H8
WAUBANSIE LN	N12
WAUPACA CT	G2
WAVERLY CT	K10
WAYEWOOD LN	O5
WAYFARING LN	M9
WAYLAND LN	J3
WAYNESBURG ST	J2
WAXWING AV	J5
WEATHERFORD LN	I3
WEBSTER LN	F1
WEBSTER ST	E13, I12
WEDGEFIELD CIR	H11
WEDGEWOOD CT	P7
WEDGEWOOD DR	I2
WEEPING WILLOW DR	M9
WEHRLI DR	I8
WEHRLI RD	M6
WELLINGTON	N11
WELLINGTON AV	M11
WELLINGTON CT	L4, M11
WELLNER RD	J7
WELTON CT	J4
WENDOVER	J2
WENDY RD	H2
WENTWORTH CT	J2
WESLEY	I3
WEST BRANCH CT	K2
WEST ST	H6, I11
WEST WOOD	K3
WESTBROOK	J2
WESTBROOK DR	D6
WESTBURY CT	J4
WESTERN AV	N12
WESTERN CT	N12
WESTGLEN LN	I5
WESTMINSTER RD	E11
WESTMORELAND CT	L8
WESTMORELAND LN	L9
WESTON RIDGE DR	D9
WESTOVER CT	L10
WESTWIND CT	C10
WEXFORD CT	L7
WHIRLAWAY AV	K7
WHISPERING HILLS CT	G8, G9
WHISPERING HILLS DR	G7
WHISPERING WINDS	C10
WHITE EAGLE DR	C3
WHITE OAK	N8
WHITE OAK DR	K8
WHITE PINE CT	H12
WHITE WATER	F6
WHITEBARK CT	G7
WHITTINGHAM CIR	L8
WHITTINGTON CIR	F2
WHITTINGTON LN	F2
WICKFIELD CT	M7, K11
WICKHAM CT	M7
WILCREST RD	G8
WILBUR AV	H13
WILD CHERRY RD	H8
WILD ROSE CT	L4
WILDEN LN	G3
WILDWOOD	N8
WILLIAMSBURG DR	H6
WILLOW RD	D10, J7
WILLOWAY DR	H9
WILMINGTON CT	I2
WILSHIRE DR	G9
WILSON AV	H9
WINCHESTER LN	F10
WINDEMERE AV	G2
WINDHAM	J10
WINDING CREEK	J5
WINDJAMMER LN	F2
WINDRIDGE CT	F7
WINDRIFT DR	D6
WINDSOR CT	M5
WINKLER CT	O9
WINOLA CT	L4
WINSLOW CT	L4
WISCONSIN ST	K11, N11
WISHING WELL LN	H2
WISTERIA CT	K4
WOOD CT	M12
WOOD DR	O7
WOODBINE CT	L7
WOODBROOK CT	M9
WOODCLIFF CT	N8
WOODCREST CT	P7
WOODCREST DR	M9
WOODEWIND	C10
WOODFIELD CT	J4
WOODLAND	G13
WOODLAND CIR	J3
WOODLAWN	G13
WOODLAWN AV	J7
WOODSTOCK CT	L10
WOODVIEW CIR	J3
WOODVIEW CT	J3
WOOSTER CT	M3
WORTHING DR	I3
WRIGHT ST	J7, J11
WYDOWN CT	M7
XAVIER CT	M3
YACKLEY AV	O5, N10
YALE CT	L4
YENDER AV	N12
YORK CT	I2
YORKSHIRE DR	N8, K10
ZAINNINGER AV	H10
4TH AV	J9
4TH ST	A9
5TH AV	H10
5TH AV	I10
6TH AV	I10
7TH AV	J10
8TH AV	J10
10TH AV	I10
11TH AV	I11
12TH AV	I11, J11
13TH AV	I11
14TH AV	I11
39TH ST	L13
46TH ST	I11
48TH ST	I12
49TH ST	I11
75TH ST	**E6, N6**
77TH ST	N5
79TH ST	E5, I5, O5
80TH ST	I5
81ST CT	I4
81ST ST	E4
82ND CT	I4
82ND PL	H4
83RD CT	G4, I4
83RD CT	C4
87TH ST	H3, L3
91ST ST	M2
95TH ST	G1, H1
96TH ST	I1

© DonTech Chicago, Il. 1992

Street Guide

ALCOA AV-N D4	FULLERTON AV-W C4	**LAKE ST-E** **D1**	MEDILL AV-E D3	SANDRA AV-N C4
ALVIN AV-N E2	GAIL AV-S C1	**LAKE ST-W** **B1**	MORSE AV-E E1	SOFFEL AV-E E1
ARMITAGE AV-E E3	GARNET DR A4	LAKEWOOD AV-S C1	MORSE DR-E D1	SOFFEL AV-W C1
ASHBEL AV-S B1	GENEVA AV-N E3	LA PORTE AV-N C4	MT PROSPECT RD A2	**TRI-STATE TOLLWAY** **A3**
BELLE DR-E D2	GOLFVIEW DR-W B2	LA VERGNE AV-N C3	**NORTH AV-E** **C2**	VICTORIA DR-E D1
BERNICE DR-E D2	**GRAND AV-E** **B4**	LA VERGNE AV-S C1	**NORTH AV-W** **C2**	VILLAGE DR-E C3
CARYL AV-N D2	HABER CT-N D3	LE MOYNE ST-E E1	NORTHWEST AV-N A2	WAGNER DR-E C4
CARYL AV-S D1	HAROLD AV-N D4	LE MOYNE ST-W E1	PALMER AV-E D3	WEST DR-W C2
CHARLES DR-E C2	HAROLD AV-S D1	LIND AV-S C1	PALMER AV-W C3	WESTWARD HO DR-N B2
COUNTRY CLUB DR-E D2	HARVARD AV-S B1	LONGFIELD AV-W C3	PARKVIEW DR-E D2	WESTWARD HO DR-W B2
DERROUGH B4	HAYES DR-E C4	LYNDALE AV-E D3	PEARL B4	WHITEHALL AV-E D2
DEWEY AV-E C3	HERBERT ST A1	MAC ARTHUR DR-E C4	PRATER AV-N C4	WILLIAM AV-N E2
DICKENS AV-E D3	HILLSIDE AV-N C3	MAJOR DR-E D3	PRATER AV-S D1	WILTSE PKWY C2
DIVERSEY AV C4	HILLSIDE AV-S B1	MANNHEIM RD E2	RAILROAD AV-N B2	WINTERS DR-E E1
DODD AV-S C1	HIRSCH ST-E E1	MAPLEWOOD ST-S C1	RHODES AV B4	**WOLF RD-N** **C4**
EAST DR-N C2	HIRSCH TERR E1	MARILYN AV-N D2	ROBERTA AV-N D3	**WOLF RD-S** **C1**
EDWARD AV-N E2	IRVING AV-S B1	MARILYN AV-S D1	ROBERTA AV-S D1	43RD AV-S E1
ELM ST-S C1	JEROME DR-N C3	MARION C4	ROY AV-N D4	44TH AV-S E1
FRANKLIN DR-W B2	JOYCE AV-N D4	MARTIN B4	ROY AV-S D1	45TH AV-S E1
FULLERTON AV-E E4	KING ARTHUR CT B4	MC LEAN AV D3	ROWLET AV D4	46TH AV-S E1

Postal ZIP Code Information

ZIP Code 60164

For additional ZIP Code information
see ZIP Code pages or call 562-1948

Village or City Boundary

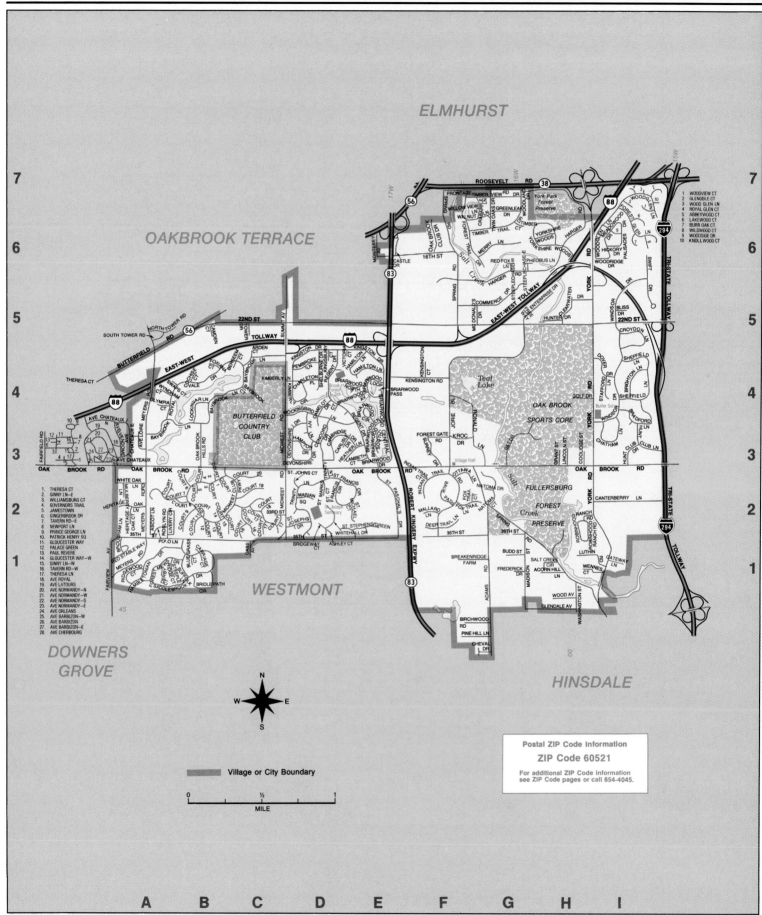

ELMHURST

OAKBROOK TERRACE

Numbered street index (left side):

1. THERESA CT
2. GINNY LN–E
3. WILLIAMSBURG CT
4. GOVERNORS TRAIL
5. JAMESTOWN
6. GINGERBROOK DR
7. TAVERN RD–E
8. NEWPORT LN
9. PRINCE GEORGE LN
10. PATRICK HENRY SQ
11. GLOUCESTER WAY
12. PALACE GREEN
13. PAUL REVERE
14. GLOUCESTER WAY–W
15. GINNY LN–W
16. TAVERN RD–W
17. THERESA LN
18. AVE ROYAL
19. AVE LATOURS
20. AVE NORMANDY–N
21. AVE NORMANDY–W
22. AVE NORMANDY–S
23. AVE NORMANDY–E
24. AVE ORLEANS
25. AVE BARBIZON–W
26. AVE BARBIZON
27. AVE BARBIZON–E
28. AVE CHERBOURG

Numbered street index (right side):

1. WOODVIEW CT
2. GLENOBLE CT
3. WOOD GLEN LN
4. ROYAL GLEN CT
5. ABBEYWOOD CT
6. LAKEWOOD CT
7. BURR OAK CT.
8. WILDWOOD CT
9. WOODSIDE DR
10. KNOLLWOOD CT

WESTMONT

DOWNERS GROVE

HINSDALE

N W E S

Village or City Boundary

0   ½   1
MILE

Postal ZIP Code Information
ZIP Code 60521
For additional ZIP Code information
see ZIP Code pages or call 654-4045.

A   B   C   D   E   F   G   H   I

© DonTech Chicago, Il. 1992

© DonTech Chicago, Il. 1992

Street Guide

ADAMS ST	A2	IOWA ST	C5
AUGUSTA ST	B6	JACKSON BL	A2
AUSTIN BL-N	D6	KENILWORTH AV-N	B4
AUSTIN BL-S	D2	KENILWORTH AV-S	B1
BELLEFORTE AV	A6	LAKE ST	B4
BERKSHIRE ST	A7	LE MOYNE PKWY	B7
BISHOP QUARTER LN-E	B4	LENOX ST	C7
BISHOP QUARTER LN-W	B4	LEXINGTON ST	B1
CARPENTER AV	B2	LINDEN AV-N	B5
CHICAGO AV	**B5**	LOMBARD AV-N	D6
CLARENCE AV	B1	LOMBARD AV-S	D1
CLINTON AV-S	B1-B3	LYMAN AV-S	D1
COLUMBIAN AV	B7	**MADISON ST**	**B3**
CUYLER AV-N	C5	MAPLE AV-N	A5
CUYLER AV-S	C1	MAPLE AV-S	A1
DIVISION ST	A6	MAPLETON AV	C7
EAST AV-N	B6	MARION CT	A5
EAST AV-S	C1	MARION ST-N	A5
EDMER AV	C7	MARION ST-S	A3
EISENHOWER EXPWY	**C2**	MILLER AV	A6
ELIZABETH CT	A5	MONROE ST	A3
ELIZABETH TER	A5	**NORTH AV-W**	**B7**
ELMWOOD AV-N	C5	NORTH BL	B4
ELMWOOD AV-S	C1	OAK PARK AV-N	B6
ERIE ST	A5	OAK PARK AV-S	B1
EUCLID AV-N	B5	ONTARIO ST	A5
EUCLID AV-S	B1	PAULINA ST	A5
FAIR OAKS AV	C6	PERCY JULIAN SQ	B4
FILLMORE ST	B1	PLEASANT PL	A4
FLOURNOY ST	D2	PLEASANT ST	A4
FOREST AV	A5	RANDOLPH ST	A3
FRANCISCO TERR-E	B4	RIDGELAND AV-N	C5
FRANCISCO TERR-W	B4	RIDGELAND AV-S	C1
GARFIELD ST	A2	**ROOSEVELT RD-W**	**C1**
GREENFIELD ST	C7	ROSSELL AV	C7
GROVE AV-N	B6	SCHNEIDER AV	A5
GROVE AV-S	B1	SCOVILLE AV-N	C4
GUNDERSON AV-S	C1	SCOVILLE AV-S	C1
HARLEM AV-N	**A6**	SOUTH BL	B4
HARLEM AV-S	**A3**	SUPERIOR ST	A5
HARLEM CT	A5	TAYLOR AV-N	D5
HARRISON ST	C2	TAYLOR AV-S	D1
HARVARD ST	B1	THOMAS ST	A6
HARVEY AV-N	C5	VAN BUREN ST	C2
HARVEY AV-S	D2	WASHINGTON BL-W	B3
HAYES AV-N	D7	WENONAH AV	A1
HEMINGWAY LN	B4	WESLEY AV-S	B1
HIGHLAND AV-S	C1	WESTGATE ST	A4
HOLLY CT	A4	WISCONSIN AV	A1
HOME AV	A1	WOODBINE AV	B6
HUMPHREY AV-N	D5	WRIGHT LN	B4
HUMPHREY AV-S	D1		

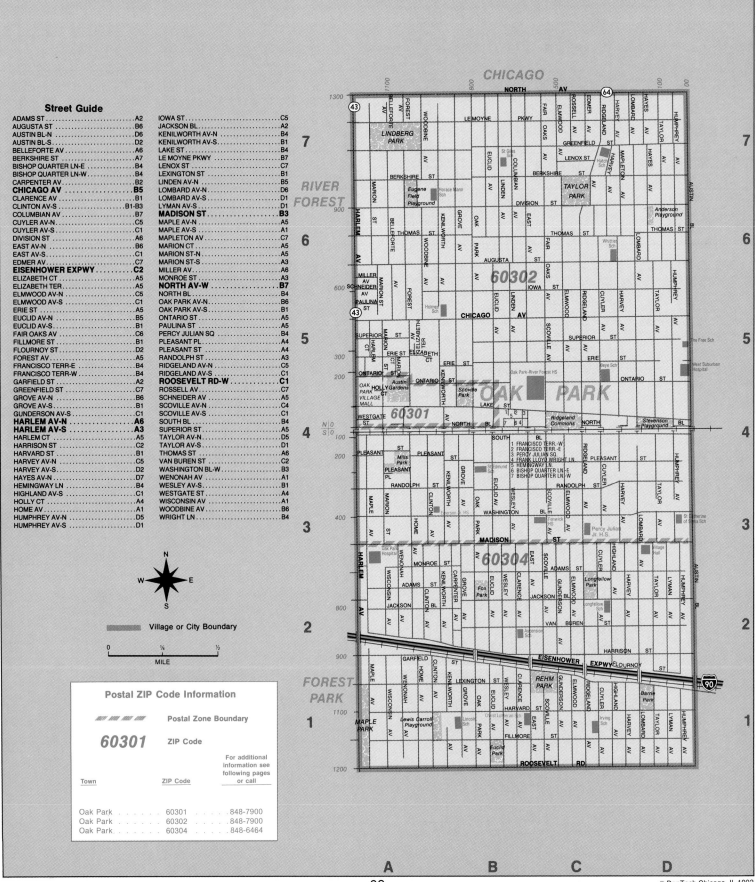

Village or City Boundary

0   ¼   ½
MILE

Postal ZIP Code Information

Postal Zone Boundary

60301 ZIP Code

For additional information see following pages or call

Town	ZIP Code	
Oak Park	60301	848-7900
Oak Park	60302	848-7900
Oak Park	60304	848-6464

© DonTech Chicago, Il. 1992

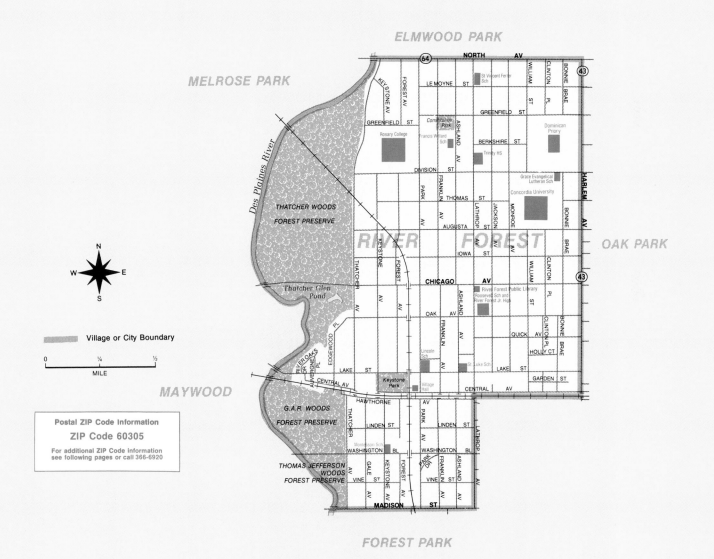

Postal ZIP Code Information

ZIP Code 60305

For additional ZIP Code information
see following pages or call 366-6920

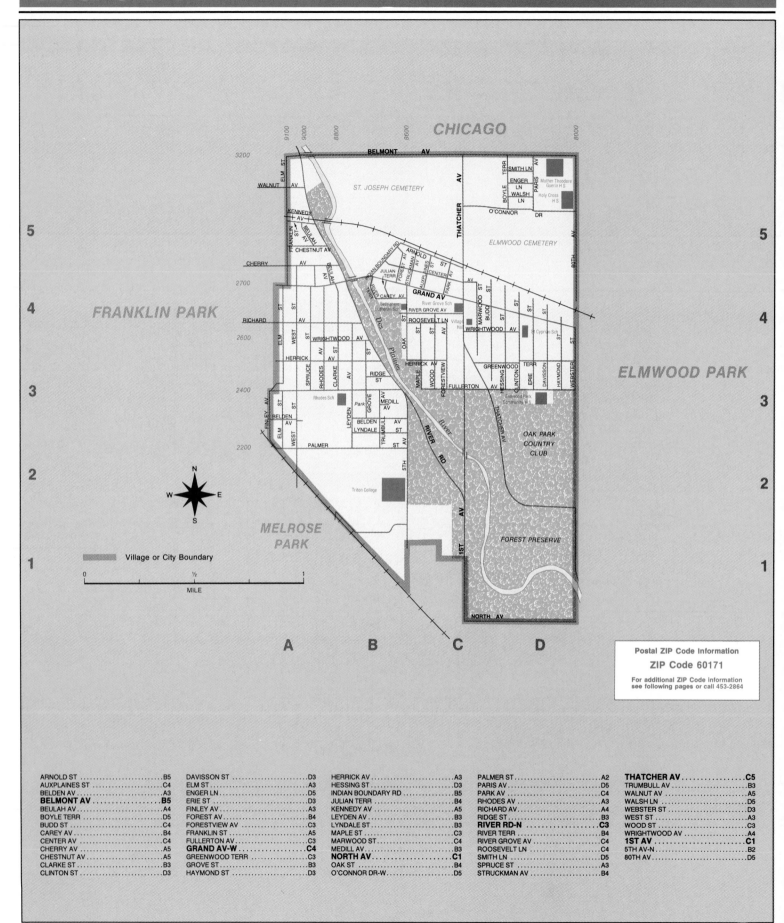

Postal ZIP Code Information

ZIP Code 60171

For additional ZIP Code information
see following pages or call 453-2864

© DonTech Chicago, Il. 1992

Riverside

Street	Grid
ADDISON RD	D3
AKENSIDE RD	D3
ARLINGTON RD	E4
AUDUBON RD	E4
BARRYPOINT RD	D1
BARTRAM RD	D4
BERKLEY RD	E4
BISMARK ST	D2
BLACKHAWK RD	D2
BLOOMINGBANK RD	C2
BLYTHE RD	E3
BURLING RD	D2
BURLINGTON ST-E	D3
BURLINGTON ST-W	C2
BYRD RD	E4
COLUMBUS BL	D2
COONLEY RD	C2
COWLEY RD-N	D3
COWLEY RD-S	D2
DELAPLAINE RD-N	D3
DELAPLAINE RD-S	E2
DESPLAINES AV	D4
DOWNING RD	E4
EAST AV	D2
EAST GROVE RD	E3
EVELYN RD	E4
FAIRBANK RD	C1
FORBES RD	C2
FOREST AV	C3
GAGE RD	D2
GATESBY RD	D4
GLADSTONE AV	D2
GROVELAND AV	C3
HARLEM AV	**E1**
HERBERT RD-N	E2
HERBERT RD-S	E2
HERRICK RD	D3
KENT RD	E4
KIMBARK RD	D3
LAWTON RD	D2
LEESLEY RD	E4
LINCOLN AV	C3
LINDBERG RD	E4
LIONEL RD	E2
LOUDON RD	D4
MAPLEWOOD RD	C3
MICHAUX RD	D3
MILLBRIDGE RD	C2
NORTHGATE CT	D4
NORTHGATE RD	D4
NORTHWOOD RD	D4
NUTTALL RD	D3
OGDEN AV	**D1**
OLMSTEAD RD	D2
PARK PL	C3
PARKVIEW AV	C2
PARKWAY RD-E	E4
PARKWAY RD-W	E4
PINE AV	C2
QUINCY ST-E	D2
QUINCY ST-W	C2
REPTON RD	D4
RIDGEWOOD RD	C2
RIVERSIDE RD	D2
ROBINSON CT	E2
SCOTTSWOOD RD	C2
SELBOURNE RD	D4
SHAKESPEARE AV	D2
SHENSTONE RD	E3
SOUTHCOTE RD	E4
STANLEY AV	D2
UVEDALE CT	E4
UVEDALE RD	D4
WASHINGTON AV	D2
WAUBANSEE RD	C2
WEST AV	C2
WOODSIDE RD	D3
YORK RD	C4
1ST AV	**C3**
39TH ST	**D2**

North Riverside

Street	Grid
BURROAK AV	D5
CERMAK RD	**D5**
COUNTRY CLUB LN	C5
DESPLAINES AV	D5
EDGEWATER RD	C4
FEDERAL DR	E5
FOREST AV	D5
FORESTVIEW DR	A5
GROVELAND AV	C4
HAINSWORTH AV	D5
HARLEM AV	**E5**
KEYSTONE AV	D5
LATHROP AV	D5
LEWE CT	C5
LINCOLN AV	C4
NORTHGATE AV	D5
PARK AV	D5
RIVER RD	C4
TRAUBE ST	D5
VETERANS DR	E4
WESTOVER AV	D5
1ST AV	**C5**
2ND AV	B5
3RD AV	B5
4TH AV	B5
5TH AV	B5
6TH AV	B5
7TH AV	B5
8TH AV	B5
9TH AV	B5
10TH AV	A5
11TH AV	A5
12TH AV	A5
13TH AV	A5
14TH AV	A5
15TH AV	A5
16TH ST	E5
17TH AV	A5
18TH AV	A5
19TH AV	A5
22ND PL	A5
23RD PL	A5
23RD ST	A5
24TH PL	A5
24TH ST	A5
25TH ST-W	B5
26TH ST	**C5**
27TH ST	C4
28TH ST	C4
29TH CT	C4
29TH ST	D8
30TH ST	C4
31ST ST	C4

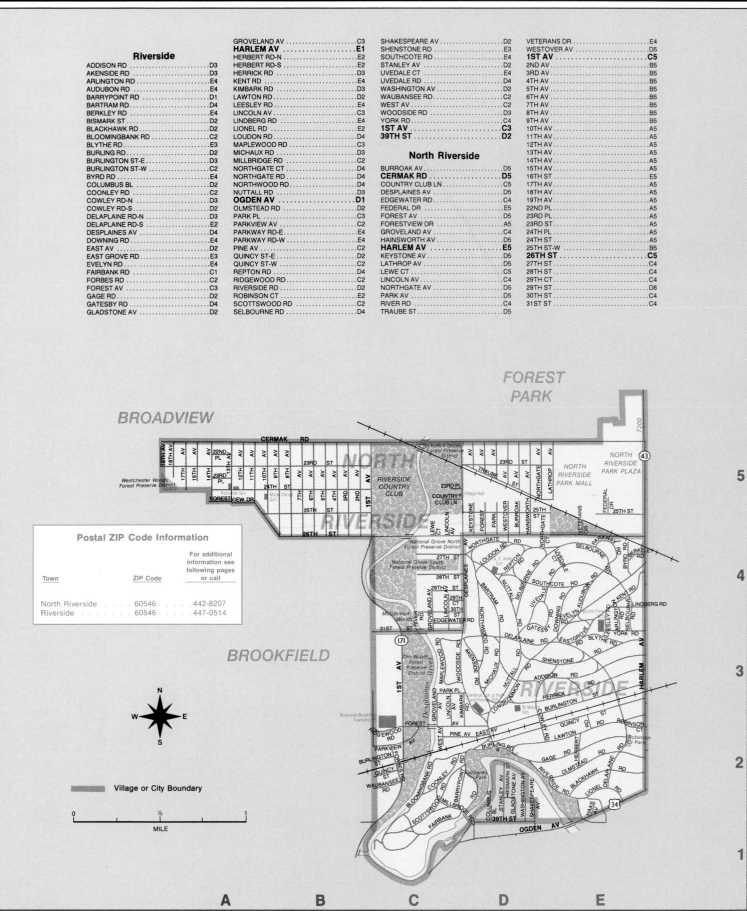

Postal ZIP Code Information

Town	ZIP Code	For additional information see following pages or call
North Riverside	60546	442-8207
Riverside	60546	447-0514

Village or City Boundary

0   ½   1
MILE

© DonTech Chicago, Il. 1992

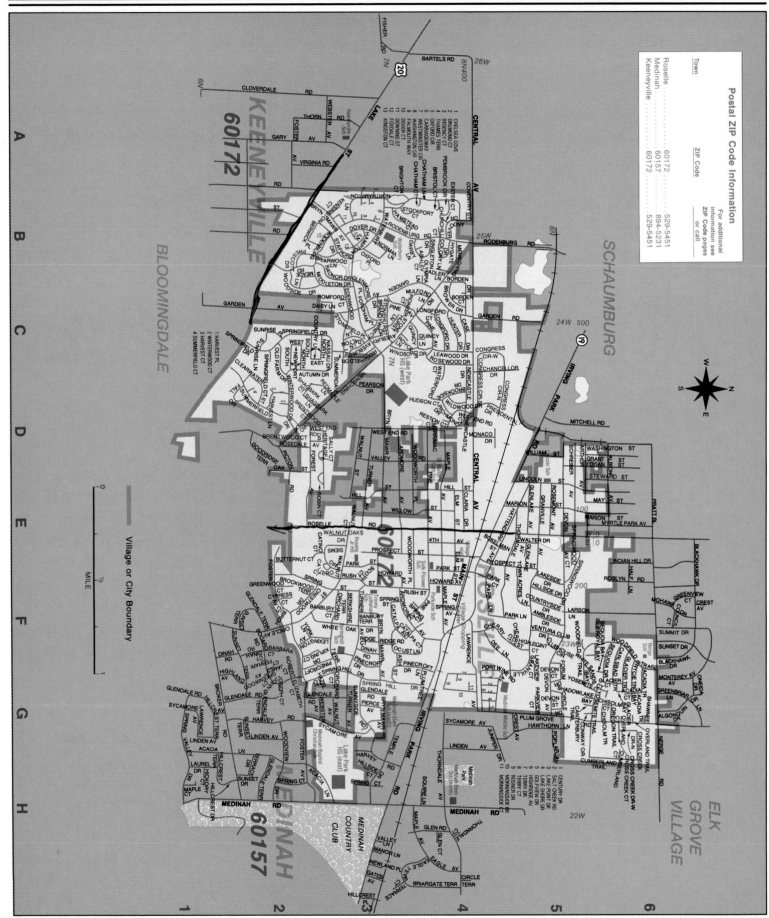

© DonTech Chicago, Il. 1992

Roselle

ACACIA LN ...H2
ACADIA BAY ...G6
ACADIA CT ...G6
ACADIA TRAIL ...G6
ADLER LN ...B4
ALBION AV ...E6
ALGONQUIN DR ...G6
ARTHUR AV-W ...E5
AMBLESIDE DR ...F5
ANDOVER DR ...B4
ARDMORE AV-E ...F3
ARDMORE AV-W ...D3
ARTHUR AV ...D5
ASH ST ...F3
ASHLEY CT ...B4
AUTUMN DR ...C2
AVEBURY CT ...C3
AVEBURY LN ...C3
BANBURY CT ...F3
BANBURY TERR ...F3
BERKSHIRE TERR ...F3
BERWICK PL ...B2
BIRCH CT ...F2
BLACKHAWK PL ...F6
BOKELMAN ST-N ...E4
BORDEN CT ...C4
BORDEN DR ...B4
BRANDYWINE DR ...C3
BRENTWOOD CT ...D2
BRIARWOOD LN ...B3
BRIGHTON CT ...B3
BRISTOL CT ...B4
BROOKSIDE DR ...D4
BROOKWOOD TERR ...F2
BROWER DR ...C6
BRYCE TR ...G6
BRYN MAWR AV-E ...D3
BRYN MAWR AV-W ...B3
BUTTERNUT CT ...E2
CALLERO CT ...F2
CANTERBURY TRAIL ...G5
CARLSBAD TRAIL ...F6
CARRIAGE WAY ...B3
CASE DR ...C4
CATALPA AV ...F3
CATALPA CT ...F3
CATINO CT ...E2
CENTRAL AV-W ...E4
CENTURY DR ...G3
CHANCELLOR DR ...C5
CHATHAM CT ...B4
CHATHAM AV ...B4
CHELSEA COVE ...B3
CHERRY CT ...F5
CHERRY ST ...F4
CHISOLM CT-N ...G6
CHISOLM TRAIL ...G6
CHURCHILL CT ...B4
CIRCLE AV ...F2
CIRCLE DR ...G5
CLARIA DR-W ...E4
CLEARWATER ST-N ...D2
CLEARWATER ST ...C2
CLUBHOUSE CIR ...F5
COLONY LN ...B4
CONGRESS CIR-N ...D4
CONGRESS CIR-S ...D4
CONGRESS CIR-W ...C4
CONWAY BAY ...G5
COUNCIL CT ...F6
COUNTY LN-E ...C2
COUNTY LN-N ...C2
COUNTY LN-S ...C2
COUNTRYSIDE DR ...F5
COVENTRY CT ...B4
CREST AV ...F6

CRESTWOOD DR ...F2
CROSS CREEK CT ...G6
CROSS CREEK DR-N ...G6
CROSS CREEK DR-S ...G6
CROSS CREEK DR-W ...G6
CUMBERLAND CT ...G6
CUMBERLAND TRAIL ...H5
CYPRESS CT ...F2
DAISY LN ...C3
DALTON LN ...C3
DARBY LN ...B3
DEE LN ...F4
DEVON AV-E ...G6
DEVON AV-W ...E6
DEVON CT ...G5
DEVON ST ...G5
DINAH RD ...F3
DOVER CT ...B3
DOVER DR ...B3
DOWNING ST ...B3
DRUMMOND CT ...B3
EDENWOOD LN ...C3
ELM ST ...E4
EXETER CT ...B4
FALL CIR ...D2
FALMOUTH LN ...B3
FORDHAM PL ...C3
FOREST AV-W ...D2
FORUM DR-E ...G5
FOSTER AV-E ...G5
FOXDALE CT ...B2
GARDEN AV ...C3
GARDEN RD ...C4
GLACIER BAY ...G6
GLACIER CT ...G6
GLACIER TRAIL ...G6
GLENDALE RD ...G3
GLENDALE TERR ...G2
GLENLAKE AV-E ...E5
GLENMORE PL ...C3
GOLFVIEW DR ...G3
GOODRIDGE TERR ...D2
GRANT ST ...D6
GRANVILLE AV-E ...G5
GRANVILLE AV-W ...E5
GREENBRIAR LN ...G6
GREENVIEW CT ...F6
GREENWOOD CT ...F6
HALF LN-E ...F6
HAMPTON LN ...B3
HAMSTEAD CT ...B3
HARVEST CT ...D2
HARVEST LN ...D2
HARVEST PL ...D2
HATTENDORF AV ...E4
HAZEL CT ...G2
HERITAGE DR ...D2
HIGH POINT CT-N ...F5
HIGH RIDGE AV-E ...G3
HILL ST-S ...E4
HILLSIDE DR ...F5
HOWARD AV-S ...F4
HUDSON CT ...D4
HUNTER CT ...C4
HYGATE DR ...B4
INDIAN HILL DR-S ...E6
IRVING PARK RD-E ...G3
IRVING PARK RD-W ...C5
ISLE ROYAL BAY ...F5
KENSINGTON CT ...B3
KINGSTON CT ...B3
KIPLING CT ...F2
LAKE ST ...B2
LAKE POINT DR-N ...G3
LAKE SHORE-N ...G3
LAKESIDE DR ...F5
LAKEVIEW CT ...G5
LARSON LN ...F5
LAWRENCE AV-E ...F4

LEAWOOD DR ...C4
LEXINGTON AV ...F2
LINCOLN ST-N ...E5
LOCUST LN ...F3
LOGAN ST ...D5
LONGFORD CT ...C4
LONGFORD DR ...C4
MAIN ST-E ...F4
MAPLE AV-E ...F4
MAPLE AV-W ...D4
MARION ST-N ...E6
MAY ST-N ...E5
MEADE LN ...B2
MEDINAH RD ...H2
MENSCHING RD ...D3
MERRIMAC CT ...D4
MIDDLETON DR ...B2
MOHAWK DR ...F6
MONACO DR ...D4
MONTEREY AV ...G6
MORNINGSIDE CT ...G3
MORNINGSIDE DR ...G3
MULFORD CT ...C4
MYRTLE PARK AV ...E6
NASSAU DR ...C2
NERGE RD ...G6
NEWCASTLE CT ...D4
NEWCASTLE DR ...D4
NEWPORT DR NORTH ...C2
NEWPORT DR SOUTH ...C2
NEWPORT DR WEST ...C2
NORMAN LN ...B3
NORTHAMPTON LN ...B3
OAK ST-S ...D2
OLD FARM DR ...C2
OLYMPIA LN ...C4
ONEIDA DR ...G6
ORCHARD CT ...G3
ORCHARD TERR ...F3
OREGON TRAIL-E ...G6
OVERLAND CT-E ...G6
OVERLAND TRAIL ...G6
OXFORD CIR ...B3
OXFORD PL ...B3
PARK CT-N ...F4
PARK LN EAST ...F4
PARK ST-N ...E5
PARK ST-S ...E4
PARKVIEW CT-E ...G5
PEARSON DR ...D3
PICTON RD-W ...D2
PIERCE AV ...G3
PINE AV-E ...F4
PINE AV-W ...C4
PINECROFT DR-S ...C3
PINECROFT LN ...F4
PIONEER CT ...G3
PLUM GROVE RD ...G5
PLUM TREE LN ...G4
PORTWINE DR-N ...G5
PRATT BL ...E6
PRESCOTT DR ...B2
PRESIDENTAL DR ...D4
PROSPECT ST-N ...E5
PROSPECT ST-S ...E3
QUINCY DR ...C4
QUINCY LN ...C4
RADNOR DR ...B3
REGENCY CT ...B3
RESTON CT ...D4
RICHMOND DR ...D4
RIDGE CT ...F3
RIDGE RD ...F3
RIDGEFIELD DR ...C3
ROBIN CT ...E2
RODENBURG RD ...B3
ROMFORD CT ...C3
ROSEDALE AV ...D2
ROSELLE RD-N ...E5

ROSELLE RD-S ...E3
ROSEMONT AV-W ...E5
ROSEWOOD DR ...C4
ROSLYN RD ...F6
ROSNER DR ...G3
ROYCE LN ...C3
RUSH ST-S ...F4
SALLY CT ...D2
SALT CREEK DR ...G3
SCHREIBER AV-W ...D5
SCOTT CT ...F3
SEQUOIA BAY ...F5
SEQUOIA TR ...F6
SEWARD RD ...E6
SHADOW LAKE BAY ...G5
SHAGBARK CT ...D2
SHAGBARK LN ...D2
SHAWNEE TR-E ...G6
SIEMS CIR ...E3
SINGLETON DR ...B4
SPRING AV ...F4
SPRING CT ...F4
SPRING ST-S ...F3
SPRING HILL DR ...G3
SPRINGFIELD CT ...C2
SPRINGFIELD DR ...C2
SPRINGWOOD CT ...E5
SPRINGWOOD DR ...F5
STAFFORD DR ...B3
STOCKPORT CT ...B3
STONEFIELD PL ...C3
STONEHURST DR ...C3
STONEHURST LN ...C3
SUMMERDALE AV ...C3
SUMMERFIELD CT ...D2
SUMMERFIELD DR ...D2
SUMMIT DR ...F6
SUNNYSIDE RD ...G3
SUNRISE LN ...C2
SUNRISE PL ...C2
SUNSET DR ...F6
SYCAMORE AV ...G3
TERRY CT ...G3
TERRY DR ...G3
THAMES TERR ...B3
THORNDALE AV ...E5
TOWN ACRES LN ...F5
TURNER AV-E ...G4
TURNER AV-W ...E4
VALLEY RD ...D3
VENTURA CLUB DR ...F5
WALNUT CT-W ...D3
WALNUT ST ...E3
WALNUT OAKS DR ...E3
WALTER DR ...E5
WANDSWORTH CIR ...D6
WATERBURY LN ...B3
WATERFORD CT ...D4
WEST END RD ...D2
WESTMINSTER CIR ...B3
WHITE OAK DR ...F3
WHITE SANDS BAY ...G5
WILDWOOD DR ...D4
WILLIAM ST ...D5
WILLOW ST-S ...E3
WINDSOR DR ...C3
WINTERWOOD CT ...D2
WINTERWOOD DR ...D2
WOODFIELD TRAIL ...F6
WOODSIDE DR ...C2
WOODWORTH PL-E ...E3
WOODWORTH PL-W ...D3
YORK LN ...F2
YOSEMITE CT ...G5
YOSEMITE TRAIL ...G5
4TH AV ...E4

Keeneyville

BARTELS RD ...A4
CENTRAL AV-W ...A4
CLOVERDALE RD ...A2
FISHER RD ...A3
FOSTER AV ...A2
GARDEN AV ...A2
GARY AV ...A2
IRVING PARK RD ...C5
LAKE ST ...A3
MITCHELL RD ...D5
THORN RD ...A2
VIRGINIA RD ...A2
WEBSTER AV ...A3

Medinah

ACACIA LN ...G1
BARBARA CT ...F2
BRIARGATE TER ...H4
CIRCLE AV ...F2
CIRCLE TERR ...H4
CREST AV ...G4
DINAH RD ...F2
EAGLE AV ...H4
EAGLE TERR ...H3
ELIZABETH CT ...G2
FERRARI CT ...F2
FOSTER AV ...G2
GATES AV ...H3
GLEN CT ...H4
GLEN RD ...H4
GLENDALE RD ...G1
GLENDALE TERR ...F2
GREENWOOD AV ...G2
HARVEY RD ...G2
HAWTHORN LN ...G5
HICKORY CT ...H1
HILLCREST DR ...H1
HILLCREST PL ...H3
HILLCREST TERR ...G1
HILLSIDE CT ...H3
IRVING PARK RD ...H3
JAMES CT ...G2
JOHN CT ...G2
JOSEPH CT ...G2
JUNIPER DR ...G4
LAUREL DR ...H1
LAWRENCE AV ...G1
LINDEN AV ...G1
MANOR LN ...H3
MAPLE CT ...H1
MEDINAH RD ...H1
NEWLAND PL ...H3
POPLAR AV ...G5
ROBERT CT ...G2
SODARO RD ...F2
SPRING CT ...H2
SPRING VALLEY RD ...G1
SQUIRE LN ...H4
SUNNYSIDE RD ...G3
SUNSET DR-S ...H2
SUNSET TERR ...F2
SYCAMORE AVE ...G1
TEMPLE DR ...G3
TERRACE CT ...H3
TERRACE DR ...H2
THORNDALE AV ...H4
THORNDALE CT ...H4
TURNER AV ...G3
VALLEY LN ...H3
WALNUT AV ...G3
WEBSTER AV ...G2
WOODVIEW DR ...G2

© DonTech Chicago, Il. 1992

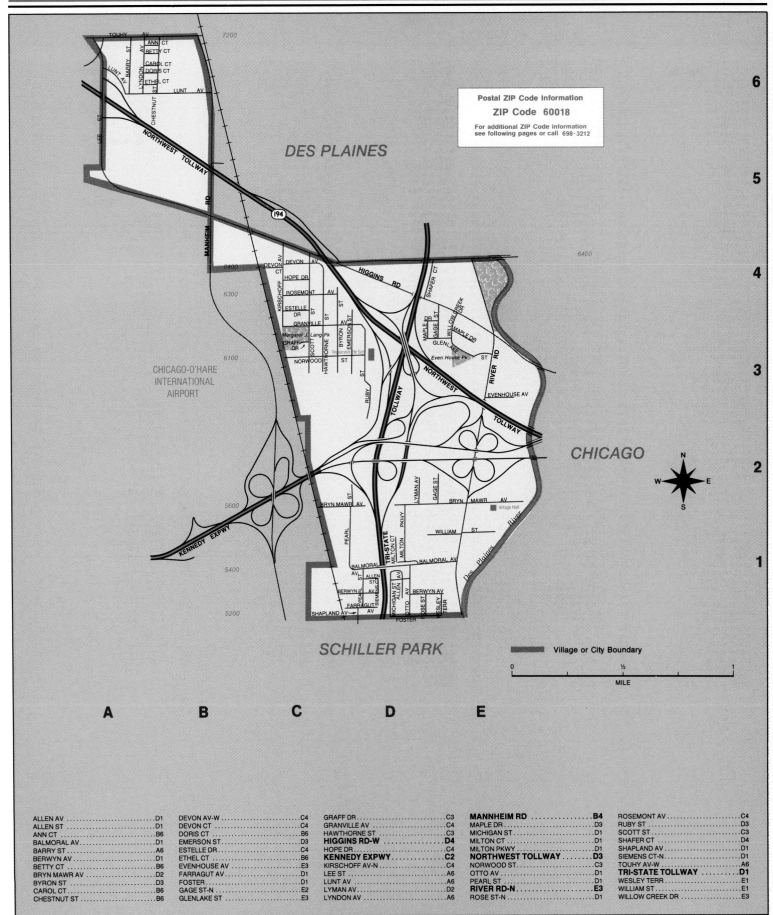

Postal ZIP Code Information
ZIP Code 60018
For additional ZIP Code information
see following pages or call 698-3212

Village or City Boundary

© DonTech Chicago, Il. 1992

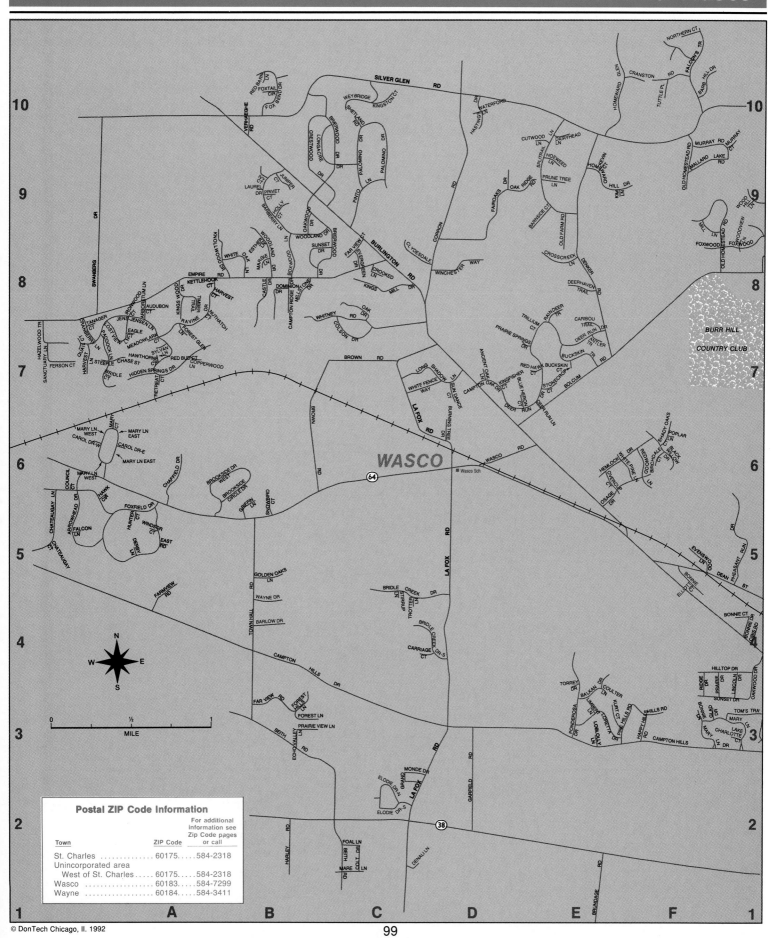

© DonTech Chicago, Il. 1992

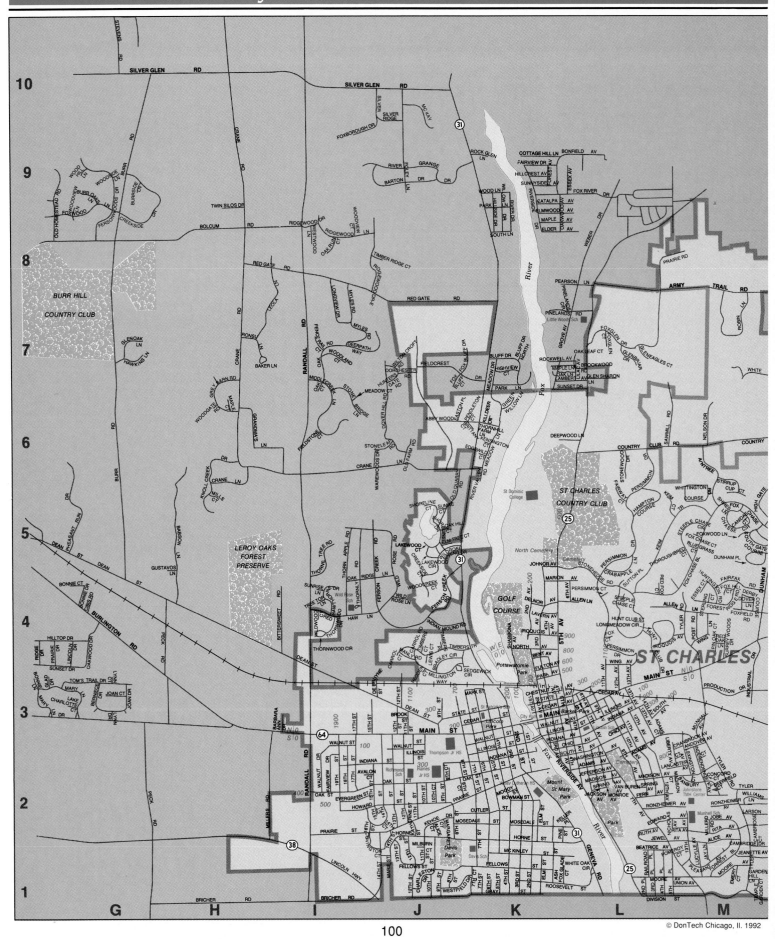

© DonTech Chicago, Il. 1992

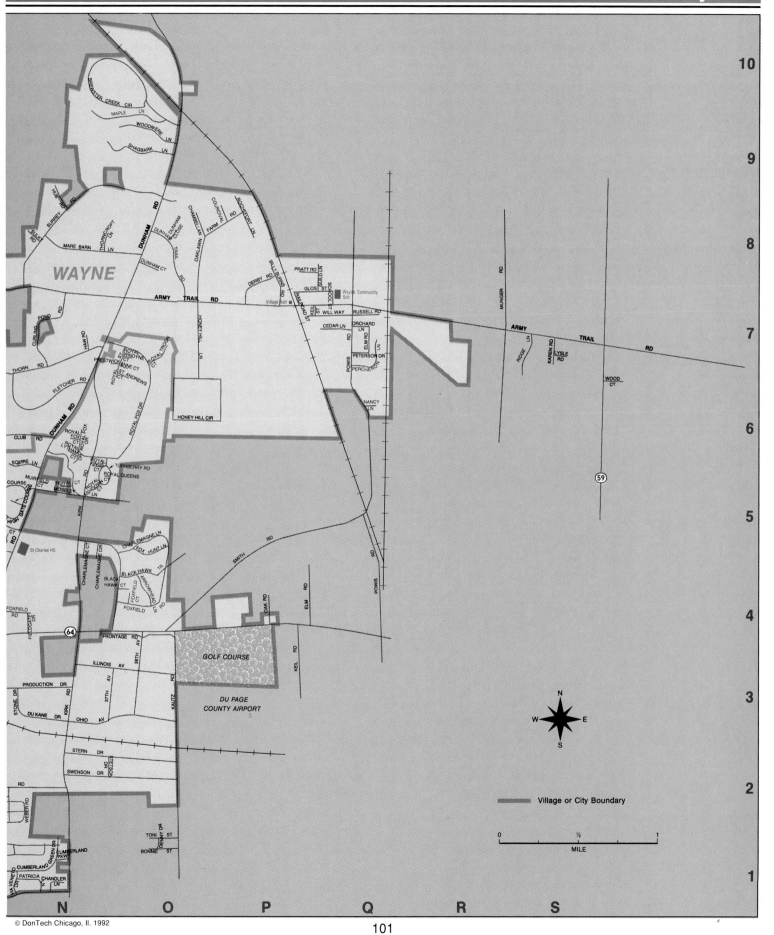

WAYNE

Village or City Boundary

0   ½   1
MILE

© DonTech Chicago, Il. 1992

St Charles

ABBY WOOD ... K6
ADAMS AV ... L2
ADAMS CT ... L3
AINTREE RD ... M5
ALICE AV ... M1
ALICE CT ... J2
ALLEN LN ... L4
ANDOVER AV ... M3
ANNE CT ... O6
ARROWHEAD LN ... O4
ASH ST ... K1
AVALON CT ... I2
BANBURY AV ... M2
BANBURY CT ... M2
BARBARA ANN DR ... H3
BEATRICE AV ... L1
BEITH RD ... B2
BENT AV ... K3
BLACK HAWK CT ... O4
BLACK HAWK TR ... O4
BLUE GRASS CT ... M5
BOWMAN ST ... K2
BRADLEY CIR ... J4
BRICHER RD ... I1
BRITTANY CT ... K6
BROOK ST ... J3
CAMBRIDGE CT ... M2
CAMBRIDGE RD ... M2
CANIDAE CT ... M5
CARROL CT ... J4
CARROL RD ... J4
CEDAR AV ... K3
CEDAR ST ... K3
CHANDLER LN ... N1
CHARLEMAGNE CIR ... N5
CHARLEMAGNE CT ... N5
CHARLEMAGNE LN ... O5
CHARLESTON DR ... J1
CHASSE CIR ... M5
CHESTNUT AV ... K3
CONCORD CT ... M2
COUNTRY CLUB RD ... M6
COVINGTON CT ... J1
CRABAPPLE LN ... L4
CRANBROOK AV ... M3
CREEKSIDE CT ... J5
CUMBERLAND GREEN DR ... N1
CUMBERLAND PKWY ... N1
CUTLER ST ... K2
DEAN ST ... J2
DE BRUYNE ST ... J3
DEERFIELD CT ... M2
DELNOR AV ... K4
DERBY COURSE ... M4
DIVISION ST ... M1
DOVER LN ... M4
DU KANE DR ... N3
DUNHAM PL ... M4
DUNHAM RD ... N4
EASTON PL ... K6
EDGEWILD CT ... K6
EDWARD AV ... M2
ELM ST ... K2
ELM TREE CT ... J5
EMERY CT ... N1
ESSEX CT ... M4
EVERGREEN ST ... I2
FAIRFAX RD ... M4
FAIRVIEW DR ... I2
FAIRWAY CT ... L5
FELLOWS ST ... K1
FERN AV ... L2
FERSON CREEK RD ... J4
FIELDGATE DR ... N3
FOREST RIDGE RD ... M4
FORREST BL ... M1
FOX CT ... L3
FOX CHASE BL ... L5
FOX CHASE CT ... M5
FOX GLADE CT ... K1
FOXFIELD RD ... M4
FOX HILL CT ... M4
FOX HUNT LN ... O5
FOXFIELD CT ... O4
FOXWOOD LN ... M5
FRONTAGE RD ... N4
FULTON AV ... K3
GARDEN HILL LN ... M1
GENEVA RD ... L1
GLENBRIAR DR ... L7
GLENEAGLES CT ... L7
GRAY ST ... K1
GREEN WILLOW LN ... K6
HAMPTON COURSE ... L5
HIGH GATE COURSE ... M5
HORNE ST ... K1
HOWARD ST ... I2
HUNT CLUB DR ... L4
HUNT CLUB ST ... L4
HUNTINGTON RD ... M4
ILLINOIS AV ... L3-N3
ILLINOIS ST ... K2
INDEPENDENCE AV ... M2
INDEPENDENCE CT ... M2
INDIANA AV ... L3
INDIANA ST ... J2
INDUSTRIAL DR ... M3
IROQUOIS AV ... L4
JACKSON AV ... L2
JAY LN ... M1
JEANETTE AV ... M1
JEFFERSON AV ... L2
JEWEL AV ... M1
JOBE AV ... M2
JOHNOR AV ... K4
KATHERINE ST ... J2
KAUTZ RD ... O2
KEHOE DR ... J2
KEIM CT ... L5
KEIM TR ... L5
KELLER PL ... K2
KENSINGTON CT ... K6
KILLDEER LN ... J6
KIRK RD ... N3
LAKEWOOD CIR ... J5
LAKEWOOD CT ... J5
LANCASTER AV ... M2
LARSEN ... M2
LAVERN AV ... K4
LEWIS CT ... J4
LEXINGTON AV ... M2
LIBERTY AV ... L2
LIBERTY CT ... L2
LINCOLN HWY ... I1
LONGMEADOW CIR ... L4
LUCYLLE AV ... M1
MADISON AV ... L2
MADISON CT ... L2
MAIN ST-E ... L3
MAIN ST-W ... K3
MANLY RD ... J4
MARGARET CT ... J2
MARIE ST ... J2
MARK ST ... K3
MARION AV ... K4
MC KINLEY ST ... K1
MEADOW LN ... J6
MILBURN CT ... J1
MILLERD RD ... M2
MILLINGTON WAY ... J4
MONROE AV ... L2
MOODY ST ... K2
MOORE AV ... M1
MOSEDALE ST ... K2
MUIRFIELD CT ... N5
MUNHALL AV ... M3
NANCY LN ... Q6
NICHOLAS AV ... M2
NORTH AV ... K3
OAK RD ... P4
OAK ST ... J2
OAK HILL CT ... J5
OHIO AV ... L2-N3
OLD QUARRY RD ... J5
PARK AV ... K3
PATRICIA LN ... N1
PENDLETON CT ... K6
PERSIMMON CT ... L4
PERSIMMON DR ... L6
PIN OAK CT ... M4
PINE ST ... K1
PLEASANT AV ... M1
POMEROY CT ... M1
POST RD ... M4
PRAIRIE RD ... L8
PRAIRIE ST ... J2
PRESTWICK CT ... O7
PRODUCTION DR ... M3
RAILROAD PL ... L1
RANDALL RD-S ... I2
RED FOX CT ... L5
RED OAK LN ... M4
REDDEN CT ... J3
RITA AV ... M2
RIVER VALLEY RD ... K6
RIVERSIDE AV ... L2
RONZHEIMER AV ... M2
ROOSEVELT ST ... K1
ROUTE 25-N ... L6
ROUTE 31 ... K7
ROUTE 38 ... I1
ROUTE 64-E ... N4
ROUTE 64-W ... I4
ROYAL ST ... O7
ROYAL ASHDOWN CT ... N5
ROYAL FOX CT ... N6
ROYAL FOX DR ... N6
ROYAL KINGS CT ... N6
ROYAL LYTHAM CT ... N6
ROYAL LYTHAM DR ... N6
ROYAL QUEENS CT ... N5
ROYAL ST. CHARLES ... N6
ROYAL TROON CT ... O7
ROYAL WINDYNE CT ... O7
RUTH AV ... L2
SEDGEWICK CIR ... J3
SHABBONA AV ... K3
SHIRES LN ... M5
SHORELINE CT ... J5
SHORELINE DR ... J5
SOUTH AV ... L2
SOUTH GATE COURSE ... M5
SPRING AV ... L2
SQUIRE LN ... M5
ST. ANDREWS CT ... O6
STATE AV ... K3
STATE ST ... K3
STEEPLE CHASE CIR ... M5
STEEPLE CHASE CT ... L4
STERN DR ... M3
STERLING CT ... M5
STETSON DR ... M2
STIRRUP CUP CT ... M5
STONE DR ... N3
STONEHEDGE RD ... L4
STONEWOOD DR ... L6
SUMAC CT ... J5
SURREY WOODS DR ... M4
SUTTON PL ... L4
SWENSON DR ... N2
TEMPLE GARDEN CT ... M1
THORNHILL FARM LN ... K6
THORNWOOD CIR ... I4
THORNWOOD CT ... I4
THOROUGHBRED CT ... M5
TIMBERS CT ... J4
TIMBERS PL ... J4
TIMBERS TR ... J4
TURNBERRY RD ... N6
TYLER RD-N ... M2
TYLER RD-S ... M1
UNION AV ... M1
VAN BUREN AV ... L2
VIA VENETO DR ... M1
WALNUT AV ... K3
WALNUT DR ... I2
WALNUT ST ... K2
WASHINGTON AV ... L2
WEBER RD ... N2
WESTFIELD DR ... J1
WHITE OAK CIRCLE ... L1
WHITTINGTON COURSE ... M6
WILDROSE SPRING DR ... J5
WILDWOOD CT ... I4
WILLIAMS LN ... M2
WING AV ... L3
WING LN ... M4
WOODCREEK CT ... J5
1ST AV-N ... K3
1ST AV-S ... K3
1ST ST-S ... K2
2ND AV-N ... K3
2ND AV-S ... L2
2ND PL-S ... L1
2ND ST-N ... K2
2ND ST-S ... L1
3RD AV-N ... K3
3RD AV-S ... L2
3RD PL-S ... L1
3RD ST-N ... K2
3RD ST-S ... K1
4TH AV-N ... K3
4TH AV-S ... L2
4TH PL-S ... L1
4TH ST-N ... K2
4TH ST-S ... K1
5TH AV-N ... K3
5TH AV-S ... L2
5TH PL-S ... L1
5TH ST-N ... K3
5TH ST-S ... K2
6TH AV-N ... L2
6TH AV-S ... L2
6TH ST-N ... K2
6TH ST-S ... K1
7TH AV-N ... L2
7TH AV-S ... M1
7TH CT ... J1
7TH ST-N ... J2
7TH ST-S ... K1
8TH AV-S ... L3
8TH CT-S ... J2
8TH ST-S ... J2
9TH AV-S ... L3
9TH CT-S ... J2
9TH ST-N ... J3
9TH ST-S ... J2
10TH AV-S ... L3
10TH CT-S ... J2
10TH ST-S ... J2
11TH AV-N ... L3
11TH AV-S ... M1
11TH ST-N ... J2
11TH ST-S ... J1
12TH AV-N ... L3
12TH AV-S ... L2
12TH ST-N ... J2
12TH ST-S ... J1
13TH AV-N ... L3
13TH AV-S ... L2
13TH ST-S ... J2
14TH AV-S ... L3
14TH CT ... J2
14TH ST-S ... J2
15TH CT-S ... I2
15TH ST-N ... I3
15TH ST-S ... I2
16TH ST-S ... I2
17TH ST-N ... I3
17TH ST-S ... I2
18TH ST-S ... I2
19TH ST-S ... I2
37TH AV-S ... N3
38TH AV-S ... O3

Unincorporated St Charles Area

ADELE LN ... G11
ANCIENT OAK LN ... D7
ANTLER TR ... E7
ARBORETUM LN ... A8
ARMY TRAIL RD ... L3
ARROWHEAD DR ... A5
AUDUBON CT ... A8
BABSON LN ... G4
BAKER LN ... H7
BALKAN DR ... E4
BARB HILL DR ... F10
BARBERRY LN ... B9
BARLOW DR ... B4
BARNSIDE CT ... E9
BARTON DR ... J9
BEITH RD ... B2
BERNIECE DR ... G3
BIRCHDALE CT ... F6
BITTERSWEET RD ... H4
BLACK WILLOW DR ... F6
BLUE HERON CT ... E7
BLUFF DR NORTH ... K7
BLUFF DR SOUTH ... K7
BOLCUM RD ... F8
BONFIELD AV ... K9
BONNIE ... F5
BONNIE CT ... F4
BONNIE DR ... F4
BONNIE LN ... F3
BONNIE ST ... O1
BRIDLE CT ... A7
BRIDLE CREEK DR ... C5
BRIDLE CREEK DR-S ... C4
BRIERWOOD DR ... C10
BROOKSIDE CIRCLE DR ... A6
BROOKSIDE DR WEST ... A6
BROOKWOOD RD ... L6
BROWN RD ... B6
BOXWOOD LN ... C9
BRUNDAGE RD ... E1

© DonTech Chicago, Il. 1992

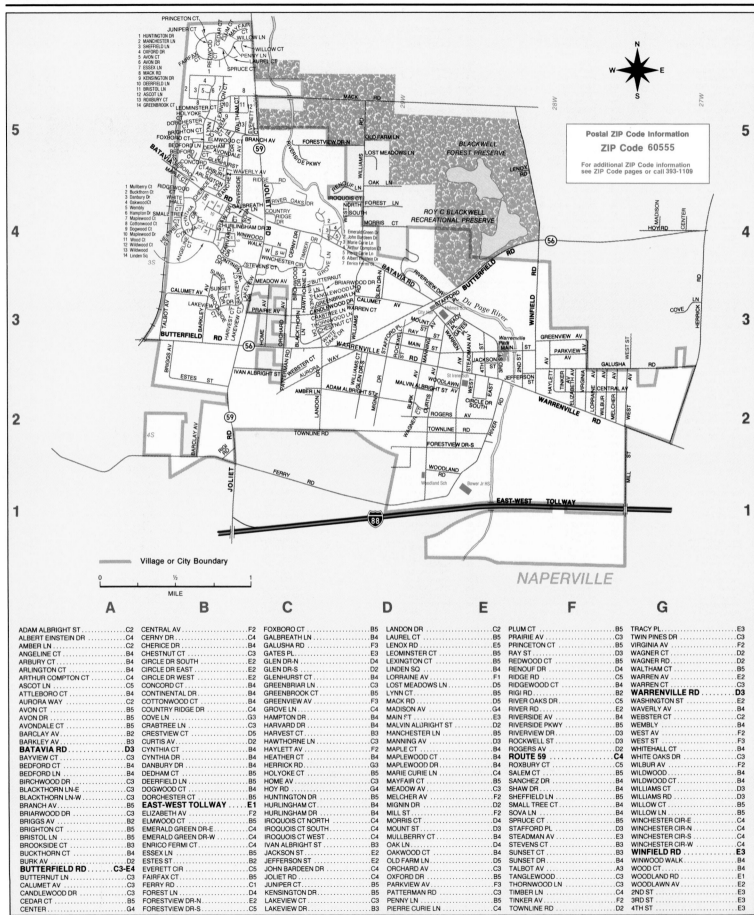

© DonTech Chicago, Il. 1992

Postal ZIP Code Information

ZIP Code 60555

For additional ZIP Code information see ZIP Code pages or call 393-1109

Village or City Boundary

0   ½   1
MILE

NAPERVILLE

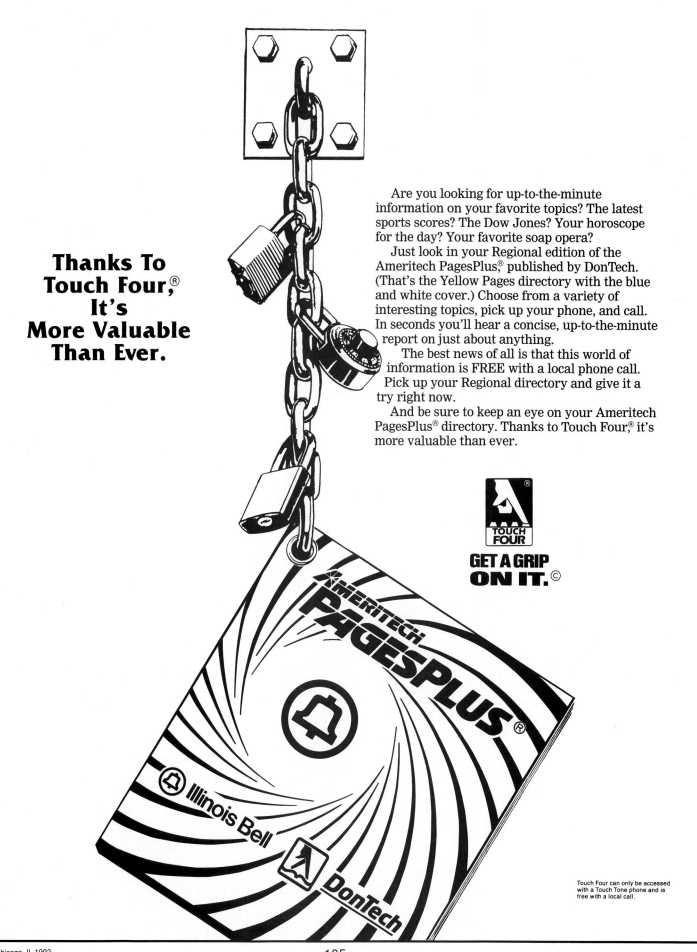

Thanks To Touch Four,® It's More Valuable Than Ever.

Are you looking for up-to-the-minute information on your favorite topics? The latest sports scores? The Dow Jones? Your horoscope for the day? Your favorite soap opera?

Just look in your Regional edition of the Ameritech PagesPlus,® published by DonTech. (That's the Yellow Pages directory with the blue and white cover.) Choose from a variety of interesting topics, pick up your phone, and call. In seconds you'll hear a concise, up-to-the-minute report on just about anything.

The best news of all is that this world of information is FREE with a local phone call. Pick up your Regional directory and give it a try right now.

And be sure to keep an eye on your Ameritech PagesPlus® directory. Thanks to Touch Four,® it's more valuable than ever.

TOUCH FOUR

GET A GRIP ON IT.©

Touch Four can only be accessed with a Touch Tone phone and is free with a local call.

© DonTech Chicago, Il. 1992

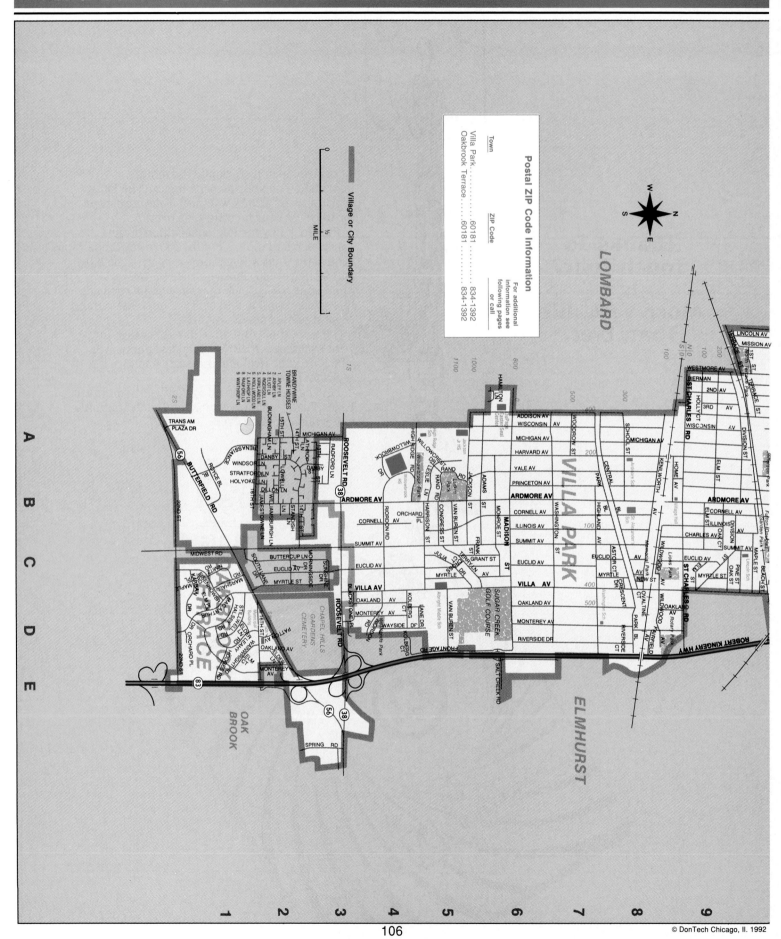

Postal ZIP Code Information

For additional
information see
following pages
or call

Town	ZIP Code	
Villa Park	60181	834-1392
Oakbrook Terrace	60181	834-1392

Village or City Boundary

© DonTech Chicago, Il. 1992

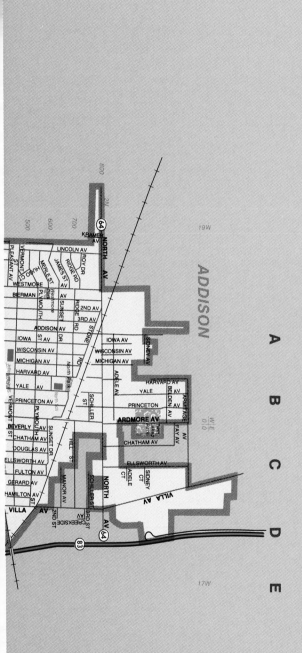

Oakbrook Terrace

BUTTERFIELD RD.	B1
EISENHOWER RD.	C1
ELDER LN.	D1-E2
ELM CT.	D1
ELM PL.	E2
FRONTAGE RD.	D1
HALSEY RD.	D4
HODGES RD.	D1
KARBAN RD.	E1
LEAHY RD.	E1
MAC ARTHUR DR.	D1
MAPLE PL.	C1
MARSHALL RD.	C1
MIDWEST RD.	C1
MONTEREY AV.	E1
NIMITZ RD.	C1
OAKLAND AV.	E1
ORCHARD PL.	D2
PATTON AV.	D2
ROOSEVELT RD.	D3
ROUTE 83	E1
SPRING RD.	E1
STILLWELL RD.	D1
SUMMIT AV-S.	C4
WAINWRIGHT RD.	E1
14TH ST.	B2
16TH ST.	D2
22ND ST.	D1

Villa Park

ADAMS ST.	B5
ADDISON RD-N.	A11

ADDISON RD-S.	A6
ADELE AV.	A12
ADELE CT-E.	D12
APLEY LN.	B2
ARMITAGE AV.	B12
ASHBY LN.	B2
ASTOR CT.	C7
BEACH ST.	C10
BELDEN AV.	B12
BEVERLY AV.	C10
BIERMAN AV.	A9
BLACKSTONE PL.	B2
BUCKINGHAM LN.	D3
BUTTERCUP LN.	C2
BUTTERFIELD RD.	A1
CENTRAL BL.	A7
CHARLES AV.	C9
CHATHAM AV.	C10
CONGRESS ST.	C10
CORNELL AV.	C6
CREEKSIDE DR.	D11
CRESCENT DR.	D8
CROSS CT.	C5
DANBY ST.	B2
DILLON LN.	B2
DIVISION ST.	B9
DOUGLAS AV.	C10
ELIOT LN.	C10
ELLSWORTH AV.	B2
ELM ST.	B9
EUCLID AV.	E8
FAIRFIELD AV.	C12
FAY AV.	C5
FRANK ST.	C5
FRONTAGE RD.	D5

FULTON AV.	C10
GERARD AV.	D10
GRANT ST.	C5
HAMILTON AV.	D10
HARRISON ST.	C8
HARVARD AV.	C5
HIGHLAND AV.	B10
HIGH RIDGE RD.	C7
HILL ST.	B5
HOLLY CT.	C11
HOLYOKE LN.	A9
HOME AV.	B8
HUGO CT.	A10
ILLINOIS AV.	C9
INGERSOLL LN.	A10-A12
IOWA AV.	A7
JACKSON ST.	C9
JAMES ST.	B5
JAMESTOWNE LN.	A11
JULIA DR.	C5
KENILWORTH AV.	A8
KIRKLAND LN.	A8
KNOLLWOOD LN.	B2
KOLBERG CT.	D4
LANE DR.	B2
LATHROP LN.	B2
LESLIE LN.	B5
LINCOLN AV.	A10
LOWELL LN.	B2
MADISON ST.	C6
MANOR AV.	D11
MAPLE ST.	A8
MERLE ST.	B11
MICHIGAN AV.	B12
MISSION AV.	A9

MONROE ST.	B6
MONTEREY AV.	D3-D6
MORNINGSIDE DR.	C2
MYRTLE AV.	D5
NEW ST.	C8
NORTH AV.	C11
OAK CT.	B9
OAK ST.	C9
OAKLAND AV.	D3-D6
ORCHARD HILL CT.	C4
OVALTINE CT.	D8
PARK BL.	B7
PINE ST.	D8
PLEASANT AV.	B10
PLYMOUTH ST.	A10
PRINCETON AV.	B9
RADFORD LN.	B2
RAND RD.	B5
RENAISSANCE BL.	A1
RIDGE RD-W.	A1
RIORDAN RD.	C4
RIVERSIDE DR.	E7
RIVERSIDE DR.	E4
RIVERVIEW AV.	D11
ROOSEVELT RD.	B3
ROBERT KINGERY EXPY.	D7
ROUTE 83	E9
ROYCE BL.	A11
ROY DR.	B1
ST CHARLES RD.	B9
SALT CREEK RD.	E6
SCHILLER ST.	B11
SCHOOL ST.	B12
SIDNEY AV.	A12
SIDNEY CT.	C12
SOUTH LANE DR.	C2

STANDISH LN.	B2
STONE RD.	A11
STRATFORD LN.	C6
SUMMIT AV.	A11
SUNSET DR.	C3
SUNSHINE DR.	A10
TERRACE ST.	A1
TERRY LN.	A5
TRANS AM PLAZA DR.	C5
VAN BUREN ST.	B10
VERMONT ST.	D6
VILLA AV.	B7
WASHINGTON ST.	D4
WAYSIDE DR.	C8
WESTMORE AV.	B2
WILDWOOD AV.	A4
WILLIAMSBURGH LN.	B5
WILLOWBROOK DR.	B2
WILLOWCREST DR.	B2
WINDSOR LN.	B2
WINTHROP LN.	A6-A12
WISCONSIN AV.	A7
WOODROW ST.	B6
YALE AV.	A9
1ST ST.	D11
2ND AV.	D11
3RD ST.	A9
13TH ST.	A3
14TH ST.	B2
15TH ST.	A2
16TH ST.	A2

© DonTech Chicago, Il. 1992

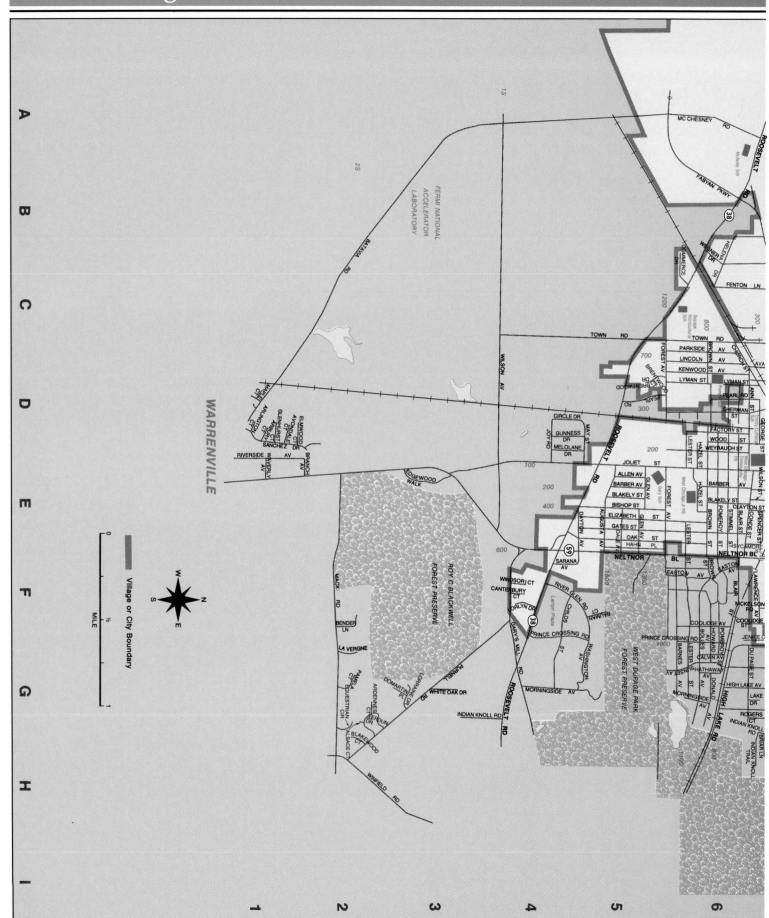

© DonTech Chicago, Il. 1992

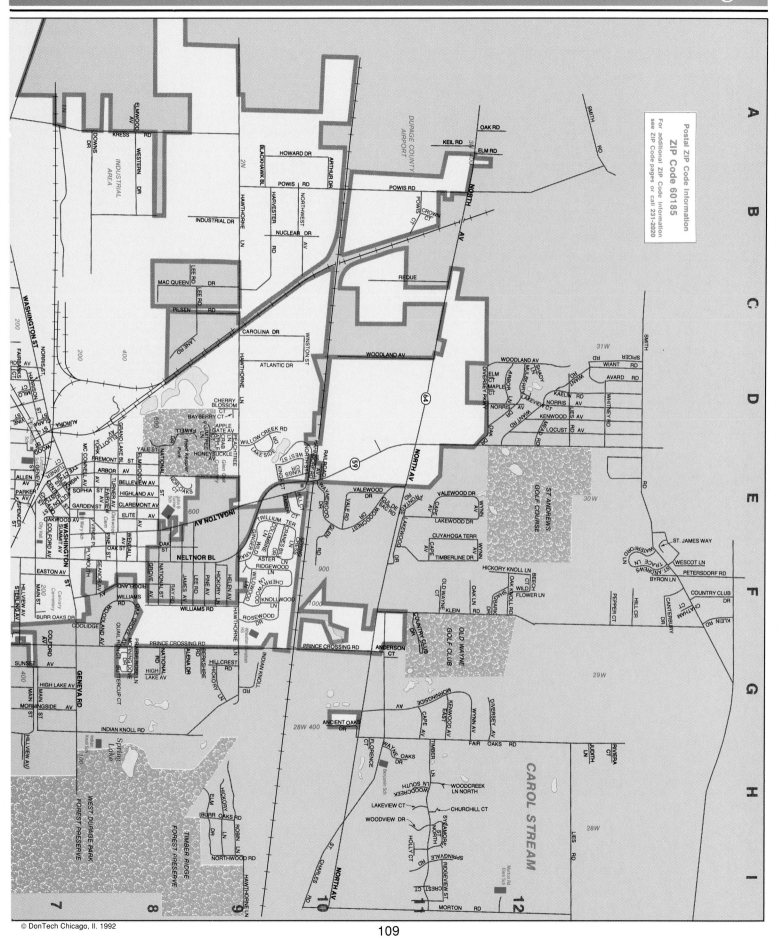

Postal ZIP Code Information
ZIP Code 60185
For additional ZIP Code information
see ZIP Code pages or call 231-2020

West Chicago

ALLEN AV	D5-D7
AMBER CT	E9
ANN ST	C6
APPLE GATE AV	D8
ARBOR AV	D8
ARTHUR DR	A10
ATLANTIC DR	C9
AUGUSTA AV	E5
AURORA ST-N	D7
AURORA ST-S	D7
AVARD AV	C6
BARBER AV	D6
BAYBERRY CT	D9
BELLEVIEW AV	D8
BISHOP ST	D5
BLACKHAWK BL	A9
BLAIR ST-E	E6
BLAIR ST-W	D6
BLAKELY ST	E6
BRENTWOOD CT	D5
BRENTWOOD DR	D5
BROWN ST-E	C6
BROWN ST-W	E6
BURR OAKS DR	F7
BUTTERCUP CT	G8
CANTERBURY CT	F4
CAROLINA DR	C9
CENTER ST	E7
CHERRY BLOSSOM CT	D9
CHERRYWOOD LN	F9
CHICAGO ST	E7
CHURCH ST	C6
CLARA ST	D7
CLAREMONT AV	E8
CLAYTON ST	E6
COLFORD AV	E7
COMMERCE DR	B6
CONDE ST	E6
COOLIDGE	F7
COOLIDGE ST	F6
CRAB APPLE CT	E9
CRANES BILL DR	F9
CROWN CT	B11
DALE AV	E5
DAYTON AV	E4
DIVERSEY PKWY	D12
DOWNS DR	A7
EASTON AV	E6
ELITE AV	E8
ELIZABETH ST	E5
ELLIOTT AV	D8
ELMWOOD AV-E	E8
ELMWOOD AV-W	A8
FACTORY ST	D6
FAIRBANKS CT	C6
FAIRVIEW AV	E7
FAWELL DR	D8
FENTON LN	B6
FOREST AV-E	E5
FOREST AV-W	C5
FREMONT ST	D8
FULTON ST	E7
GALENA ST	D7
GARDEN ST	E7
GARY'S MILL RD	E4
GATES ST	E5

GENEVA RD-W	**B7**
GENEVA ST-E	D7
GENEVA ST-W	D7
GEORGE ST	D6
GLEN AV	E5
GRAND LAKE BL-E	E8
GRAND LAKE BL-W	D8
GROVE AV	E8
HAHN PL	E5
HAHNDORF RD	D10
HARRISON ST	D7
HARVESTER RD-N	B9
HARVESTER RD-W	B9
HAWTHORNE LN-E	F9
HAWTHORNE LN-W	A9
HAZEL ST-E	E5
HAZEL ST-W	D5
HELENA AV	B6
HIGH ST	E7
HILL CT	E10
HILLVIEW AV	F7-G7
HONEYSUCKLE AV	E9
HOWARD DR	A10
INDUSTRIAL DR	B8
INGALTON AV	E8
JENICE CT	F6
JOLIET ST	D5
KENWOOD AV	C6
KINGS CIR	D9
KINGS CT	D9
KNOLLWOOD LN	F9
KRESS RD	A8
LAKE SIDE DR	D9
LAWRENCE AV	E6
LESTER ST	E6
LINCOLN AV	C6
LORLYN DR	F4
LYMAN ST	C6
MAIN ST	E7
MC CHESNEY RD	A6
MC CONNELL AV	D8
MILO CT	C7
MORNING DOVE DR	G8
NATIONAL ST-E	D8
NATIONAL ST-W	E6
NELTNOR BL-N	**E8**
NELTNOR BL-S	**E5**
NICKELSON RD	F6
NOR-OAKS CT	E8
NORRIS ST	C7
NORTH AV	**D11**
NORTH ST	D9
NORTHWEST AV	B10
NUCLEAR DR	B9
OAK DR	D12
OAK ST-N	E8
OAK ST-S	E5
OAKWOOD AV-N	E7
OAKWOOD AV-S	E7
PARKER AV	E7
PARKSIDE AV	C6
PEACHTREE LN	D9
PEARL RD	D6
PILSEN RD	C9
PINE ST	E8
PLUMTREE LN	E9
PLYMOUTH	F7
POMEROY ST-E	D6
POMEROY ST-W	E6

POWIS CT	B11
POWIS RD	A10
PRAIRIE ROSE LN	G8
QUAIL RUN CT	G8
RAILROAD ST	D10
RIDGELAND AV	F7
RIDGEWOOD LN	F9
ROGERS CT	G6
ROOSEVELT RD-E	**E4**
ROOSEVELT RD-W	**A6**
ROSEWOOD DR	F9
ROUTE 59-N	**D10**
ROUTE 59-S	**D4**
SARANA AV	E4
SEANOR AV	F7
SHERMAN ST	D6
SOPHIA ST	D7
SPENCER ST	E7
SPRING CRESS LN	F9
STERLING AV	F6
STIMMEL ST-E	D6
STIMMEL ST-W	E6
SUMMIT AV	E7
SYCAMORE ST	E6
TOWN RD	C6
TRILLIUM TER	E9
TURNER AV	E8
TURNER CT	D7
TYE CT	D7
VINE ST	D7
VIRGIE PL	E7
WASHINGTON ST-E	**E7**
WASHINGTON ST-W	**C7**
WEGNER DR	B6
WENDALL AV	E8
WESTERN DR	A8
WEST ST	D9
WEYRAUCH ST	D6
WILDWOOD LN	F9
WILLOW CREEK RD	D9
WILSON ST	E6
WINDSOR CT	E4
WINSTON ST	C9
WOOD ST	D7
WOODLAND AV NORTH	C11
YALE ST	D8
YORK AV-E	E8
YORK AV-W	D8

West Chicago Unincorporated Area

ALENA DR	F8
ALSACE CT	G2
ANCIENT OAKS DR	G10
ANDERSON CT	F11
ARBOR LN	C12
ARBURY CT	D1
ARDENNES CT	G2
ARLINGTON CT	D1
ASTER LN	F9
AVARD RD	C12
AVONDALE CT	D1
BARNES AV	F6
BATAVIA RD	B2
BAUMAN CT	F6
BEECH CT	F12
BENDER LN	F2
BERKSHIRE RD	F9
BLAKEWOOD CT	H2

BOLLES AV	F6
BRANCH AV	D2
BRIAR LN	G6
BROADVIEW	F7
BURR OAKS RD	H9
BYRON LN	F12
CALVIN AV	F6
CAMBRIDGE DR	F12
CANTERBURY DR	F12
CAPE AV	E11-G11
CHATHAM CT	F12
CHILDS ST	F4
CHURCHILL CT	H11
CIRCLE DR	D4
COLFORD AV	F7
COLUMBINE LN	E9
COUNTRY CLUB DR	F11
CREST CT	I11
CUL DE SAC RD	E11
CUYAHOGA TERR	E11
DIVERSEY AV	G12
DOMARTIN PL	G3
DONALD AV	G6
DU PAGE ST	F6
EDGEWOOD WALK	D3
ELM CT	C12
ELM DR	H9
ELM RD	A12
ELMWOOD CT	D1
EQUESTRIAN CIR	G2
FABYAN PKWY	A6
FAIR OAKS RD	G12
FLORENCE CT	G10
FRONTAGE RD	E11
GENEVA RD-E	G7
GLENHURST CT	D1
GLEN RD	E10
GUNNESS DR	G4
HAHN PL	E5
HATHAWAY AV	F6
HELEN AV	E9
HICKORY KNOLL LN	F12
HIGH LAKE AV	F7
HIGH LAKE RD	G6
HILL CR	F12
HILLCREST RD	F9
HOLLY CT	H11
HOWARD AV	F6
INDIAN KNOLL RD	G3-G8
INDIAN KNOLL TRAIL	G6
JOY RD	D4
JUDITH LN	G12
KAELIN RD	D12
KEIL RD	A11
KENWOOD AV EAST	G11
KENWOOD AV NORTH	D12
KLEIN RD	F11
LA VERGNE	F12
LAKE DR	C6
LAKEVIEW CT	H11
LAKEVIEW CT WEST	C12
LAKEWOOD DR	E11
LANE RD	C8
LEE RD	B8-E8
LIES RD	D12-H12
LOCUST AV	D12
LORRAINE DR	G3
MACK RD	E2
MAC QUEEN DR	B8

MAPLE CT	C12-D1
MAY ST	D5
MEAD RD	D12
MELOLANE DR	D4
MORNINGSIDE AV	H6
MORTON RD	I12
MULBERRY DR	C12
NORRIS AV	D12
NORTHWOOD RD	H9
OAK LN	F11
OAK RD	A12
OAK GROVE AV	F8
OAK KNOLL RD	F12
OLD WAYNE CT	F11
PAMELA CT	G2
PEARL RD	C5
PEPPER CT	F12
PETERSDORF RD	F12
PINE AV	E9
PRINCE CROSSING RD	F8
PURNELL RD	G3
RAY RD	E8
REQUE	C11
RIDGEVIEW ST	I11
RIVER GLEN RD	F4
RIVERSIDE AV	D1
RIVIERA CT	G12
ROBIN LN	D1
SANCHEZ DR	D1
ST. ANDREWS TRACE LN	F12
ST. CHARLES RD	H10
ST. JAMES WAY	F12
SHADY LN	C12
SHAGBARK DR	F11
SMITH RD	E12
SPICER RD	D12
SPRINGVALE RD	H11
SUNSET AV	F7
SYCAMORE ST NORTH	H11
TIMBER LN	H11
TIMBERLINE DR	E11
VALEWOOD DR	D10
VERDUN DR	G2
WASHINGTON AV	F5
WATERFORD LN	F12
WAYNE OAKS DR	G11
WAYNEWOOD DR	E10
WAVERLY AV	D1
WESCOT LN	F12
WHITE OAK DR	F3
WHITNEY RD	D12
WIANT RD	D12
WILD FLOWER LN	F12
WILD GINGER TRAIL	F12
WILLIAMS RD	F6-F9
WILSON AV	D4
WINFIELD RD	H3
WOODCREEK LN NORTH	H11
WOODCREEK LN SOUTH	H11
WOODCREST DR	E10
WOODLAND LN	F8
WOODVIEW DR	H11
WYNN AV	E11-G11

© DonTech Chicago, Il. 1992

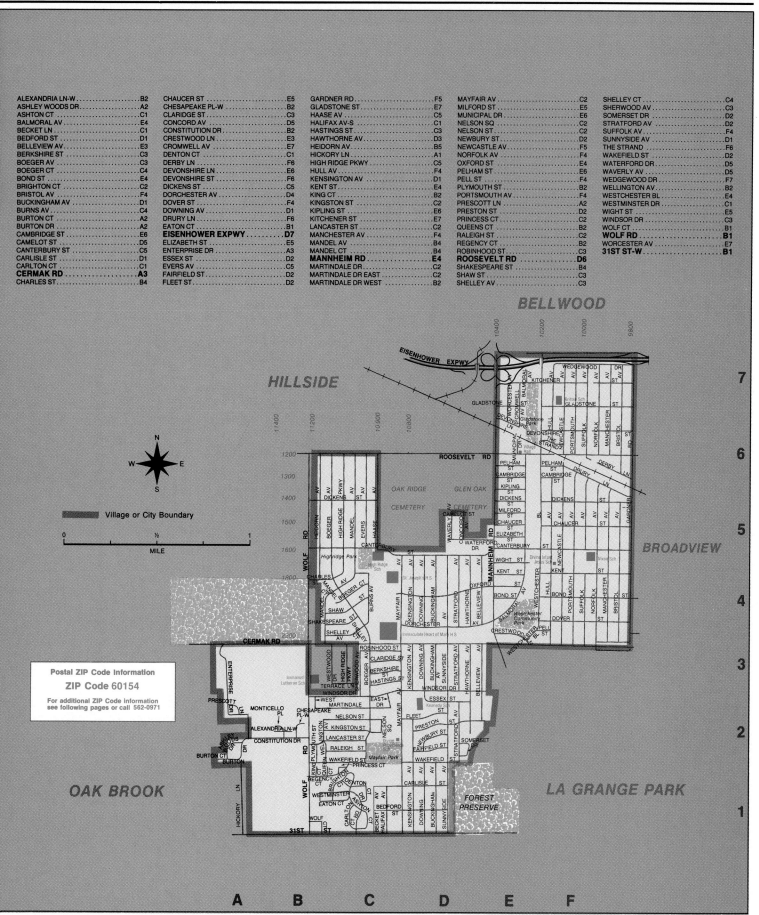

© DonTech Chicago, Il. 1992

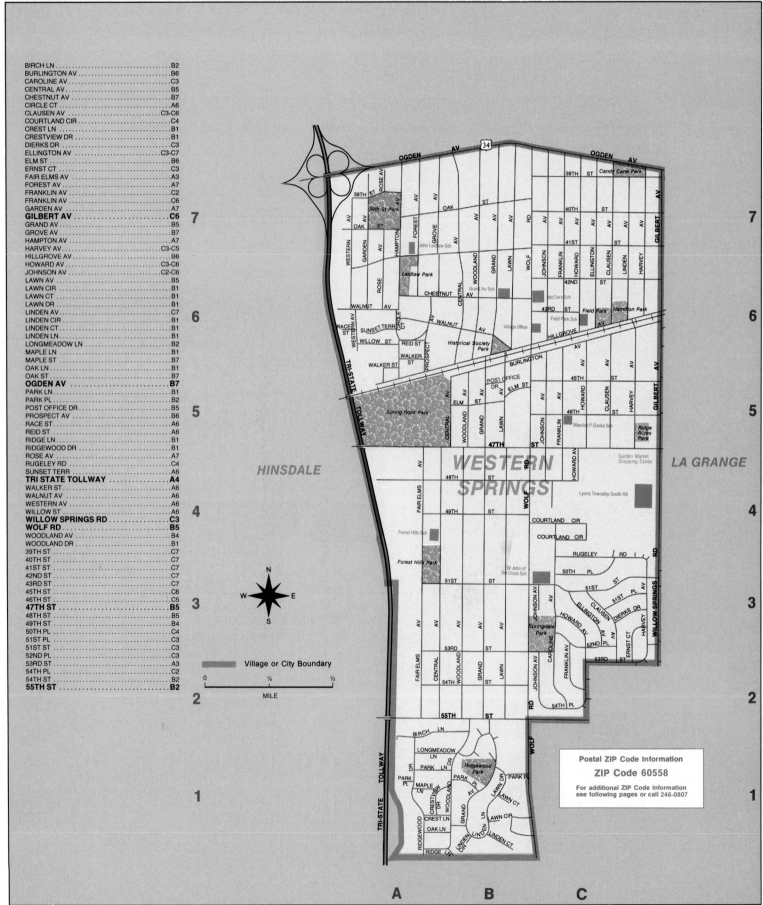

Village or City Boundary

0   ¼   ½
MILE

Postal ZIP Code Information
ZIP Code 60558
For additional ZIP Code information
see following pages or call 246-0807

HINSDALE

WESTERN SPRINGS

LA GRANGE

© DonTech Chicago, Il. 1992

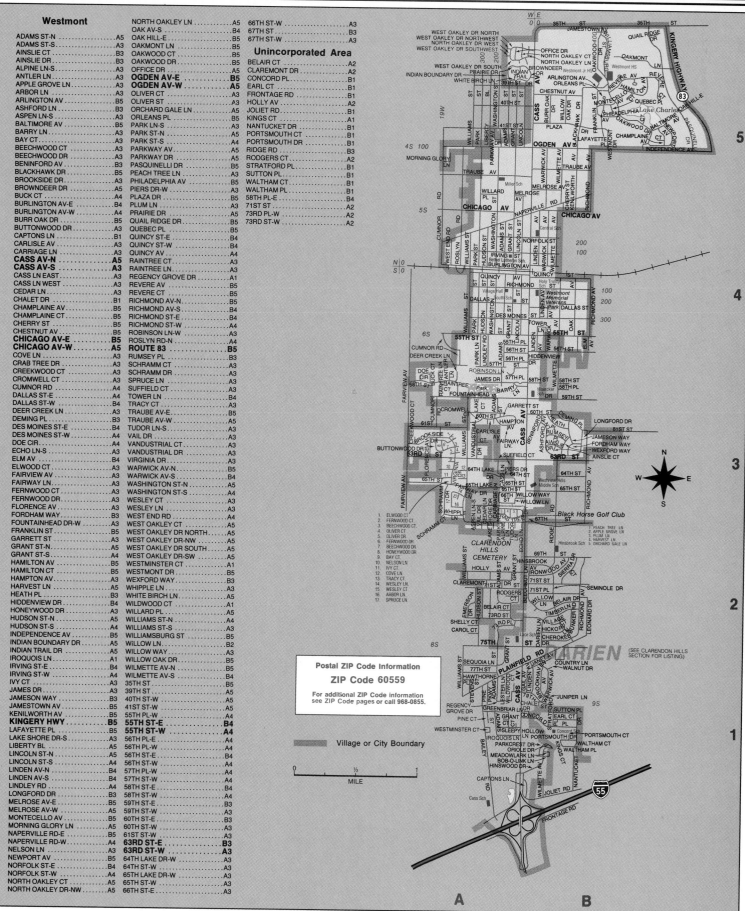

Westmont

ADAMS ST-N	A5
ADAMS ST-S	A3
AINSLIE CT	B3
AINSLIE DR	B3
ALPINE LN-S	A3
ANTLER LN	A3
APPLE GROVE LN	A3
ARBOR LN	A3
ARLINGTON AV	B5
ASHFORD LN	B3
ASPEN LN-S	A3
BALTIMORE AV	B5
BARRY LN	A3
BAY CT	A3
BEECHWOOD CT	A3
BEECHWOOD DR	A3
BENINFORD AV	B3
BLACKHAWK DR	B5
BROOKSIDE DR	A3
BROWNDEER DR	A5
BUCK CT	A4
BURLINGTON AV-E	B4
BURLINGTON AV-W	A4
BURR OAK DR	B5
BUTTONWOOD DR	A3
CAPTONS LN	B1
CARLISLE AV	A3
CARRIAGE LN	A3
CASS AV-N	**A5**
CASS AV-S	**A3**
CASS LN EAST	A3
CASS LN WEST	A3
CEDAR LN	A3
CHALET DR	B1
CHAMPLAINE AV	B5
CHAMPLAINE CT	B5
CHERRY ST	B5
CHESTNUT AV	B5
CHICAGO AV-E	**B5**
CHICAGO AV-W	**A5**
COVE LN	A3
CRAB TREE DR	A3
CREEKWOOD CT	A3
CROMWELL CT	A3
CUMNOR RD	A4
DALLAS ST-E	A4
DALLAS ST-W	B4
DEER CREEK LN	A3
DEMING PL	B3
DES MOINES ST-E	B4
DES MOINES ST-W	A4
DOE CIR	A4
ECHO LN-S	A3
ELM AV	B4
ELWOOD CT	A3
FAIRVIEW AV	A3
FAIRWAY LN	A3
FERNWOOD CT	A3
FERNWOOD DR	A3
FLORENCE AV	A3
FORDHAM WAY	B3
FOUNTAINHEAD DR-W	A3
FRANKLIN ST	B5
GARRETT ST	A3
GRANT ST-N	A5
GRANT ST-S	A4
HAMILTON AV	B5
HAMILTON CT	B5
HAMPTON AV	A3
HARVEST LN	A5
HEATH PL	B3
HIDDENVIEW DR	B4
HONEYWOOD DR	A3
HUDSON ST-N	A5
HUDSON ST-S	A4
INDEPENDENCE AV	B5
INDIAN BOUNDARY DR	A5
INDIAN TRAIL DR	A5
IROQUOIS LN	A1
IRVING ST-E	B4
IRVING ST-W	A4
IVY CT	A3
JAMES DR	A3
JAMESON WAY	B3
JAMESTOWN AV	B5
KENILWORTH AV	B5
KINGERY HWY	**B5**
LAFAYETTE PL	B5
LAKE SHORE DR-S	A3
LIBERTY BL	A5
LINCOLN ST-N	A5
LINCOLN ST-S	A4
LINDEN AV-N	B4
LINDEN AV-S	B4
LINDLEY RD	B3
LONGFORD DR	B3
MELROSE AV-E	B5
MELROSE AV-W	A5
MONTECELLO AV	B5
MORNING GLORY LN	A5
NAPERVILLE RD-E	B5
NAPERVILLE RD-W	A4
NELSON LN	A3
NEWPORT AV	B5
NORFOLK ST-E	B4
NORFOLK ST-W	A4
NORTH OAKLEY CT	A5
NORTH OAKLEY DR-NW	A5

NORTH OAKLEY LN	A5
OAK AV-S	A4
OAK HILL-E	B5
OAKMONT LN	B5
OAKWOOD CT	B5
OAKWOOD DR	B5
OFFICE DR	A5
OGDEN AV-E	**B5**
OGDEN AV-W	**A5**
OLIVER CT	A3
OLIVER ST	A3
ORCHARD GALE LN	A5
ORLEANS PL	B5
PARK LN-S	A3
PARK ST-N	A5
PARK ST-S	A3
PARKWAY AV	A5
PARKWAY DR	A3
PASQUINELLI DR	B5
PEACH TREE LN	A3
PHILADELPHIA AV	B5
PIERS DR-W	A3
PLAZA DR	B5
PLUM LN	A3
PRAIRIE DR	A5
QUAIL RIDGE DR	B5
QUEBEC PL	B5
QUINCY ST-E	B4
QUINCY ST-W	B4
QUINCY AV	A4
RAINTREE CT	A3
RAINTREE LN	A3
REGENCY GROVE DR	A1
REVERE AV	B5
REVERE CT	B5
RICHMOND AV-N	B5
RICHMOND AV-S	B4
RICHMOND ST-E	B4
RICHMOND ST-W	A4
ROBINSON LN-W	A3
ROSLYN RD-N	A4
ROUTE 83	**B5**
RUMSEY PL	B3
SCHRAMM CT	A3
SCHRAMM DR	A3
SPRUCE LN	A3
SUFFIELD CT	A3
TOWER LN	B4
TRACY CT	A3
TRAUBE AV-E	B5
TRAUBE AV-W	A5
TUDOR LN-S	A3
VAIL DR	A3
VANDUSTRIAL CT	A3
VANDUSTRIAL DR	A3
VIRGINIA DR	A3
WARWICK AV-N	B5
WARWICK AV-S	B4
WASHINGTON ST-N	A5
WASHINGTON ST-S	A4
WESLEY CT	A3
WESLEY LN	A3
WEST END RD	A4
WEST OAKLEY LN	A5
WEST OAKLEY DR NORTH	A5
WEST OAKLEY DR-NW	A5
WEST OAKLEY DR SOUTH	A5
WEST OAKLEY DR-SW	A5
WESTMINSTER CT	A1
WESTMONT DR	B5
WEXFORD WAY	B3
WHIPPLE LN	A3
WHITE BIRCH LN	A5
WILDWOOD CT	A1
WILLARD PL	A5
WILLIAMS ST-N	A4
WILLIAMS ST-S	A3
WILLIAMSBURG ST	B5
WILLOW LN	B2
WILLOW WAY	A3
WILLOW OAK DR	B5
WILMETTE AV-N	B5
WILMETTE AV-S	B4
35TH ST	B5
39TH ST	A5
40TH ST-W	A5
41ST ST-W	A5
55TH PL-W	A4
55TH ST-E	**B4**
55TH ST-W	**A4**
56TH PL-E	B4
56TH PL-W	A4
56TH ST-E	B4
56TH ST-W	A4
57TH PL-W	A4
57TH ST-W	A4
58TH ST-E	B4
58TH ST-W	A4
59TH ST-E	B3
59TH ST-W	A3
60TH ST-E	B3
60TH ST-W	A3
61ST ST-W	A3
63RD ST-E	**B3**
63RD ST-W	**A3**
64TH LAKE DR-W	A3
64TH ST-W	A3
65TH LAKE DR-W	A3
65TH ST-W	A3
66TH ST-E	A3

66TH ST-W	A3
67TH ST	B3
67TH ST-W	A3

Unincorporated Area

BELAIR CT	A2
CLAREMONT DR	A2
CONCORD PL	B1
EARL CT	B1
FRONTAGE RD	B1
HOLLY AV	A2
JOLIET RD	B1
KINGS CT	A1
NANTUCKET DR	B1
PORTSMOUTH CT	B1
PORTSMOUTH DR	B1
RIDGE RD	B3
RODGERS CT	A2
STRATFORD PL	B1
SUTTON PL	B1
WALTHAM CT	B1
WALTHAM PL	B1
58TH PL-E	B4
71ST ST	A2
73RD PL-W	A2
73RD ST-W	A2

Postal ZIP Code Information

ZIP Code 60559

For additional ZIP Code information
see ZIP Code pages or call 968-0855.

Village or City Boundary

0   ½   MILE

© DonTech Chicago, Il. 1992

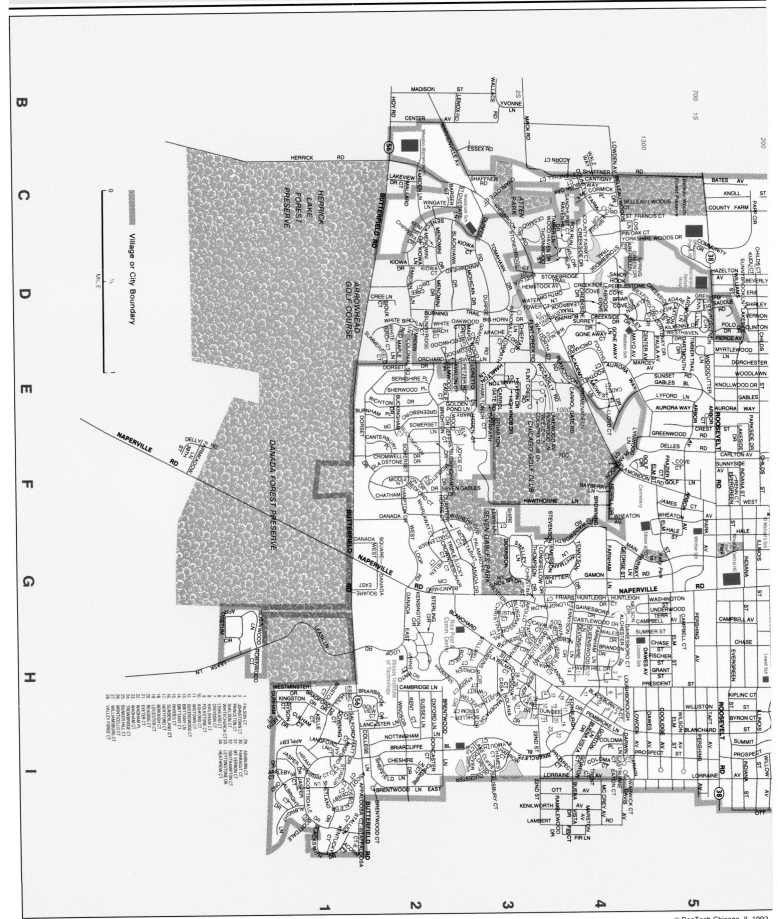

© DonTech Chicago, Il. 1992

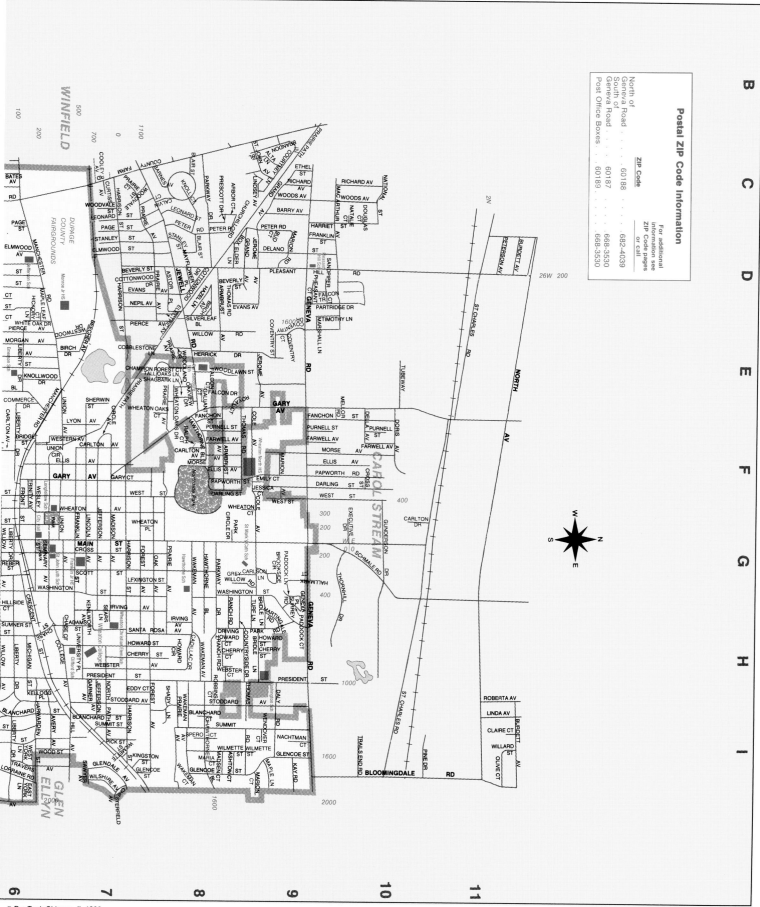

© DonTech Chicago, Il. 1992

© DonTech Chicago, Il. 1992

© DonTech Chicago, Il. 1992

Winfield

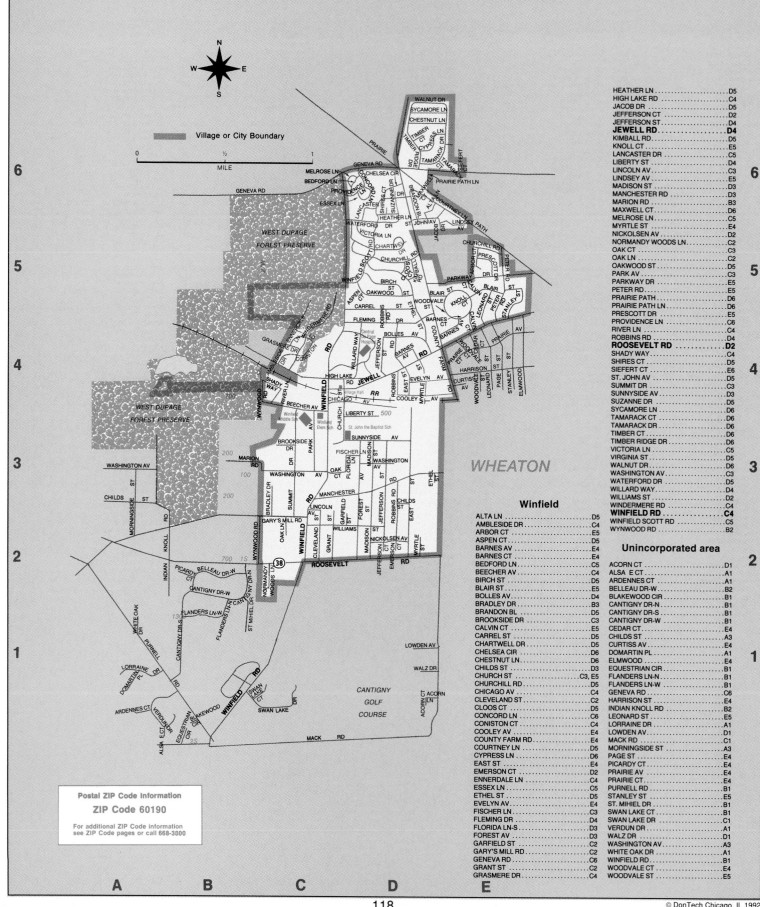

Village or City Boundary

Postal ZIP Code Information
ZIP Code 60190
For additional ZIP Code information
see ZIP Code pages or call 668-3800

WHEATON

© DonTech Chicago, Il. 1992

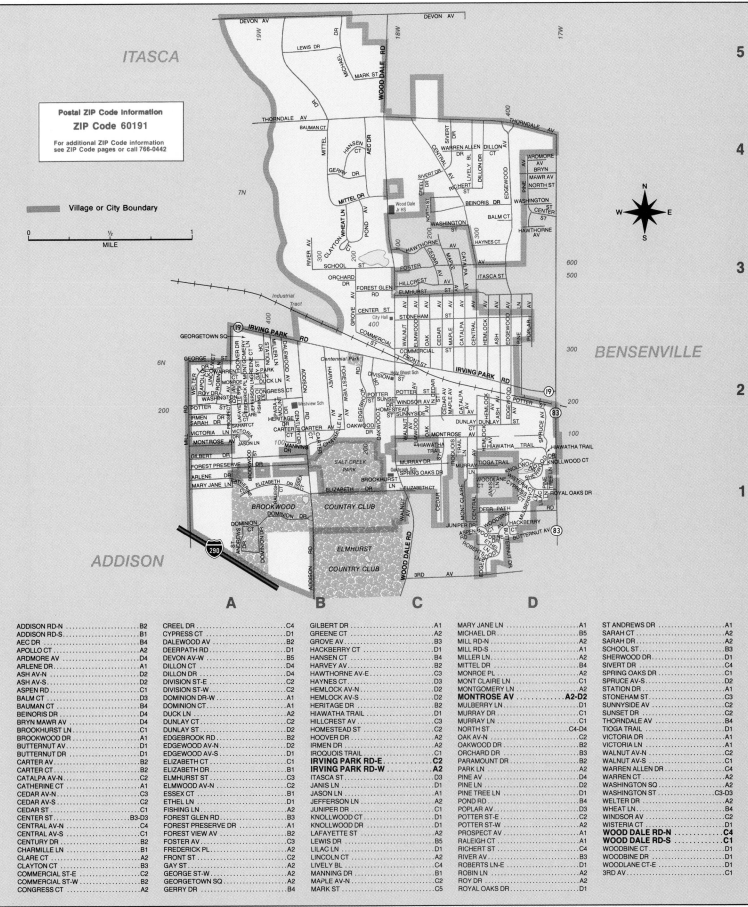

Postal ZIP Code Information
ZIP Code 60191

For additional ZIP Code information
see ZIP Code pages or call 766-0442

Village or City Boundary

© DonTech Chicago, Il. 1992

Woodridge

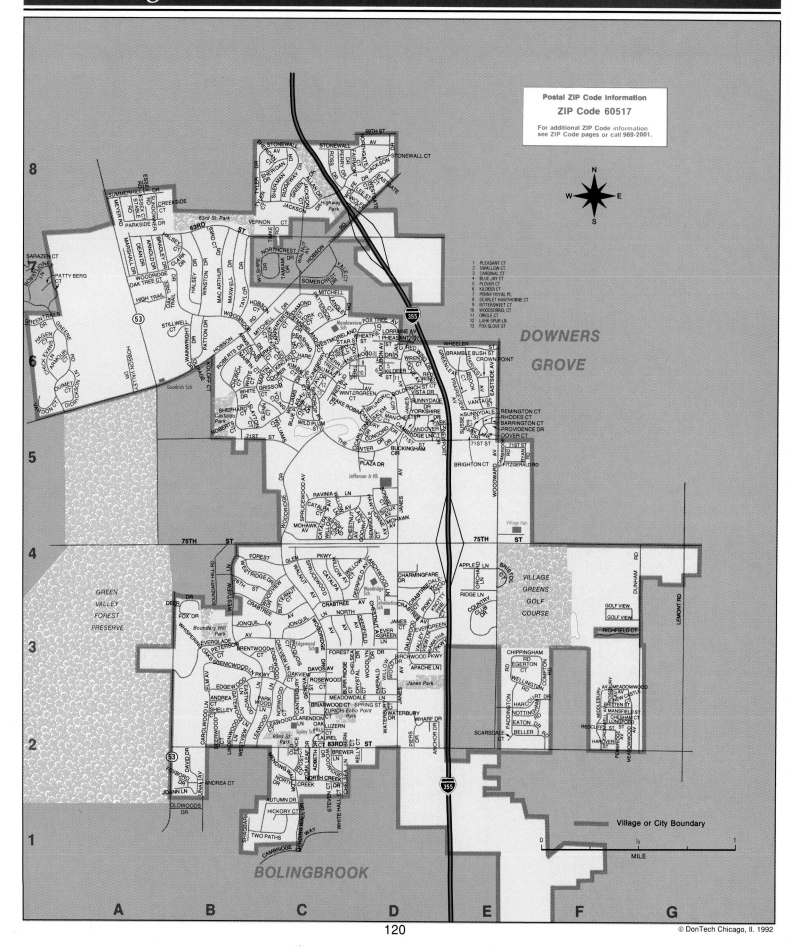

© DonTech Chicago, Il. 1992

Postal ZIP Code Information
ZIP Code 60517

For additional ZIP Code information
see ZIP Code pages or call 969-2001.

1 PLEASANT CT
2 SWALLOW CT
3 CARDINAL CT
4 BLUE JAY CT
5 PLOVER CT
6 KILDEER CT
7 PENNY ROYAL PL
8 SCARLET HAWTHORNE CT
9 BITTERSWEET CT
10 WOODSORREL CT
11 ORIOLE CT
12 LARK SPUR LN
13 FOX GLOVE CT

DOWNERS GROVE

BOLINGBROOK

Village or City Boundary

MILE

© DonTech Chicago, Il. 1992

Yellow Pages advertising has

Impact

Inexpensive
Priced lower than most other advertising

Market coverage
Your message is carried into homes and offices that a salesperson could not ordinarily reach

Permanent
It's never lost or discarded. Very often, it's the ONLY source of information for the buyer

Availability
It's as near as the phone, ready to put your sales message to work

Constantly working
Relays your message, 24 hours a day, 365 days a year

Total usage
Surpasses all other mediums of advertising

DonTech
A Partnership between Ameritech Publishing and Donnelley Directory

For additional information contact DonTech at 312-861-2551

© DonTech Chicago, Il. 1992

Reach Buyers, Not Just Prospects!

Now your business can benefit from this truly unique advertising medium where buyers seek sellers.

Buyers:
Unlike creative advertising where sellers seek buyers, people using the Yellow Pages have made the decision to buy.

Frequency:
Your sales message is visible and working all the time...24 hours a day, 7 days a week, 365 days a year.

Reach:
Complete market coverage is easier than you think. The Yellow Pages is delivered free to virtually every home and business as well as to new movers throughout the year.

Usage:
Next to recommendations of family & friends, consumers & businesses turn to the Yellow Pages most often to find the products and services they need.

Results:
For over 100 years, the Yellow Pages has been a proven advertising source for reaching new customers.

Value:
Yellow Pages is the sensible communications vehicle for companies seeking cost-effective advertising with frequency and complete market coverage.

DonTech

A Partnership between Ameritech Publishing and Donnelley Directory

For additional information contact DonTech at 312-861-2551

© DonTech Chicago, Il. 1992

WATCH YOUR MAILBOX FOR MONEY-SAVING COUPONS!

Brought To You By

DonTech
A Partnership between Ameritech and Donnelley Directory

For advertising information contact DonTech at **708-449-1350**

© DonTech Chicago, Il. 1992

W9-COS-090

My name is Orlando.
    This is how I used to look
when I met someone for the first time.

HEAD LOW →

EYES
SQUEEZED
SHUT

ARMS
WRAPPED →
AROUND

HANDS CLASPED
TOGETHER

AND...

one foot standing on top of the other. My
parents called it "being shy".

In those days I never
had any friends.

That was not much fun.

It happened one day on the playground. Sitting by myself I wondered, how does one make friends? What should I say? Will it be scary? Maybe it won't work. ?????

This is me when I made my first friend. "Hi," I said to the next person who walked by, "my name is Orlando."

"Want to be my friend? Want to play ball?"

And he did! We played and played every day, in sun, rain, sleet, or snow. We were good friends. We shared everything together.

After I made one friend, it was easy to make others. We played together every day. Some of us went to the same school, some of us were in the same soccer team. We even spent the night with each other. Having friends was much better than being alone. We were <u>long-time</u> friends.

Here is our super-shiny travel-anywhere van, ready to take off on a Summer adventure.

"Good-bye everyone," I said. "See you when school starts. I'll send you a post card."

Take care of my pet turtle.

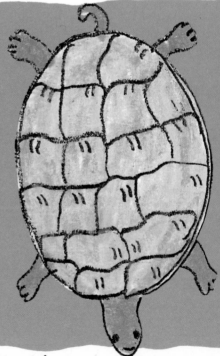

Good-bye everyone, good-bye.

"Think of all the nice places we are going to visit," my parents said, "won't this be fun..."

... but I could only think about my friends, they had each other...

...my parents had each other...

...who would I have on this long, long trip? My stomach had an empty feeling in it, even after eating three bananas.

"Never mind," my parents said, "it will only be for a little while."

We stopped for the night at a camping park. There were lots of children there, swimming, sliding and making sand castles.

Orlando, Mother said, "why don't you play with the children dear? They look like they're having so much fun. We are sure they would like to be your friends."

I climbed up a nearby tree. Peeping through the leaves I watched the children below.

How could they be friends with me?

No one here lived near my house, or went to my school. No one here would ever play in my team, or even see me again after tomorrow.

Hiding in the leaves I made up a song. It
went like this:

Long-time friends how I miss you,
Long-time friends the world is grey and
   stony and filled with gorillas and
   monsters when you are not around.
I'm a sad space cowboy,
I've lost my rocket pony,
How will I ever cross the starry prairie?

This is me nearly falling out of the tree when I had an IDEA!

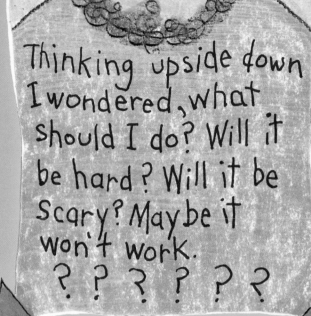

Thinking upside down I wondered, what should I do? Will it be hard? Will it be scary? Maybe it won't work.
? ? ? ? ? ?

"Hi!" I said to the next person who walked by, "my name is Orlando. Want to be my little-while friend?"

Her name was Leana. She is special because she is

the first little-while friend I made in the world.

Leana climbed up. We hung from the branch and played bats-in-a-tree. We laughed, talked, and sang a few songs together.

The tree began to fill with bats. We made funny faces and scary or silly or strange sounds. Leana gave me a tiny metal car she had found buried deep in the sand.

I gave her a tattoo sticker of a dove. She stuck it on her forehead.

"Children, come home. Bed time," all the parents called. We ran in every direction back to our tents, trailers, tee-pees or travel vans.

Sitting around our campfire I sang another song. My parents thought it was very good.

Oh little-while friend your eyes were as green as the sea, I'll never forget ol' bat-hanging tree, You didn't last long, we'll never meet again, But it was fun while it lasted, Oh little-while friend.

Having little-while friends is much better than being alone.

The next day...

on the road, watching trees and cows and fences whiz by, our super-shiny travel-anywhere van broke down.

My Father called Mr. George. He fixes vans.

Mr. George pulled our van away with his red tow truck.

I got to ride in the truck.

me ?

You will never guess what happened.

This is George Junior. George Junior likes to fish. He knows how to catch tadpoles with his bare hands.

Fish

While George's Father fixed our van, we became little-while friends.

George and I ran across a nearby field. George showed me a hole that went all the way to China.

We found a big log.

It became a spaceship so we landed on Mars and said "Hello" to the Martians.

Down at the stream George scooped up tadpoles in his bare hands, we watched them swim away through the water.

"Good-bye, George Junior," I said when my Father called, "your Father sure knows how to fix a van fast. Good-bye."

Stopping beside the road for a picnic, the day hot, buzzing with insects, and

birds singing loudly.

I ate a sandwich and watched a bicycle far, far away come closer and closer and closer.

The bicycle came to a stop "Hi," I said, "my name is Orlando. Are you thirsty? How long have you been riding? Would you like a drink of water? Would you like to be a little-while friend?"

His name was Brian. He took a long drink from my canteen.

"I have raced all the way from town," he said. "I am on my way to the best swimming hole in the world. It's not far from here. Like to come along?"

"Forward," my parents happily shouted. "To the swimming hole we go!"

We quickly packed up our picnic and followed Brian down a bumpy, dusty road.

My parents swam with us, we played water-
ball and water hide-and-seek. Brian let
me use his underwater-seeing goggles. I
pushed him on my yellow raft. We swung
together on an old tire hanging from a tree
over the stream. When it was time to go,
Brian showed me how he could crack his
knuckles. I will always remember Brian.
He was a fine little-while friend.

On to skyscraper city. Mother wanted to shop, so we found a store and went inside.

In the shoe department I had to sit and wait and wait.

Mother tried on brown, green, orange, purple, polka-dotted and zebra-striped shoes.

A girl sat in a seat across from us. Her hands were in her lap, her face looked down and her feet were crossed.

She did not look happy, she looked very sad.

Hi. My name's Orlando.

Want to be little-while friends?

For a moment nothing happened, I wondered if she was going to cry.

But when she looked up, she smiled, and I was glad.

"Sumi's my name," she said.

Can you play ball and jacks?"

We sat on the floor near our Mothers.

We played every ball and jack game we could think of, pigs-in-the-pen, pick-a-cherry, double-jacks, hot-jacks, and around-the-world jacks.

My Mother bought polka-dot shoes.

Sumi's Mother bought Zebra-striped shoes.

I swapped Sumi a smooth water pebble for an old rubber ball she had in her pocket.

Good-bye Sumi, little-while friend.

The great museum, where paintings are hanging on every wall, and white and cold and smooth statues of men and women sit on blocks of stone, was so big I thought it would never end.

We stopped for a drink at a water fountain. We had to wait in line. A boy stood in front of me.

Why not try it, I thought, so I said, "Hi, my name is Orlando. Want to be a little-while friend?"

Was I surprised when he turned around and said...

Me llamo Pablo. No hablo Inglés.

"What did he say?" I asked my Father.

"He said, 'My name is Pablo. I do not speak English.'"

Our parents walked ahead, leaving us behind.

I could not speak Spanish, he could not speak English. **?**

Suddenly Pablo grabbed my arm. When he pointed across the big room our eyes nearly popped out of our heads. In a corner, under a light, a knight in shining armour sat on top of a black wooden horse.

The knight and the horse were not real, but his shield, armour, and lance were. Pablo made signs with his hands. He pointed at the horse and knight.

I knew at once what he was trying to say.

Without a word we both put on our pretend armour, picked up our shields and lances, and hopped on our pretend horses. Riding by paintings and statues we made faces and hand signs so each could tell what the other was thinking.

When the tour ended, we had both learned how to speak a little English or Spanish.

Hasta luego Pablo.

Good-bye Orlando.

Sitting in the wet sand, Rachel showed me how to make a water-sand castle. Taking a little water and a little sand, drop by drop we built a fairy-drip castle. I made a bridge and a wall out of shells. Rachel thought that was a very good idea.

We found a piece of rubbery sea-weed near the water, and carried it on our heads.

I wrapped the seaweed around a driftwood stick.

It became a dragon that wanted to eat our castle.

Rachel and I dug a deep hole in the sand, we put our dragon in it and told him to behave.

When my parents called me saying, "Orlando, it's time to go now dear," I asked Rachel a serious question.

How many little-while friends have you made this Summer?

Oh, about 199!

Here we are driving down our very own street. Our trip is over now. I'll see all of my old long-time friends, we'll play everyday, spend the night on weekends, begin a new year at school together. I wonder how my tortoise is doing? I wonder where I put my soccer ball?

"Look Mother and Father," I said. "Someone has bought the house next to ours."

Moving men were carrying lamps, tables and chairs from a big truck into the house.

We stopped in our driveway. After I helped my parents unload our van, I walked down the street, hoping to get a look at our new neighbors.

I raced around to the backyard,
toys were scattered everywhere,
but no one was there.

Something strange
made a noise in a
nearby leafy tree.
It sounded like a
"beep", it sounded
like a growl, then it
sounded like an owl. "Whoo
whoo! Who who?" I
walked over to
take a look.

A girl swung down from the
tree, she hung by her knees
swinging back and forth.
"Hi," she said, "remember me?
My name is Leana.
We played bats-in-a-tree.
I'm your new neighbor.
Want to be a long-time friend?"